Daubier

P9-BBT-654

A HISTORY
OF THE
CHINESE
CULTURAL
REVOLUTION

A HISTORY
OF THE
CHINESE
CULTURAL
REVOLUTION

·

JEAN DAUBIER

TRANSLATED FROM THE FRENCH

BY RICHARD SEAVER

PREFACE BY HAN SUYIN

VINTAGE BOOKS
A Division of Random House
NEW YORK

VINTAGE BOOKS EDITION,
February 1974

Library of Congress Cataloging in Publication Data

Daubier, Jean.
A history of the Chinese cultural revolution.

Translation of Histoire de la révolution culturelle
prolétarienne en Chine, 1965-1969.
1. China (People's Republic of China, 1949-   )—
Politics and government.   I. Title.
[DS777.55.D3713   1974b]   951.05   73-4733
ISBN 0-394-71843-7

To the memory of Jean Baby

PREFACE

O f all the books that have appeared concerning the Great Proletarian Cultural Revolution, the book by Jean Daubier reflects most accurately the twists and turns of this historic event as seen and endured from within China itself. Jean Daubier was in China, and he has chronicled with exactness the varied course, the multiple facets, of those perplexing years. For perplexities they are, and will remain, although we grasp far better now the mainstream of the policies which guided it.

One of the main difficulties in trying to gauge the Cultural Revolution is that it is unprecedented. There has been nothing like it in history, ever before. It is this uniqueness which makes it an inexhaustible source of assumptions, and especially of surprising conclusions which may appear valid but which time invalidates. Hence, as Daubier says himself, many of the things which appeared firmly assured, an end to one phase of the Cultural Revolution, have revealed themselves evanescent and part of that process of attrition of which I was so aware, and which I lectured about at Yale in October 1971.

For in this acceleration of history which we now live, the Cultural Revolution is the most accelerated, the swiftest process which one has ever seen, and in this process "a day is like twenty years," as one cadre, who had undergone humiliation in the early days of the Revolution, was afterward fully rehabilitated, and is now honored, said to me. It is therefore not surprising that whole lifetimes seem to have been lived, for some of the political figures that emerged through the Cultural Revolution sank again into obscurity. And it is this rapidity, this swiftness of a "great leap" in consciousness, which we must always remember when we deal with persons or aspects of this extraordinary process. It is because Jean Daubier has captured, in his book, the swiftness of change from one event to the next, that his book is a most useful adjunct to anyone studying the history of China. I hope it will attract a great many readers.

HAN SUYIN

CONTENTS

A HISTORY
OF THE
CHINESE
CULTURAL
REVOLUTION

· THE ORIGINS OF THE ·
· PROLETARIAN CULTURAL ·
· REVOLUTION ·

The tradition of all dead generations weighs
like an Alp on the brains of the living.
—Karl Marx

The Chinese Communists have never offered a complete or detailed analysis of the causes of the Cultural Revolution and the
various forms it has taken. There have been a vast number of
articles and editorials on the subject, but these have been scattered
and fragmentary, appearing as the various needs and demands of
propaganda required, and even taken together give only a partial
picture, not an overall theory. What follows is an attempt to synthe-
size and to offer an interpretation which obviously does not pretend
to exhaust the multiple facets of the subject.

I intend first of all to show how certain distortions and contradictions which any socialist regime inherits from capitalism (and, in
the case of China, from both capitalism and feudalism) can furnish
the basis for a new class struggle for power, which in fact the
Chinese Cultural Revolution typifies.

In theory, the socialism that follows the overthrow of bourgeois
capitalism is a transition regime whose role is to prepare for the
advent of communism, which is viewed as an egalitarian social system in which each person will receive a portion of the social product
in accordance with his needs, and where the division of classes will
be abolished, as will its corollary, the state.

But this transition does not seem to occur very rapidly, and the
Chinese Communists themselves today affirm that this phase will

necessarily cover a very long period of history. There is nothing unusual about the fact that in the phase of socialism that precedes the arrival of communism various inequalities and social contradictions remain. This basic fact is also readily admitted by the Chinese Communists.

These contradictions and inequalities essentially derive from a social factor whose origins are lost in the mists of time: the division of labor. Over the centuries, by separating city from country, separating the branches of industry and the professions, creating specialties, specializers, and stereotyped, mechanical thinking, this division of labor, which has reached its highest point in our time, has caused deep schisms in human societies. Separating man from himself, it is basically responsible for every kind of alienation. It is also responsible for this plain, unadulterated, irrefutable fact, to which we have grown so accustomed that we are no longer in a position to fully measure its enormous consequences: the separation of manual and intellectual labor. It was this dissociation which led certain men to conceive of and study the methods of production, while others became the fragmented performers who carried them out but were cut off completely from the intellectual aspect of their efforts. This schism assumed gigantic proportions with the arrival of big industry within the framework of capitalism, which pressed science into its service, together with scientists and technicians, and made it a productive power independent of work. It was accompanied by a more than secular tradition of contempt for manual labor on the one hand, and of privileges for intellectual labor on the other. The division of labor has therefore led to the inequality of workers. These aftereffects of feudalism and capitalism still persist in the socialist regimes, which find them impossible to eliminate with one fell swoop, and we shall here make a rapid survey of their specific manifestations.

The university is one of the prime areas where the vestiges of the division of labor still exist. Indeed, the university sanctifies a distinct division between science and labor. It sets the bearer of knowledge at the opposite pole of production from the worker. Since socialist countries quite naturally need engineers and technicians of all kinds, they obviously cannot do without universities; but unless the universities in socialist countries undergo profound changes they will be incapable of contributing to the depolarization of labor. If they do not change they will simply reproduce the polarization inherited from the preceding regime, that opposition between the bearers of knowledge on the one hand and the mass of workers—deprived of science—on the other. Then, even though the capitalist method of production will have disappeared, an institution which reproduces the contradictions and distortions it engendered will remain.

There is, in fact, a good chance that if this separation continues to exist, intellectual labor will by force of habit continue to be fraught with privileges and considered an occupation nobler than manual labor. Intellectuals will therefore continue to form a coveted elite to which only a privileged few gain access. Teaching will remain selective, founded on competition, and will tend to stimulate individual ambitions rather than devotion to the collective good. In which case the regime can give all praise to the proletariat and proclaim that the workers are the masters of the country, but the real power of decision will nonetheless begin to slip into the hands of a social stratum of administrators and technicians whose concepts and interests may be diametrically opposed to those of the workers.

This same phenomenon persists as well in the realm of literature and the arts. In capitalist and feudal societies, culture is a privilege. The fact that in the large capitalist countries today culture is available to certain portions of the population besides the members of the ruling class does not radically alter this basic premise. Powerful structural and ideological strictures are such that the mass of manual workers will never have access to that culture. To be cultured, therefore, is to benefit from an advantage that eludes most of the population.

Thus, even if an artist emerges from the people, even if he remains poor (which is not all that unusual), his work becomes part of the heritage of the propertied class: either materially, because only the wealthy have the means to buy it, or because the knowledge this art contains is accessible only to members of the upper class or to those, more numerous today, whom this class has included in its cultural pale but who are rarely, if ever, members of the working class.

Socialist regimes therefore often inherit a considerable number of intellectuals who have acquired under the former system a culture founded ultimately on a notion of class superiority. Even if these intellectuals accept the new form of government—which is not necessarily the case—their habits and psychology remain far re-

moved from those of the workers. So there is a risk that their pur-
suits may well remain foreign to the interests and concerns of the
workers, both because of the more or less esoteric qualities of what
they produce and because they are expressing—and transmitting—
traditional values molded in an ideological context different from
that of revolutionary socialism. This division has a strong tendency
to solidify, to ossify into an establishment, by the concession of
various material advantages—higher salaries, better living quarters
—all of which combine to make the artists and writers in socialist
countries members of a privileged group whose way of life and
concerns become ever farther removed from those of the people in
general.

But the weightiest consequences of the division of labor may well
be in the relationships between the governed and those who govern.
Between those entrusted with the exercise of power and those whose
task it is to carry it out, there is obviously a difference. Any difference is a contradiction, and this contradiction exists in socialist
regimes as it does in others.

The origin of this difference also derives from the division of
labor. In early societies work productivity was very low, and most
men were fully occupied with the task of culling from nature whatever it took to keep body and soul together. But alongside this vast
majority there grew up a group who, freed from this directly productive work, were given the task of organizing the affairs of the
collectivity: distribution of jobs, organization of political affairs,
justice, science, the arts, etc. Little by little this group, by the very
fact of having been given the responsibility for apportioning the
products of labor among the members of the social group, began to
abuse this privilege, to live at the expense of the workers, to augment their resources and possessions above and beyond the average of what was needed in the society and what was strictly necessary for the exercise of their particular functions. Thus was born
exploitation, and society split up into antagonistic or opposing
classes.

Socialist forms of government are capable of suppressing exploitation by applying the principle of giving to each according to his
labor. But even the strict application of this principle is not enough
to do away with inequalities. Indeed, aside from the fact that in
modern economies capacities for work vary greatly, even when
there is equality of work and equal apportionment of the social

product, men nonetheless remain unequal in needs, therefore unequally rich from the same income. As long as society cannot give to everyone according to his needs, it will remain a society of relative scarcity and therefore of inequality.[1] The division of the gross national product remains a source of internal tensions, and men will continue to oppose one another. Certain social groups will make a special effort to try to obtain a larger share of the total for themselves. Those who have the best training or education, who are the most qualified, those whose work capacity is larger than most, will tend to increase their demands above and beyond what their work allows them, and thus to obtain privileges. One of the reasons for the continued existence of the state in socialist countries is, in fact, the need to enforce the proper division of the gross national product on the basis of work.

But the existence of the state then preserves another inequality, that of the rulers and the ruled. Those who exercise power are in the best position to obtain privileges and to exempt themselves from the principle of each according to his labor. This tendency cannot fail to exist among certain elements of the Communist Party and the state in whom individualism and egoism remain dominant characteristics. If it develops and grows, the struggle against it can turn into a major conflict which, since it occurs within the very framework of the administrative and political apparatus, will directly involve the power of the state.

In this context, the Great Proletarian Cultural Revolution launched in China in 1965 by Mao Tse-tung seems like a perfectly logical Marxist endeavor. As a Marxist, Mao Tse-tung believes that human societies will evolve toward communism, but he also thinks that, toward that end, any socialist government must bend its every effort to create conditions favorable to such a change.

The first task, in order to create the possibility of one day giving to each according to his needs, is obviously to develop the productive capacity of the country as much as possible. But in Mao's thinking such an undertaking will move toward fruition only as social inequalities are progressively eliminated, for if on the con-

---

[1] A society of inequality does not necessarily mean a society of privilege. If one strictly applies the principle of "to each according to his labor" there will be inequalities issuing from the diversity of capacities and needs, but no privileges. In such a case social differences would necessarily remain small. This distinction is indispensable to an understanding of the analysis which follows.

trary they were to increase they would bring about a regression toward exploitation, which in turn would play havoc with the planned structures, impede economic progress, and reintroduce the anarchy of the market.

That implies a struggle against the deeply rooted individualistic traditions which have been part and parcel of men's habits and mores for thousands of years and tend to make them conceive of their happiness in terms of individual rather than collective satisfaction. These ideological factors are a powerful stimulus to the growth of inequalities. To combat them calls for a complete disruption of customs and ways of thinking to eradicate from them any vestiges of mental attitudes carried over from the past, and requires also that the entire body of administrative, pedagogical, and cultural superstructures, where this influence is most likely to materialize to varying degrees, be recast.

The term "Cultural Revolution" must therefore be construed in its largest sense—that is, in the sense of all the various components that make up a civilization.

So it would appear that there are several lines of force involved in this Chinese Proletarian Cultural Revolution. One involves the transformation of teaching, so that it not only no longer makes a point of favoring intellectual labor to the detriment of manual labor, but attempts to erase any distinction between them. The ultimate aim of teaching, then, is not the immediate goal of preparing administrators needed by the society but the creation of a new man, prepared both physically and morally, who is both a worker and an intellectual. This transformation of teaching methods is actually being done in China today, where stress is being put on the concrete and pragmatic as it applies to production and work. Students are no longer drawn primarily from a particular social stratum, but from among workers and peasants who already know the meaning of work, and who will follow a relatively short training course. These innovations are experimental and are based essentially on two notions: one, that the best teaching derives from the practical application of any given work, and ought to take priority over so-called book learning; two, that promotion of students should not be made according to any elitist standards, that is, judging them by how much they know as individuals, but rather according to their political and ideological level and their measure of devotion to the collective enterprise.

In the realm of literature and the arts, the Cultural Revolution seems above all to have eliminated from their posts of responsibility those intellectuals who were judged to be still under the influence of bourgeois thought. The result has been the elimination of privileges which intellectuals formerly enjoyed, and many spend time in factories and people's communes where, it is presumed, extended contact with the workers is giving them a new way of looking at life and at their fellow men. The Chinese press makes a constant point of reminding its readers how vital it is to create a new art and literature extolling strictly proletarian and revolutionary values. The new Peking opera productions offer at least one concrete proof of the success of this effort.

At the heart of the Cultural Revolution was the relationship between the rulers and those they ruled, between those in power and the people. Mao Tse-tung emphasized that it was a political revolution, and all during its development the press kept pointing out that that was the basic question. This inherent aspect underlies the historical events themselves.

We noted earlier that in socialist regimes the lingering persistence of inequalities tends to result in a struggle for the division of the social product, and in the stubborn effort of certain social groups to abrogate to themselves a number of privileges. This tendency has the best chance of taking hold with some degree of efficacy among people in positions of authority. Their authority can, in fact, help them consolidate the advantages of their position. What happens then, with a small fraction of Communists in positions of authority, is that certain privileged groups appear. If this phenomenon is not eliminated by the Party leaders who have remained faithful to the revolutionary line, there is a risk that little by little a real social elite will grow up. This privileged group will then try to do away with the socialist norms of division according to one's labor, with the result that inequalities will increase rather than decrease and a neo-bourgeoisie will appear. The differences between the rulers and those they rule will become greater and solidify, instead of withering away and thus creating a basis for communism—in which the state, being useless, disappears. The importance of this phenomenon depends on a variable time factor. In China before the Cultural Revolution it was of minor importance. In the U.S.S.R., however, the growth of inequalities in the period after World War II was considerable, and during the past fifteen years has been even more marked.

The cause of this phenomenon has not been, as certain Trotsky-ists have somewhat dogmatically declared,[2] the poverty of a given country. It is not because the U.S.S.R. in the twenties was poor, or that China today is relatively poor, that privileged social strata tend to form. In a collective effort, on the contrary, poverty can act as a powerful stimulant for equalitarianism, which will give it a co-herence, whereas inequality would be divisive and could ultimately decimate its least privileged echelons.

The advent of socialism in the so-called wealthy nations would probably not have prevented the social product from being divided not according to one's need but according to one's labor. These societies would have remained societies of relative scarcity. The fact that their gross national product was high would not necessarily engender equality and could, on the contrary, serve to exacerbate the chase after privileges.

It is a question of what standards of division are utilized, and this is not an economic element but ultimately depends on ideological factors, and on the ability of the socialist regime to overcome indi-vidualistic tendencies which tradition and habit have implanted in people's minds, and to replace them with the basic notion of collec-tivism. This is a difficult task which involves a daily struggle, con-stantly renewed, and it is doubtless one of the bases of Mao's theory which pictures the revolution as a never ending battle. It is also, in my opinion, the underlying reason for the battle Mao and his fol-lowers had to wage against another group of Party leaders, espe-cially Liu Shao-ch'i, who was then the head of state, a struggle for which the Cultural Revolution is best known abroad.

The men who make up the ranks of the Communist Party are no different from other men, and men, according to what Mao is

---

[2] Trotsky himself, in a book quite representative of his thinking, *The Revolution Betrayed*, clearly says so, as do the following quotations from Publications of the Fourth International: "Bureaucratic tendencies which impede the workers' move-ment will also necessarily appear after the proletarian revolution. But it is quite obvious *that the poorer the society* whence the revolution has come, the more this 'law' will apply, and the more violent will be the forms that bureaucratic tendency assumes; and the more dangerous it may be for the development of socialism" (p. 48). "*The basis* of bureaucratic authority is the paucity of articles of consump-tion, and the struggle on the part of everyone that results therefrom" (p. 96). "The sense and substance of the Soviet Thermidor is beginning to become clear to us. *Poverty* and the uncultivated state of the masses materialize once again in the menacing forms of a leader armed with a powerful cudgel" (p. 97).

reported to have told André Malraux, don't like to carry on the revolution all their lives.[3]

Once power has been seized, the Communist leaders who are going to exercise it are confronted with a new and insidious test to which some, no matter how brilliantly they have performed under other circumstances, will succumb. The rigors of clandestinity, the harsh demands of partisan life, are no more than a memory. There are some who acquire a taste for comfort and an easy life. They slip into work habits characterized by a mixture of unimaginative routine, smugness about themselves, and toughness with their subordinates. Material and wage privileges are sought after, at times obtained, and these tendencies are on their way to becoming institutions. Between the simple workers and this segment of the Party leadership the close liaison, the permanent dialogue, the equality which marked those heroic times when the revolution imposed the same dangers and communicated the same hopes to all, tend to weaken.

At this stage there is still only bureaucratism, an evil which is not yet generalized; serious for the regime, but not yet really alarming. But if this process continues, the accumulation of bad habits can corrupt and even ruin the revolutionary faith of certain leaders. The taste for pleasure, the increasing individualism, lead to another stage. In the very midst of the revolutionary regime there appear new mandarins who no longer see in other men anything but either means or obstacles, and who place their responsibilities in the service of selfish goals. For men such as these, revolutionary politics, with its equalitarian resonances and the militant abstention that it demands, becomes in the long run intolerable, and they bend their every effort to thwart it.

The Chinese Communists' assertion that the Cultural Revolution was a struggle between the proletariat and the bourgeoisie may have come as a surprise to many. Some people expressed astonishment that a second revolution was necessary in a Communist regime against a bourgeoisie which for more than twenty years had been deprived of political and economic power. The statement would be false if it referred to the traditional Chinese bourgeoisie, which

[3] An interview published in *Le Figaro littéraire*, under the title "My Meeting with Mao," and incorporated into his volume *Antimemoires* (published in France by Editions Gallimard, and in the United States by Holt, Rinehart & Winston, 1967). The text of this conversation was disseminated unofficially by various revolutionary groups throughout 1967.

today is indeed but a shadow of its former self. This assertion can, however, be understood if one realizes that it refers to a neobourgeoisie made up of those who, thanks to the continuing existence of inequalities, have been able to acquire certain privileges which they attempt to augment and which they defend by trying to impose political views opposed to Mao's militant rigorousness.

Socialist regimes preach, and practice, the dictatorship of the proletariat. They brook no opposition, and whatever opposition may exist in principle does not enjoy freedom of action or expression as the West understands the term. But since social contradictions do remain, it is obvious that antagonistic political currents cannot fail to exist. Opposition to the official Party line is inevitable, but it is obliged to resort to clandestine or underhanded methods to impose itself. The only way it can survive and operate is by making full use of the only path still open to it—by nibbling patiently at the zones of power in the very midst of the Communist Party, carefully dissimulating its real views beneath an appearance of political and ideological loyalty. The strict regime and the doctrinaire rigor that the Communist parties establish in those societies where they hold power tend to render their opponents much more insidious.

In a socialist country, political life is the result of a specific series of factors, and it appears as a sum of conflicts which, for the reasons just mentioned, are concentrated within the framework of the Party itself and which, depending on circumstances, are of varying intensity. From without, these various oppositions may seem to be a conflict among proletarian revolutionaries equally motivated by Marxist faith, but in fact they are *the expression of a new form of the class struggle.* Beneath the apparently monolithic edifice of the Communist Party, beneath the seeming adherence to Marxist ideology, an unending series of concealed struggles is ferociously going on.

Lui Shao-ch'i's opposition to Mao Tse-tung must be viewed in this context. It cannot be thought of as a quarrel between two people any more than it can be considered a doctrinaire conflict pure and simple. It was, in fact, the political expression of a whole complex of class contradictions in which both social and ideological factors were involved, and which were nurtured by a substratum of material privileges, bureaucratic tendencies, and difficulties in adapting to the accelerated rhythm of Maoist policies.

This makes it possible for us to understand that the tactics adopted by Mao Tse-tung during the Cultural Revolution were far more complex and subtle than simply stripping his opponents of their functions and influence by administrative or strong-arm methods. Mao Tse-tung fought his opponents while at the same time trying to undermine the ideological and social base of their policies.

The Chinese Cultural Revolution set as its basic and ultimate goal the remaking of the human spirit. It is in this light that the watchword should be understood: *Dousze*—Combat individualism. It was a question of assuring the preeminence of a collectivist conception of the world in place of the traditionally egocentric vision that man has had of himself and the society he lives in.

To transform people's minds in this sense is to dry up at the wellspring the force of the tradition which, deeply rooted in man's mores and secular customs, impels him to the primordial search for his own satisfaction; it is also to discourage the ambition, the "careerism" which contributes so importantly to the increase in inequalities.

As soon as a socialist regime consciously tries to eliminate inequalities, it must bend every effort to make certain that there are as few social differences as possible. This brings up a very delicate point. Men no longer have the incentive to work that they formerly had, that is, the prospect of material improvement. The absence of privileges for minorities does away with the compass that they constituted for the majority. Therefore Mao Tse-tung declared that these material incentives would be replaced by moral incentives. By which he meant simply that both the workers and the people in positions of authority should be working for socialism, out of revolutionary conviction. This implied a complete reversal of ideas and the disappearance of egotism. It was a challenge offered to money and the fetishism of material goods—not to man himself, as some Western commentators have maintained, I believe without having thought the matter through. On the contrary, it strikes me as indicating great confidence in mankind, since the entire premise is based on the conviction that humanity can rid itself of its ideological chains.

To transform mental attitudes consists of implanting revolutionary ideas in social life. We should not be misled into believing that this operation consists merely of learning Mao's doctrine through a study of his writings, as the dissemination of millions of copies of his works during the Cultural Revolution might lead one to think.

The politicalization of the Chinese masses was accomplished above all by a tough, practical struggle which was very complex and often very bitter. The study of Mao's work was conceived of as a guide to clarify concrete problems as they arose in the course of that struggle, and what was learned from them had to be applied as quickly as possible. It was therefore not a question of "indoctrination" based on the constant repetition of a certain number of themes, although that aspect did exist: it consisted above all of learning the revolution as you went along.

What it amounted to, really, was that the population was mobilized to comment on and criticize anything and everything in the society which had been subjected to the influence of tradition, including teaching, art, and literature. It was also necessary for the people to be able to criticize the workings of the state, since the distance between the rulers and the ruled was one of the crucial problems. This led to a movement of critical comment on the people in positions of authority whose purpose was to bring the rulers and the masses closer together. It was an effort to recast the structures of power—founded at first on the principles of the Paris Commune, but later using another, more elaborate formula, that of the "revolutionary committee of the three-in-one combination"[4]— in a way that would give the people a greater say in the affairs of state and to buttress the democratic and revolutionary aspect of the regime. The goal of the undertaking was to institutionalize the right of the ruled to criticize their rulers and to integrate representatives of the ruled, chosen directly by them, into the new forms of power.

Such an undertaking is in itself a revolution, because it inevitably meets with some kind of resistance, which must be overcome by vigorous effort. This resistance comes from all those who, relying on the persistence of inequalities, have already managed to carve out for themselves a privileged or a relatively privileged situation, and it is made all the stronger by the fact that they include people in authority in both the Party and the administration. Contrary to what has often been said abroad, these people have never been more than a minority in China, but their positions enabled them to maneuver with considerable effectiveness. They were also able to make good use of the comparative unwieldiness of the Party appa-

[4] These committees were to have equal numbers of elected representatives of the people, of Party cadres, and of military representatives. See Chapter 5.

ratus, as well as to utilize various bureaucratic and conservative tendencies.

The presence of dissidents in the very seat of Party authority and in the different divisions of the Communist organization made Mao's task considerably more complicated, all the more so since this opposition continued to declare itself not only Marxist but also Maoist, mouthed the official Party slogans, and kept its real opinions carefully to itself. A classic purge of high-echelon officials would have served to cut back the most obvious branches. It was much more difficult to locate the regional branches of the opposition, and those of the middle hierarchy. Administrative inquiries were virtually helpless to find this level of opposition in all its ramifications. Mao Tse-tung therefore opted for a tactic whose purpose was to force the enemy to give up some of its entrenched positions and to reduce it to less advantageous ones. He tried to break up the opposition's slow but steady "nibbling," which had the weight of custom on its side, in an effort to bring it out into the open.

Since the distance between the rulers and those they ruled threatened to let the power slip imperceptibly into the hands of the political representatives of a neobourgeoisie, Mao had the idea of calling upon the masses to examine the conduct of the leading cadres at all levels. It was they themselves who would have to determine which of their rulers were still worthy of their trust and which were acting like new mandarins; it was they who would have to denounce their flagrant excesses and, where it existed, their corruption.

The cadres' reaction to this movement would enable one to judge their real feelings; one would soon see which of them had not lost contact with the people, still considered themselves servants of the people, and had retained both democratic work methods and a simple mode of life. The opposition could not fail to be denounced, and in reacting to the denunciations would reveal itself to the world.

As a matter of fact, the initial phases of the Cultural Revolution were marked by vigorous efforts, through a variety of pressures, to prevent the population from voicing its criticisms, to keep it in as passive a state as possible. Later this tactic on the part of the opposition changed as the population's involvement in the mass criticism increased. At that point the dissidents made every effort to foment or exploit divisions and, by many and often devious means, to muddy the waters and break up the unity of the Maoists. As a result they were forced to take certain risks and reveal more openly their hostility to Mao's political programs. Mao then took advantage of the situation to neutralize them and progressively strip them of whatever power they possessed.

In tracing the beginnings of the Cultural Revolution I have up to this point refrained from mentioning the external factors that influenced it. At this juncture it will be useful to consider the most important of them: the Sino-Soviet conflict.[5]

A case can be made for dating the origin of the split as 1956, the year in which Khrushchev in a "secret" but world-famous report condemned the Stalinist era and set Soviet policy on a new course. The Chinese Communist Party never accepted the repudiation of Stalin, and never concealed its hostility toward Khrushchev's theses.

As we know, Sino-Soviet dissension grew more and more acute, passing from the problems of how to build socialism to the problem of foreign policy toward other Communist countries, until in 1962 it became so bitter that it exploded in public. Worsening ever since, it has affected relationships not only between the two Communist parties but also between the two states.

Although Mao Tse-tung has never resorted to the same methods used by Stalin, and although in Stalin's day China suffered from his errors, Mao saw Khrushchev's "de-Stalinization" program in the Soviet Union as a pernicious phenomenon.

In the West a poorly informed part of public opinion often sees Khrushchev's attempt to "liberalize" the Soviet regime with a certain degree of sympathy. It inspires quite different feelings and judgments in China. We must clarify this point if we are to understand fully the underlying causes of the Cultural Revolution.

The Chinese Communists view Khrushchev's policy as an abandonment of the revolution characterized by the explicit rejection of the idea of the dictatorship of the proletariat and other important Marxist tenets. In the eyes of the Maoists, Khrushchev's efforts resulted in a dismantling of the collectivistic economy, as well as in a betrayal of proletarian internationalism by the proclamation of peaceful coexistence and, what is more, collaboration with the United States, which the Peking press called a "New Holy Alliance" whose global goal was to maintain the status quo and prevent revo-

---

[5] There were two other very important external factors: First, the intensification of the class struggle on a world scale, which led Communist China to assume new and greater responsibilities toward the world revolution. Second, the evolution of the Communist camp, which was marked by the decreased role of Russian leadership.

lutions. But Khrushchevism, in the eyes of the Chinese Communists, is also, and perhaps especially, the rupture of that close and delicate bond which is supposed to unite the Communist Party and the masses; it is the constant, uncurbed growth of a privileged caste among the functionaries and dignitaries of the Soviet regime: the moderate, conciliatory foreign policy of the Russian leaders is, according to the Chinese, simply the extension of their tendency to backslide into bourgeois habits and a corruption that has henceforth spread to their internal policies.

The disastrous evolution of the Soviet Union during these past few years has been, for Mao Tse-tung, an alarm signal. China could also fall into the same rut, thus seriously compromising the revolution.

Weren't there a number of disconcerting symptoms of middle-classism among a certain faction of the Chinese leaders, indicative of at least the possibility of a phenomenon similar to Soviet revisionism? True, the difference between the lowest and the highest salary scales had never been very great under Mao, but that was only one aspect of the matter. The fact was, the Chinese had clearly drifted away from the situation that existed during the war against Japan and during the struggle for national liberation. At that time, of course, the cadres had no salaries but only basic foodstuffs and other absolute necessities; their way of life had been extremely simple and had hardly differed from that of the masses. They had no special privileges, unless moving constantly from one end of China to the other—to fight wherever the situation required, under the most difficult circumstances imaginable—can be called a privilege.

For two or three years after the liberation of China the situation of the cadres was essentially the same; and then, little by little, certain elements managed to arrogate to themselves certain material advantages. True, in post-Liberation China there had never been the flagrant attribution of privileges among the high functionaries which had become so widespread in the Soviet Union over the past several years. There had never been, in China, any "white-curtain stores."[6] Chinese officials, except when their state duties demanded otherwise, bicycled or took buses from one place to another, and ate their meals in the workers' canteens. It was

---

[6] In Eastern Europe the term "white-curtain stores" applies to those stores reserved exclusively for high functionaries and their families, where it is possible to obtain high-quality merchandise, often imported, which is not generally available on the open market.

usual to see them playing ping-pong or basketball with the workers in the two fifteen-minute breaks, at 10:00 A.M. and 4:00 P.M., during the working day. Nevertheless, some things are obvious and others less obvious. Beginning in 1951 a system of salaries for functionaries had been instituted. Modified and enlarged in 1955 and 1956, this system created a large number of salary categories. For some functionaries seniority and merit meant higher pay and, on occasion, better housing. Special schools were set up for the children of certain high functionaries, in spite of Mao Tse-tung's opposition. All this may seem a tempest in a teapot—and in fact even the most privileged functionaries were not all that much better off materially than the workers—but the tendency for these differences to grow and wax ever greater was present. Whereas Mao was saying that the cadres ought to be the people's servants and enjoy no special privilege, Liu Shao-ch'i could be found proclaiming in one of his books that the Party ought to "create every facility" for the members of government, thus allowing them to work and exercise their functions under optimum conditions.

In some publishing houses the cadres were paid extra for translating foreign works outside the scope of their normal functions. Certain writers and journalists augmented their salaries by free-lancing for various periodicals. In the film industry there were cases of actors and scenarists claiming, and obtaining, higher than normal salaries and private houses replete with every comfort, which they said they needed because of the creative nature of their work. Some requested and obtained soundproof apartments, again citing the demands of their work as the overriding reason for their special needs.

This is hardly comparable with the extravagance and luxury evident among the "bourgeoisie" in the Soviet Union or the capitalist countries, but the way was open, and some were ready and waiting to set out upon it at full speed, with all the attendant consequences.

In addition to these limited but tangible phenomena of social differentiations there were the psychological elements which accompany the exercise of responsibilities. Considerations of rank and grade often went hand in glove with notions of prestige. Some persons in positions of authority became authoritarian, overweening, without the least consideration for their subordinates but bowing and scraping to their superiors. Progressively, conditions were being created whereby power, and those who exercised it, were separated

more and more from the people, thus opening up the route to
Khrushchevism.

After the Sino-Soviet rupture of 1960, and Khrushchev's withdrawal of Soviet experts from China, the Maoist regime could no
longer look to the outside world for help and henceforth had to do
battle on two fronts. To move forward China had only its own
forces to rely upon. Mao Tse-tung was counting heavily on the
enormous capacity for work of the vast Chinese population, then
some 700,000,000 strong. For that a high pitch of excitement and
militant enthusiasm were necessary; Mao needed the country kept
at a level of uninterrupted revolution. However, the presence within
the confines of the Party itself of certain neobourgeois elements
more concerned about their own privileges and special favors than
about the revolution, tending toward moderation and conciliation,
represented a real obstacle to Maoist policy. Every stage of the
endeavor, in fact, would be impeded by people in positions of
authority who, weary of the heady excitement of major revolutionary campaigns, had become proponents of more traditional methods. As early as 1958 the Great Leap Forward had suffered from
the effects of certain bureaucratic brakes, and since that time Mao
had watched the opposition grow constantly hardier and bolder.

The reestablishment of the people's militia in 1958 and the new
military policy had been the occasion for a conflict with the Minister
of Defense, P'eng Teh-huai, who advocated building a Chinese
army along more or less classic lines, emphasizing technology and
armaments to the detriment of the guerrilla-type army that had sur-
vived up to then. But to follow this policy would have required
massive aid from the Soviet Union, hence good relations with
Khrushchev. On that Mao was adamant. The showdown on the
matter occurred in September 1959, when P'eng, defeated in a fate-
ful meeting of the Central Committee at Lushan, was dismissed
from his post, to be replaced by Lin Piao.[7] (This event was closely
related to the beginning of the Cultural Revolution.)

But that did not put an end to the opposition. The vicissitudes of
the Great Leap Forward, the difficult years that followed, which
were made even harder by a series of natural calamities and the
withdrawal of the Soviet experts, all gave the opportunity for certain
Party leaders to question the policy Mao Tse-tung had followed so

---

[7] Lin was to be, until 1971, head of the armed forces and Mao's "close comrade-
in-arms."

far. Accusations of "subjectivism" were made, and of excessive haste. The charge of demagogy was leveled, and of the "itch" for revolution. The people's communes were likened by some to Fourier-like socialistic communities. There was talk of a return to utopian socialism. In the concert of voices three stood out: that of Liu Shao-ch'i, chairman of the government of the People's Republic of China; that of Teng Hsiao-p'ing, general secretary of the Chinese Communist Party; and that of Peking's mayor, P'eng Chen.

In 1962, judging the time to be propitious, P'eng Teh-huai requested his rehabilitation. Various literary works offering thinly veiled satire of the Party were published. For his part, Liu Shao-ch'i had printed a new edition of his book *How to Be a Good Communist*, in which he made scathing attacks on "leftists" he avoided naming and at the same time called for peace within the Party. There were also a great number of insinuations clearly aimed at Mao Tse-tung, which in China today are believed to have been meant to prepare public opinion for a political campaign similar to Khrushchev's denunciation of Stalin. On another front, Lu Ting-yi, director of the Central Committee's propaganda bureau, roundly criticized certain measures taken at Mao's suggestion during the Great Leap Forward, in particular the creation of schools in which students divided their time between academic work and manual labor. Lu Ting-yi, who in the past had often recommended China's following the example of Soviet teaching, lent his weight from 1960 on to reducing the roles of manual labor and political studies in the curriculum. It was at his behest that the study of classics and of calligraphy was reintroduced into the primary schools.

Had Mao at that time lost power, as has sometimes been suggested abroad, quite unreliably, to my way of thinking? It is highly unlikely, for during this entire period the policy of the Chinese Communist Party, be it internal or external, remained basically the same. What is more, we know that at the Tenth Plenary Session of the Central Committee, in September 1962, Mao succeeded in having his censors' tendencies criticized as right-wing deviations. Nonetheless, for reasons still not completely clear, this opposition, which had shown both its tenacity and strength, was neither eliminated nor purged, and Mao continued to govern surrounded by these dissident elements.

Mao must have suspected that this hardening of the opposition, these indications of dissidence which had been multiplying, had something to do with the offensive that Khrushchev had publicly launched against his regime toward the end of 1961. He doubtless lived in the shadow of the hated Khrushchevian revisionism. His prestige and agility had enabled him thus far to cope with this current, but after his death, could a new Khrushchev be prevented from appearing in China to repeat what had happened in the Soviet Union?

Mao Tse-tung's reaction was not long in coming. In 1963 he was to launch the Socialist Education Movement, a forerunner of the Cultural Revolution and partially founded on similar principles. This movement aimed at combating the influence of both tradition and individualism, and at minimizing the possibility of the corruption of the revolutionary regime known as revisionism.

There were, in fact, certain alarming signs. During the "difficult years," 1959–61, a number of deviations had appeared. There were reports of embezzlement and malfeasance, as well as an upsurge of private enterprise in certain rural districts, with the aid and encouragement of a faction of Party officials.

In 1964 a great number of exhibitions were arranged in rural areas, some of which were meant to correct cases of injustice or fraud, while others told of life under the old regime, to educate the youth as well as to remind people of all ages of the dangers of a reversion to that state of affairs if the practices in question were not checked. At the same time administrative officials and intellectuals were sent out into the countryside as part of an overall campaign. They had a threefold purpose: they were to draw up reports on life in the rural areas; they were to enlarge their views through contact with the concrete realities of rural life; and taking part in physical labor would contribute to their own proletariatization, in both the political and moral sense of the term.

In the cities the Party newspapers began to publish a large number of theoretical articles. Time and time again it was stressed that every revolutionary, as well as counterrevolutionary, effort starts from some literary or artistic terrain. All sorts of arguments were developed on this score to demonstrate the character of class culture and the primacy of political over artistic criteria. The transformation of the art form known as Peking opera dates from this time. This art form became the vehicle for modern revolutionary themes. In June 1964 a festival of the new Peking opera took place in the Chinese capital. In the period just preceding, plays such as *The Raid on the White Tiger Regiment*, which illustrates an episode from the Korean War, and a ballet entitled *Red Detachment of Women*, based on an episode on Hainan Island during the Civil War, had been created.

Throughout the country scenes of the old society were reproduced with life-size clay statues. The bitter memories of the past were thus brought back to life for new generations. One of these exhibitions was called *Rent Collection Courtyard*: in it one saw peasants obliged to hand over a portion of their harvest to the landlord, who forced them to submit to all kinds of humiliations. These works were widely publicized. Reproduced as illustrations, filmed, collected and used as traveling exhibitions, they formed an important part of ideological education, an example of art as a public service.

It would appear that the Socialist Education Movement was one element of an overall plan whose first aim was to consolidate the bases of socialism in rural areas.[8] This was also the goal of the "four clean-ups"—in the political, ideological, economic, and organizational areas—which were an integral part of the SEM and took place mainly in the rural areas. The movement's purpose was also to counteract the growth of material incentives, nepotism, the misappropriation of public funds, the black market, and favoritism, insofar as they inevitably led to the growth of rich, or relatively rich, peasants. Cases of arbitrary and immoral conduct by some people in authority were brought out. Bureaucratic excesses were being committed. The increasing number of hierarchical levels of authority proved that the power was escaping from the people. In certain communes some authorities had got into the habit of allocating work points to themselves by taking the figures for the three peasants with the best scores, dividing by three, and giving themselves the corresponding figure.

Thus the mass organizations were brought back to life, including the associations of poor peasants and the women's organizations. In his report of January 1, 1964, Chou En-lai reminded the People's Congress that the basic point of the Socialist Education Movement was to mobilize the masses. It was the people who, from top to bottom, had to examine the conduct of the authorities and, in cases of abuse, denounce them. Cadres of the army and the Party were divided into teams and sent into rural communes to check and see

---

[8] The Cultural Revolution, which succeeded it, aimed specifically at resolving urban problems. See point 13 of the Sixteen-Point Party Decision, a vital document of the Cultural Revolution which is reproduced as Appendix 3 in this book.

how they were being run. They gathered the people together to hear and assess their complaints and act on their unresolved differences. If necessary, they dismissed corrupt cadres or those whose revolutionary ardor was insufficient. At the same time this practical application of class struggle was taking place, a vast movement was undertaken to study the works of Mao Tse-tung, in order to assure a lively and complete education.

Morality, which the difficult years had put to the test in certain areas, was encouraged, as was criticism of certain aspects of the cultural conditioning of society which had feudal origins. Typically, the *People's Daily* cited a card game that was enjoying a certain success among young peasants. The game was called "lord." Whoever went out first was called "lord"; the next person out was the wealthy peasant; and the last person out was the poor peasant, who had to ante up to the others.

During the time of the Socialist Education Movement the battle against superstition, which was still more or less strong, was stepped up. In 1964 the sale of objects having to do with its implementation or practice was forbidden.

It was also in 1964 that the SEM began to spread to the cities. There were a number of critical articles dealing with literary and artistic matters. The works of poets such as Tu Fu and Tcheu Houcheng came under attack, and at the same time numerous essays and articles were published on the problems of literature and cinema from the beginning of the twentieth century. In schools and universities more and more time was devoted to ideological discussion and to the struggle against revisionism.

Control teams were sent into the factories. A goodly number of people left the city to go and work in the country, to participate in the "four clean-ups" for periods of up to a year. In some cases up to two-thirds of certain production units were sent into the countryside. In all, nearly five million people took part in these activities.

It is not surprising that this vast political and ideological campaign met with some resistance from Mao Tse-tung's opponents. The internal struggles of that time are difficult to detail with any degree of accuracy. I have relied for information on texts published by revolutionary groups during the Cultural Revolution, but these texts suffer from the double shortcoming of being too sketchy and lacking in nuances. Furthermore, they are not official texts and in principle are only the responsibility of those who wrote them. In spite of these reservations, however, they do offer one interesting piece of information: in particular, they seem to demonstrate that the conflicts that appeared during the Socialist Education Movement were the forerunners of those that would later arise during the Cultural Revolution itself.

In May 1963 Mao Tse-tung had written a ten-point document intended to guide the Socialist Education Movement. In it he emphasized that two interlocking problems were involved: on the one hand the class struggle, and on the other the dissidence of a handful of people in authority whose orientation was not toward socialism but toward a return to capitalism. In his view it was necessary to mobilize the masses, who, guided by the true revolutionaries of the Party, could unmask those authorities. Thus according to Mao's concept—which we shall see developed during the Cultural Revolution—the masses would educate themselves by confronting concrete problems and by forcibly immersing themselves in the practical matters of the class struggle, at the same time cleaning up the Party organizations and reinforcing the revolutionary aspects of the regime. To attain the latter goal by resorting to the mobilization of the masses, rather than through measures adopted by the Central Committee of the Party, is characteristic of Mao's thinking, and it was this notion that was to preside over the beginning and evolution of the Cultural Revolution.

According to the published texts, the authorities in question were not long in reacting. Their principal political representative, Liu Shao-ch'i, personally took charge of the SEM in the region of Taoyuan. In keeping with a method current in China, his goal was to carry out an experiment there that he intended to implement later in other areas. His tactic was not to fight the Socialist Education Movement head-on, but to influence wherever possible the direction it took, at the same time diverting it from the targets it had set up. We shall see similar situations arising throughout the Cultural Revolution.

From these same texts it emerges that the work team operating in Taoyuan under the personal direction of Liu Shao-ch'i's wife, Wang Kuang-mei, was not following the precepts of Mao's "ten points" and in fact had set itself quite different goals. The work team was carefully avoiding any involvement of the commune peasants in the discussions or investigations. Meetings were held quasi-clandestinely behind closed doors; Wang Kuang-mei herself was there under an assumed name. What the group did in this instance was investigate a considerable number of middle- and lower-echelon Party cadres, some of whom were attacked and removed from their posts. Thus the real targets were cleverly made to disappear, and as soon as the Taoyuan experiment became known, the same tactics were used in other places. At this point Mao Tse-tung had to step in. He drafted a second, twenty-three-point document on the problems of the Socialist Education Movement in the rural areas, in which he again emphasized the class nature of the struggle, called on the peasants to mobilize themselves, and reminded the people that only a tiny minority of revisionist cadres were the target of the present attacks. Liu Shao-ch'i's methods were described in the document and condemned as "left in appearance but right in essence."

The articles of the Red Guards and various revolutionary groups make clear the diametrically opposed viewpoints expressed by the two highest-ranking Party leaders, and their radically different methods. It is fairly safe to assume that Liu Shao-ch'i used his considerable influence to impede or subvert, sometimes directly and sometimes indirectly, Mao's policies. It is also highly likely that by the end of 1965, on the eve of the Cultural Revolution, this conflict between the two Chinese leaders had reached the stage of thinly disguised warfare.

In Mao's mind the future of the regime had not been secured, nor was vigilance against foreign enemies enough to assure it: everything depended on which direction the Party would take in the future.

The struggle between Mao Tse-tung and his opponents crystallized and took the form of a repeated series of attacks and counterattacks. From then on a decisive confrontation was inevitable. The curtain was rising on the Great Proletarian Cultural Revolution.

Postscript 1973

Since the Ninth Party Congress, held in April 1969, Ch'en Po-ta[9] has been purged and certain aspects of the late Lin Piao's policies have been reexamined. For the past two years there has been a vigorous political and ideological campaign against ultraleftism. None of this, however, has made the above analysis of the origins and goals of the Cultural Revolution obsolete. In the realms of art and education revolutionary innovations are proceeding apace.

[9] Mao's former secretary, who came to prominence as adviser to the Group in Charge of the Cultural Revolution.

Nonetheless, one can see that the antileftist campaign has been accompanied by a lessening of ideological tension, especially in the literary area, where a certain pluralism is once again allowed.

Similarly, the effort to prevent the resurgence of a privileged class among the Party cadres is still going on, but here it is hard to tell whether the Chinese leaders have any precise policy aside from the cadres' systematic participation in manual labor. This policy, which is of major importance, sends the cadres to May Seventh schools[10] for relatively long periods of time—generally two years—to alternate intensive courses in Marxism-Leninism with equally intensive stints in production.

The question of reducing the cadres' salaries and eliminating the few material advantages they enjoyed—which never amounted to very much—was not clearly resolved during the Cultural Revolution. The argument most often heard was that putting such measures into effect could possibly lead to some sort of "economist" deviation.

The other continuing problem is that of the relationship between the cadres and the masses, and the tendency on the part of the former to be authoritarian. One thing which clearly emerged from the Cultural Revolution was that workers and students alike harbored deep resentment against many cadres, and this hostility nurtured ultraleftist movements. The tendency to sweep great numbers of cadres aside, and the workers' considerable resistance to reinstating those who were ultimately guilty of no more than political peccadilloes, created a problem which Mao in 1967 admitted was serious. In fact things got so out of hand in this area that at one point the authorities spoke of "anarchy." It was this situation which led to the condemnation of the ultraleft.

Today in China the emphasis is on discipline, and efforts are obviously being made to restore to the cadres an authority which they all but lost in 1967. The revolutionary committees have tended increasingly to remain in the background, and it is difficult to say just how the "grass-roots" control of the cadres, which was one of the chief objectives of the Cultural Revolution, really works. However, it can be seen that the press constantly reminds the cadres

---

[10] The name comes from the date of a 1966 directive in which the Chairman outlined a program for furthering socialist education through "military-educational, military-agricultural, military-industrial, and military-civilian work." Generally this means that people from the cities, especially those in professional and "white-collar" occupations, go to work in the countryside with the peasants and soldiers.

to maintain a simple life style and keep in close touch with the masses. A number of articles stress the necessity for the cadres to make sure to avoid the "four airs": the bureaucratic air, the apathetic air, the smug air, and the stuck-up air. The lessons of the Cultural Revolution are still very much with the Chinese people, but it is still too early to fully evaluate their lasting effect.

In the latter half of October 1972 a movement was started to have the cadres send their children to share the workers' life. This was but another manifestation of the continuing effort to try to avoid the creation of hereditary privileges in this part of the population. The November 1966 episode of the *Lien Tung*[11] has shown how dangerous any "lineage theory" could be.

Paris, April 1973

[11] See Chapter 3.

I

NOVEMBER 1965 TO JANUARY 1967:

THE CONFLICT GROWS CLEARER

Revolution is a drama filled with passion.
—Mao Tse-tung

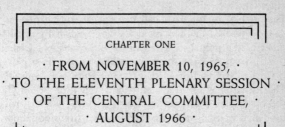
· FROM NOVEMBER 10, 1965, ·
· TO THE ELEVENTH PLENARY SESSION ·
· OF THE CENTRAL COMMITTEE, ·
· AUGUST 1966 ·

1. The First Battles

The Attack on Wu Han and P'eng Chen's Resistance

The initial phases of the Cultural Revolution were not spectacular. Until May 1966 they consisted primarily of a struggle within the Communist Party hierarchy and revolved around the repercussions caused by a series of attacks on the writer Wu Han. The upshot of this struggle was the elimination of a group of important personalities in the regime, in April 1966, which caused a considerable stir. The active period of the Cultural Revolution can be dated from these events.

Official Chinese Communist Party texts give the beginning of the Cultural Revolution as November 10, 1965. It was on that day that a Shanghai daily, *Wen Hui Pao* (*Evening News*), published an article violently attacking a play entitled *Hai Jui Dismissed from Office*. Written in 1961 by Wu Han, a former history professor, a leading non-Party intellectual, and until 1964 a deputy mayor of Peking, the play described the suffering of Soochow peasants at the hands of unjust Ming Dynasty officials who had confiscated their lands. Hai Jui, a fair-minded official, intervened on the peasants' behalf and appealed to the emperor for the return of their land. For his efforts he was removed from office. Denouncing the abuses of autocracy and exalting Hai Jui's steadfastness of soul under trying conditions, the play was clearly alluding to the conditions of the peasants under the commune system, and to the protests and subsequent dismissal of P'eng Teh-huai in 1959. It is interesting to note that it was in 1961, when P'eng was requesting his rehabilitation, with the support of a number of Party members, that the play was produced.

The attacks on Wu Han had come at the instigation of Mao Tse-tung himself. Mao had asked a young Shanghai journalist and member of the propaganda section of the Municipal Committee, Yao Wen-yuan, to write the article which appeared on November 10, "On the New Historical Play *Hai Jui Dismissed from Office*."[1]

The attack on Wu Han was only the first part of a carefully conceived battle plan drawn up by Mao Tse-tung. Basically, what the Chairman was trying to bring about was a transformation, in a revolutionary sense, of the superstructures of Chinese society. He knew that in so doing he would meet some stiff opposition within the Party, and he was fully prepared to cope with it. It is therefore safe to say that his choice of terrain for the initial offensive was a conscious one: the literary and artistic areas. During the spring and summer of 1965 a vast debate covering many works and authors had been launched, of which the November attack on Wu Han was simply the most important. Indeed, it is always in the intellectual milieus, which are ultrasensitive to doctrinaire conflicts, that revolutionary struggles begin. Ideological influences are widely and subtly exerted in these milieus, where calls to revolution generally tend to find their most ready responses. Lively discussions and debates are easily provoked over literary and ideological problems.

Since Wu Han's play was a eulogy to P'eng Teh-huai, any attack upon it could not help but involve some deeply rooted political problems that had existed within the Chinese Communist Party since 1958. Mao's opponents were quick to perceive this fact, which must have upset them greatly. The prospect that certain questions debated by the Central Committee of the Party at Lushan in 1959, at the Tenth Plenum in 1962, were to be brought up again for further discussion could hardly have overwhelmed them with pleasure. In 1962, specifically, their tendencies had been criticized as

<hr/>

[1] Eight years earlier, in 1957, Yao had also acted as Mao's spokesman, in an attack on *Wen Hui Pao* for its publication of "rightist" criticism of Party rule. The piece appeared in the *People's Daily*. Later Yao became a member of the Group in Charge of the Cultural Revolution and one of the heads of the Shanghai Revolutionary Committee, created in 1967. Today he is one of the most important, and also one of the youngest, high-ranking members of the Chinese Communist Party. Fate, which chose him to launch the attack against Wu Han, made him famous overnight.

Some specialists in Chinese affairs believe that Yao Wen-yuan is Mao's son-in-law. That may be, but I never heard it when I was in China.

"rightist," but no sanctions had been taken against them, nor had they been dismissed from their posts. It must have gone through their minds that if these same files were reopened now, the results might not be so favorable for them this time.

Thus they did their best to limit the discussion about the transformation of literature, and in particular the attack on Wu Han which was central to it, to academic debates. P'eng Chen, mayor of Peking and first secretary of the Peking Party Committee, was the focal point of this maneuver.

In the introduction I spoke especially of Liu Shao-ch'i as the leading adversary of Mao Tse-tung. Subsequent events have amply shown that he was indeed the principal opponent of the Party Chairman. And yet during the period I am about to describe, from November 1965 to the beginning of June 1966, Liu Shao-ch'i does not appear. It seems that he reacted very cautiously to the events of the time, during which P'eng Chen assumed the role of major opponent. This may well stem from the fact that Mao's offensive tactics (and specifically his choice of Wu Han, a close colleague of the mayor of Peking, as his principal target) were calculated to provoke a reaction from P'eng Chen rather than from Liu Shao-ch'i. Mao doubtless preferred to deal with each of them separately rather then together.[2]

P'eng Chen was one of the leading figures among those who, tacitly opposing Mao during the preceding few years, had grown increasingly bold and open later on. P'eng rightly reasoned that Yao Wen-yuan's indictment of *Hai Jui Dismissed from Office* was only the beginning of a much broader offensive that would involve those for whom Wu Han had served as spokesman and for whom he was now, at least for the time being, serving as scapegoat.

In 1966 P'eng Chen was still very much a leading luminary in the Chinese Communist Party. His name was familar to all those who kept a close watch on the Chinese political scene. He always held a high-ranking position in the hierarchy of the Party and made frequent public appearances. He often traveled abroad, and it was he who in 1960 denounced Khrushchev in Bucharest for attacking Mao and for advocating accommodation with the United States. In

---

[2] Liu Shao-ch'i has often been accused of supporting P'eng Chen. During the years preceding the Cultural Revolution both often did oppose Mao. It would nonetheless appear that during the early months of 1966 Liu left the initiative to P'eng, then abandoned him to his fate. The Chinese describe this maneuver with an image borrowed from chess, "Sacrifice your pawns to save the king."

1965 he went to Indonesia, where he made a long speech bitterly denouncing Russia and calling for world revolution under Mao's banner. Before 1966 no one outside China seems to have suspected that P'eng's policies deviated from those of Mao. On the basis of his many public speeches a number of Western newspapermen considered him a hard-line Maoist. Actually, nothing is more tenuous than an evaluation based on such elements. In China, when any high-ranking official makes a public statement it inevitably follows the Party line, for to do otherwise would be to lay oneself open to the accusation of betrayal of Party discipline.

It is in the course of internal discussions, when Party leaders solicit frank opinions, that differences are made known much more obviously than in any public displays. The opposition of people such as P'eng Chen is expressed by obstructive maneuvers, by failures to perform, by clandestine efforts to water down or undermine the application of official policies, but it would be naïve to expect this opposition to be openly expressed in public.

P'eng Chen had all the more reason to believe that others besides Wu Han were targets of the offensive, and in particular himself, because of the fact that the November 10 article was published in Shanghai rather than Peking. The first salvos had been fired in the provinces rather than in Peking for the obvious reason that Mao was concerned about what P'eng might do to subvert his attack, since P'eng was secretary of the Peking Party Committee and had a long arm in the capital.

Therefore P'eng had good reason to be on his guard. He tried to stem the tide, to limit the influence of the attack on Wu Han without openly opposing it, which would have been foolish. It was a question of trying to minimize the publicity over the attack on Wu Han and at the same time do everything in his power to keep the discussion out of politics and on a purely academic level. In this effort P'eng could count on the collaboration of Lu Ting-yi, like himself a member of the Politburo, as well as director of the propaganda bureau. Also responsible for cultural and educational institutions, Lu had often championed Soviet methods in this area, thus bringing himself into conflict with Mao, especially after the Great Leap Forward. He too, therefore, had good reason to hope that the recent past would not be disinterred for close scrutiny.

The obstructive maneuvers by P'eng Chen and Lu Ting-yi were many and varied. The most important was to use influence to limit the widespread publication of Yao Wen-yuan's article. It is customary in Chinese political life for an important article to be republished in many newspapers, both national and local, to give it maximum impact. But Yao Wen-yuan's article was republished only in newspapers and magazines of eastern China. Lu Ting-yi had managed to get the papers in the rest of the country not to run it.

It was not until three weeks later, on November 30—at the insistence of Chou En-lai, it was later reported—that the *Peking Daily* republished it. But the editor prefaced the article by stressing that the matter at issue was academic and the Wu Han affair was a historical rather than a political debate.

Two weeks later, in mid-December, Teng T'o, a colleague of P'eng Chen and cultural director of the Peking Municipal Party Committee, published in the *Peking Daily* an article called "From *Hai Jui Dismissed from Office* to the Problem of the Inheritance of Moral Values." In it he attempted to show that the debate raging around not only Wu Han's play but literature in general had little or no political relevance and ought to be limited to a certain number of problems relating to historical research. Teng T'o and Wu Han had for several years jointly directed not only the *Peking Daily* but also the magazine *Front Line*, and both were closely associated with P'eng Chen.

P'eng Chen and Lu Ting-yi forbade the publication of several articles revolving around the attack against Wu Han, and more specifically suppressed the publication of an article by Ch'i Pen-yu,[3] "The Reactionary Nature of *Hai Jui Dismissed from Office*."

Wu Han Seems to Weather the Storm—P'eng Chen Disseminates the "February Report"

The opposition of P'eng Chen and Lu Ting-yi to the wider dissemination of the attack on Wu Han is in itself hardly surprising. What is much more difficult to explain is the ease with which this opposition was able to develop over the next few months, roughly from December 1965 to the end of February 1966, to such an extent that one might well assume that P'eng and Lu had managed to impose their views. This is one of the unexplained mysteries of the Cultural Revolution. On December 27 Wu Han published a long self-criticism for the political errors in his play which appeared in

[3] Who was to become editor of *Red Flag*, the theoretical organ of the Party Center.

both the *Peking Daily* and the *People's Daily*, which might well have been construed as putting a period to the debate. The fact is, given the political habits of Communist China, the simple fact of having published a self-criticism in the official press indicates that one's repentance has been accepted and that one should henceforth be held blameless for the past sins committed.

In the directives that he issued and in political conversations he held in January 1966, P'eng Chen declared that it would be possible to come to some conclusion concerning Wu Han in two months' time. What he meant to imply was that the problem raised was not all that serious and could be resolved in a relatively short period of time. P'eng Chen assumed the responsibility for sending Wu Han away from Peking. He was shipped off to a rural commune to participate in the "four clean-ups." It was not really a vacation, but it was not all that far from it. Everything seemed to indicate that he had been exonerated and was authorized to find a little peace and quiet to recover from his emotions. In February P'eng Chen affirmed that the investigations under way had "proved that no link existed between Wu Han and P'eng Teh-huai."

The controversy over Wu Han's play was part of a vaster movement whose beginnings we saw in 1965, aimed at criticizing a certain number of artistic and literary manifestations considered faulty or pernicious. This movement was itself part of an ever larger movement whose goal was to analyze and evaluate bourgeois ideology and the vestiges of tradition. People were already beginning to talk about "Cultural Revolution," although the term was not widely used prior to April 1966. It was used, however, within the confines of various Party organisms, and as early as the beginning of 1966 there existed a "Group of Five in Charge of Cultural Revolution."

What is even more surprising when one takes a close look at this period is that not only did P'eng Chen apparently succeed during January and February in virtually whitewashing Wu Han, but also that he was at the head of the "Group of Five." Why was the Cultural Revolution, begun at the behest and desire of Mao Tse-tung, put under the direction of a man who at the time was actually his adversary? And why, among the other members of the group, were Lu Ting-yi, Chou Yang,[4] and Wu Leng-si,[5] three men whose

---

[4] A deputy director of the propaganda department of the Central Committee and a close collaborator of Lu Ting-yi.

[5] Wu Leng-si was the director of the New China News Agency.

orientation was strikingly similar to that of the mayor of Peking, whereas only the last, K'ang Sheng,[6] could be considered a truly faithful follower of Mao?

In an attempt to explain these strange circumstances some Western commentators have advanced the theory that at this or that moment Mao had lost control of power, which is pure fantasy. Actually, one can understand this kind of problem only by taking into careful consideration all the peculiarities of Chinese political life and by constantly referring to the principles and methods that Mao advocates. For him, it is best not to attack an enemy head-on but to let him come forward and reveal himself, after which there is time to counterattack. Mao applies the principles of guerrilla warfare to political life. He allowed P'eng Chen to assume certain directorial responsibilities, going on the assumption that P'eng would indeed commit errors and demonstrate in practice the revisionist aspect of his policies. In any other country such an explanation might well appear incredible. But it will come as no great surprise to those who know how greatly political practices in China differ from those of the West.

It is unthinkable that P'eng Chen could have been at the head of the Cultural Revolution without Mao's express approval. Every document, every official and nonofficial text, reveals that the start of the movement with the spectacular article of November 10 in Shanghai was the work of Mao Tse-tung. We also know that important meetings of the Central Committee took place in September and October, with Mao present and actively chairing the sessions, which laid the groundwork for the Cultural Revolution. It is therefore highly unlikely that this movement which he instigated could have escaped from his control during the first two months of 1966, since we know that in April of the same year he was once again firmly in charge. The fact is, P'eng Chen was put in charge of the Group of Five only because Mao Tse-tung knew full well that the mayor of Peking was bound to hook himself on the insoluble contradiction of having to guide an undertaking which in his heart of hearts he detested. As we proceed we shall see a number of similar situations in which the most outspoken opponents of Mao found themselves at certain times in charge of organizing or implementing

---

[6] An ex-functionary of the Comintern, K'ang rejoined Mao in Yenan during the anti-Japanese war. At the start of the Cultural Revolution K'ang was an alternate member of the Politburo. As of 1966 he was a full-fledged member and a member of its Standing Committee.

his policies—Liu Shao-ch'i and T'ao Chu[7] come immediately to mind—which in every instance proves to be the prelude to their fall.

Thanks to his prominent position in the Group of Five, and despite the probable opposition of K'ang Sheng, P'eng Chen had drawn up, in February, an "Outline Report on the Current Academic Discussion Made by the Group of Five in Charge of the Cultural Revolution," a written document intended to serve as a guide to the future development of the Cultural Revolution. This text once again tended to stress the academic nature of the various discussions under way, especially those of Wu Han's play, and contained various recommendations which were later roundly criticized.[8] This document was widely circulated among various Party organizations.

P'eng Chen's Resistance Is Broken

With this report, P'eng Chen had committed a fatal error. Indeed, there now existed a written document, in which he clearly outlined in considerable detail his restrictive conception of the Cultural Revolution, which could be used against him. This was precisely what Mao Tse-tung had had in mind when he gave him free rein during the months of January and February 1966.

Starting in March, Mao shed his reserve of the preceding months and moved swiftly to curb the activities of Peking's mayor. The February Report became the target for his attacks. At the request of the Party Chairman a meeting of the Secretariat was held, probably including some outside high-ranking officials, during which P'eng Chen was subjected to criticism. Meanwhile Mao had summoned a number of cadres and expressed to them his dissatisfaction with both P'eng Chen and Lu Ting-yi. He castigated the censorship of several articles attacking Wu Han and the harassment of their author, Ch'i Pen-yu, by P'eng Chen.

He also roundly attacked the propaganda department of the Central Committee for its support of these maneuvers. It was at this juncture that he offered the following slogan, which today is famous in China, and which at the time had profound repercussions among the organizations concerned. "You must overturn the King of Hell and set all the little devils free!"[9] What he clearly

---

[7] See Chapter 2.

[8] See Appendix 2, "The May 16 Circular."

[9] A rough translation of a very idiomatic Chinese formula.

implied was that the propaganda department (the King of Hell) and its leaders ought to be subjected to critical evaluations on the part of the cadres and the branches dependent upon them (the little devils). It was this same method that Mao constantly advocated to rectify the work in any branch of the Party: submit the upper echelons to criticism by the middle and lower echelons. This threat was put into effect, and was accompanied by the revocation of the February Report. In the course of a subsequent Central Committee meeting, with more members present, P'eng Chen was accused of opposing Mao Tse-tung's policies. Other personages with whom he was associated were also implicated: Lu Ting-yi, director of the propaganda department, about whom we have already spoken; Lo Jui-ch'ing, Chief of Staff and Vice-Minister of Defense; and a member of the Secretariat of the Central Committee, Yang Shang-k'un. As is generally the case in China, the problem remained internal; the four men in question were relieved of their responsibilities, but for the moment no decision as to their dismissal was forthcoming. The Party press published attacks against the theses contained in the February Report, but without citing the author's name or those of his fellow defendants. It was only about a year later that they were designated by name. During this entire period their theories, their ideas were the subject of criticism, but not them personally, at least officially.

About this same time, in mid-April 1966, the *Peking Daily*—which was still under the direction of P'eng Chen's friends, all profoundly concerned about how they could keep the lightning from striking them—hurriedly began to publish self-critical articles concerning two series of newspaper essays called *Evening Chats at Yenshan* and *Notes from Three-Family Village*.[10] These columns had for several years been the work of Wu Han, Teng T'o, and Liao Mo-sha, all friends of P'eng Chen, and all holding positions of high authority in the Peking Municipal Committee. Over the years they had played within the Party a rather important oppositional role to Mao's leadership. These self-criticisms were an effort on their part to build themselves a shelter against the storm they knew was brewing now that Mao and his followers had made up their minds to move the Cultural Revolution from the theoretical to the action phase of the struggle.

---

[10] See Appendix 1, "Teng To's *Evening Chats at Yenshan* Is Anti-Party and Anti-Socialist Double Talk."

Starting in April 1966 an ideological offensive was opened against the policies promulgated up to this time by P'eng Chen. This campaign was based on a document entitled: "Summary of the Forum on the Work in Literature and Art in the Armed Forces." The text summarized the conclusions to which this meeting, held under the leadership of Chiang Ch'ing,[11] Mao Tse-tung's wife, had come.

Without alluding directly to the Wu Han affair, this document stressed the priority of the political over the academic. It pointed out that the persistence of a "black line" in matters literary and artistic had, over the past seventeen years, prevented these arts from becoming truly proletarian. Also emphasized were the need to combat these insidious bourgeois influences and, in these areas, to lead an uncompromising struggle. Taking the opposite tack from P'eng Chen's theses, this text underscored the political aspects of literary and artistic creation. Widely distributed in the spring of 1966,[12] this summary served the propaganda department, whose director, Lu Ting-yi—the "King of Hell"—had been dismissed, as the source for a series of articles published throughout the country in which the main themes of the Summary were utilized.

2. The Cultural Revolution Moves into High Gear

Concerning Notes from Three-Family Village

The end of April and the month of May brought with them a new phase of the Great Proletarian Cultural Revolution. From this point onward it was to discard the quiet, rather imprecise rhythm that had typified its evolution since 1965 and to be loudly proclaimed by every arm at the disposal of the propaganda department. As its pace increased, so did its goals and its scope.

On April 18 the *Liberation Army Daily* ran an editorial called "Hold High the Great Red Banner of the Thought of Mao Tse-tung and Take an Active Part in the Great Socialist Cultural Revolution." Following the same line as that given in the Summary, this editorial

---

[11] Chiang Ch'ing, Mao's third wife, was formerly an actress. She secretly joined the Party in 1933, and in 1938 made the dangerous trek to Yenan, where she met Mao. She played only a very limited political role until recently, but during the Cultural Revolution she was suddenly given great power in the cultural area. In 1966 she was declared "First Deputy Leader within the Cultural Group of the Central Committee." At the Ninth Party Congress she was elected to full Politburo membership.

[12] The Summary was published in *Peking Review*, No. 23, June 2, 1967.

recalled that since Liberation in 1949 a fierce class struggle had been raging without letup in the realm of arts and letters, an area considered vital and one through which the whole socialist regime could degenerate. On May 8 various articles were published naming and criticizing Wu Han, Teng T'o, and Liao Mo-sha. On May 10 the already famous Yao Wen-yuan published another article in Shanghai attacking the three journalists. On May 11 an article entitled "On the Bourgeois Position of the *Peking Daily* and *Front Line*" appeared in *Red Flag*. Its author was Ch'i Pen-yu, whom P'eng Chen had banned from the pages of the Peking press a few months earlier.

Yao Wen-yuan's second article is the most important of this period. Entitled "Concerning *Notes from Three-Family Village*," and bearing the subtitle "The Reactionary Character of *Evening Chats at Yenshan* and *Notes from Three-Family Village*," the article was a long indictment of Wu Han, Teng T'o, and Liao Mo-sha, who were accused of having long opposed both the revolutionary line of the Party and Mao Tse-tung. It began by attacking the self-evaluations published on April 16 in the *Peking Daily* and in *Front Line* in which the two papers had admitted their lack of revolutionary vigilance and confessed to having been influenced by bourgeois ideology. Yao Wen-yuan set out to demonstrate that in his opinions these self-criticisms were in fact false criticisms.

What these people are trying to do, he said in essence, is to minimize their responsibilities and convince people that their revolutionary lucidity and perspicacity were less than they should be, whereas in fact they acted deliberately, consciously, and systematically.

The article also mentioned the fact that Teng T'o and Liao Mo-sha both defended Wu Han's play *Hai Jui Dismissed from Office*, which had been another way of reindicting the Lushan meeting and the decisions made there in 1959. According to the article, taking as a pretext the three "difficult years" 1959–61 which the country had undergone, and in collaboration with the revisionist thinking propagated by the leaders of the Soviet Union, the three men under indictment chose to follow a line different from that laid down by the Party. Using insidious innuendos and veiled allusions, and taking full advantage of their positions as journalists, they had advocated a clearly revisionist-oriented reversal of policy: renouncing mass movements as the way to build socialism, abandoning the priority of politics, relying on specialists and technocracy, and so on. Moreover, at a time when the ideological conflict with the Soviet leaders was growing more acute, they had widely advocated maintaining relations with the U.S.S.R., and even following their example, specifically in an article entitled: "How to Make Friends and Receive Guests."

The May 16[13] Circular

With this series of articles, the offensive against the group of men allied to P'eng Chen, whom the Chinese press at the time described by the somewhat picturesque term of "The Black Gang"—supporters of the "black line," a line opposed to that laid down by Mao Tse-tung—was sharply emphasized. Henceforth, this conflict which up to this time had been essentially a Party affair, began to be widely publicized. Still, the information given was limited and carefully phrased. In fact the press had not yet associated P'eng Chen, Lu Ting-yi, Lu Jui-ch'ing, and Yang Shang-k'un by name with the "black line" it was denouncing. Only Wu Han, Teng T'o, and Liao Mo-sha—who were really only second-echelon figures— had been named. This is customary in Communist China: the higher the rank of the person involved, and the greater the problems his case raises, the longer the period of time taken to settle it. This phenomenon was to occur again and again in the course of the Cultural Revolution, most especially in the case of Liu Shao-ch'i.

Nonetheless, within the Party organizations the indictment was much more precise, and internal documents specifically named P'eng Chen as a "representative of the bourgeoisie." That is clearly shown in a Circular of the Central Committee dated May 16, 1966. At that time circulated only within the Party, this text is thought to have been written by Mao Tse-tung himself. It announces the canceling of the Report drawn up in February by P'eng Chen in the name of the Group of Five, and sets out to refute it in a ten-point rebuttal. This document, with its extremely well-thought-out theoretical basis, is written in a language far clearer than the ordinary political tract and indeed sets forth the basic orientation for the Cultural Revolution.

The Circular castigates P'eng Chen's report for having falsified the problems under discussion and for having blurred the goals of the Great Proletarian Cultural Revolution. The attack on Wu Han's

[13] See Appendix 2.

play, which was undertaken within the framework of the revolutionary transformation of art and literature, had been turned into a formal debate concealing the real basic political problems involved in *Hai Jui Dismissed from Office*. The Circular openly stated that the whole point of the struggle was in fact to attack Wu Han and others like him—and it stated that they were a "considerable number"—who were accused of being anti-Party and antisocialist representatives of the bourgeoisie.[14] It went on to say—and this is an important point—that a certain number of these elements were still operating within the Central Committee itself and within the Party at various provincial and municipal levels.

P'eng Chen, the Circular went on, wanted to stifle political debate and reduce it to a purely academic level. What is more, using freedom of speech as a pretext, he wanted to give these "representatives of the bourgeoisie" every possibility of answering the attacks made upon them, and even of counterattacking. Whereas the struggle in which we are engaged, the text went on, is a class struggle wherein no compromise whatsoever is possible, P'eng Chen came up with this reactionary truism: "Everyone is equal before the truth." To which the Circular responded: "Our relationship with them [the representatives of the bourgeoisie] can in no way be one of equality. On the contrary, it is a relationship in which one class oppresses another, that is, the dictatorship of the proletariat over the bourgeoisie." Finally, in point 9, the Circular reveals this interesting bit of information: it suggests that in many places the battle has not yet begun and that, where it has, the vast majority of the Party Committees only vaguely understand their leadership role. Now, doesn't P'eng Chen recommend that the struggle be conducted "under direction," "with prudence," "with caution," and "with the approval of the leading bodies concerned"? All of which, the Circular concludes, "serves to place restrictions on the proletarian left, to impose taboos and commandments in order to tie its hands, and to place all sorts of obstacles in the way of the proletarian cultural revolution."

By the end of this document the Cultural Revolution had acquired a different dimension, which is what gives the Circular its great historical importance. It was no longer simply a question of making sure that the literary and artistic realms took a more revolutionary turn. The rather lively opposition that it encountered among

[14] See Appendix 1.

at least a certain faction of the Party led the movement to include among its goals first the uncovering, then the elimination of this group.

It was also necessary for the proletariat to reaffirm the primacy of its conceptions and methods in the administration and functioning of the Party. That was why the May 16 Circular ended by asserting that representatives of the bourgeoisie who had infiltrated the Party, the government, the army, and different cultural milieus were a collection of revisionists and counterrevolutionaries, and it contained this sentence which would only take on its full meaning at a later date: "Some of them we have already seen through, others we have not. Some are still trusted by us and are being trained as our successors, persons like Khrushchev, for example, who are still nestling beside us."

The dissemination of this Circular within the Party immediately cast a new light on the Cultural Revolution.

The series of articles published starting in April attacking the "Black Gang," as well as the Circular of May 16, was an appeal to the masses, a call to arms to acquaint them with the problems and to involve them in the discussions. Their purpose was also to bring into play forces outside the Party, in order to frustrate, if necessary, the maneuvers of certain authorities intent on obstructing Mao's policies. Also involved was an effort to make the masses more vigilant, so that they would be better able to detect in their places of work, and in their schools, any indications of revisionist activity and, in the event they did, single out the Party authorities responsible for their existence.

In many places this is the direction the movement took. In particular, the Chinese custom of using "big-character posters—*ta-tzu-pao*—through which everyone could make his opinions known to everyone else and candidly criticize those in positions of authority, became widespread.

The "First National Marxist-Leninist Ta-tzu-pao"

On May 25, 1966, one of these big-character posters was put up at Peking University.[15] Its repercussions were to be enormous. It was signed by seven people, including a philosophy teacher, Nieh

---

[15] See *Peking Review*, No. 37, September 12, 1966.

Yuan-tzu, who would later become a leader of the Revolutionary Committee of Peking before she was injured in the spring of 1968.[16] The *ta-tzu-pao* was a violent attack on two members of the Peking Municipal Government responsible for university affairs, and on the university president, Lu P'ing, all three of whom were high-ranking Party officials and collaborators of P'eng Chen. The seven signers of the poster listed the various restrictions imposed on the Cultural Revolution movement at the university by the three people cited, specifically the attempt to minimize its political aspect and turn it into a purely academic affair; their refusal to allow the posting of *ta-tzu-pao*; and their constant reference to the need for reinforcing the "leadership" and giving it a "just" orientation. This *ta-tzu-pao* denounced these maneuvers and declared that it was indispensable to mobilize the masses unreservedly, to develop to the highest point possible the use of posters and the unrestricted right of meetings for debate and discussion. It also affirmed the necessity to stoutly combat the revisionist plots of those in power who opposed socialism and Party policy.

This poster, which revealed an exemplary revolutionary attitude of decision and boldness, with its ringing assertion concerning the right to criticize people in high places, became widely known, for Mao Tse-tung heard about it and asked that it be broadcast over the radio and printed in the papers on June 1. Thus the revolt against Party authorities suspected of following a bourgeois line was given an added impetus from the top, and became an example to follow on the national level. This event without doubt constitutes a turning point in the Cultural Revolution. The level of the criticism was stepped up. The Chinese universities were in a state of effervescence, and conflicting posters covered every inch of wall space. This *ta-tzu-pao* signed by the seven was termed the "first Marxist-Leninist *ta-tzu-pao*."

The Reorganization of the Peking Municipal Party Committee

On June 3 the Central Committee of the Chinese Communist Party announced a significant measure: the modification of the Peking Municipal Committee. With no mention of P'eng Chen by name, and no announcement of his removal, his fiefdom was taken

16 See Chapter 11.

away from him and new nominations were made. Li Hsueh-feng[17] was named first secretary of the Municipal Committee, and Wu Teh[18] deputy secretary.

Other decisions were simultaneously made public: the *Peking Evening News* and the *Peking Daily* were reorganized and the editorial staffs revamped; the publication of *Front Line* was temporarily suspended while it too was undergoing a thorough restaffing. The links between the Teng T'o group and the Peking municipal authorities therefore appeared through the decision taken. At the same time, it was revealed that President Lu P'ing of Peking University had been dismissed and that a work group had been dispatched to the university to direct the Cultural Revolution there. This last decision eventually proved to be extremely controversial.

Since the beginning of June, Peking University had been in a state of turmoil. Situated at the West of the capital, the university is in a park not far from the Summer Palace of the former Empress Tz'u Hsi. At that time the courses of study were basically literary: philosophy, literature, history, languages. . . . In these subjects the custom was to deal with ideas in their pure state, whereas the students were very politically oriented. Since 1960 there had been a feeling of uneasiness in the university. After the period of the Great Leap Forward Lu Ting-yi—at the time chairman of the Central Committee's Pedagogical Commission—had turned his back on the principles of Mao Tse-tung which stressed the primacy of politics in the academic areas. There had been a return to more traditional formulas, which many students contested, criticizing them for being based on classical studies derived exclusively from books. The *ta-tzu-pao* of the seven signers came like a spark on dry tinder. Wave after wave of attacks ensued: days were spent making posters, printing handbills, meeting, discussing endlessly. Everything was passed through a rigorous screening process. Students, in some cases backed by their professors, held meetings virtually every day, attacking and condemning their former president. He was blamed not only for having opposed the mobilization of the masses and for having tried to squelch the Proletarian Cultural Revolution, but also for having advocated certain teaching methods.

---

[17] First secretary of the Bureau of the Central Committee for North China. After a period of eclipse during which he was roundly criticized, Li Hsueh-feng was reaffirmed in positions of authority and became head of the Revolutionary Committee of Hopei. He was in eclipse again, however, after the Lin Piao affair in 1971.

[18] First secretary of the Party Committee for the province of Kirin.

Teaching Challenged

Revision of teaching methods and curriculum became a subject of prime importance. Many voices began to be raised in the schools against a system which, it was said, was hardly any different from, or any better than, the teaching methods employed under the old bourgeois regime.

A few weeks earlier, on April 12, a conference of teaching cadres had been held at Tsinan during which the necessity of bringing politics to the fore had been stressed. Since then there had been various criticisms in the streets and in the schools of the curricula offered, the system of exams, and the teaching methods. The students declared that current teaching had little or nothing to do with reality, that the students had no real contact with the life of the people, with practical scientific practice, with politics, or with the processes of production; they claimed that the bourgeois students enjoyed a number of advantages unknown to the sons of peasants and workers, who were often neglected or persecuted; they further charged that the system fostered an emulation of individualism and of bourgeois-style choice, that it favored servilism and careerism, and, in fact, tended to form new "men of letters" rather than servants of the people. In short, the teaching then current was, in their eyes, still rife with vestiges of the past and needed a thorough revamping from top to bottom.

In a letter to the Central Committee reprinted in the press, a number of high-school students asked for a transformation of this system which, they said, augmented the differences between manual and intellectual labor, between workers and peasants, between city and country, in other words did just the opposite of what socialist teaching was supposed to, namely to reduce these differences and open the way to a truly communist society.

In Peking, other high-school students, in a letter seconding what their fellow students had said, further accused the teaching system of relegating politics to a secondary position, of favoring the making of technocrats, and therefore, in the final analysis, of fostering the return of capitalism. Recalling the necessity for socialism to form a new kind of intellectual who would have close links with the people and a proletarian consciousness, they declared: "What we are destroying is not only a system of examinations but also the cultural yoke which has weighed upon the Chinese people for thousands of years; it is the birthplace of the intellectual aristocracy and the highly paid upper social strata, the springboard leading to modern revisionism."

The schools and universities, then, formed the outposts of the Cultural Revolution, at least in its early period. It was among the students, as well as among others in the cultural milieus, that the movement found its staunchest advocates. History offers many examples of this phenomenon—the important role of students and intellectuals at the beginning of a revolutionary movement. In China itself there was a fairly recent precedent: the May Fourth Movement of 1919, which had found the intellectuals in the vanguard during the early days of a revolution which would, in three decades, transform the country.

On June 13 a decision of the Central Committee and the government was made known whereby examinations were postponed and matriculation in the schools set back for a semester.

The schools and universities suspended their classes. High-school students, university students, and their teachers nonetheless went every day—and often every night—to their classrooms, where there were endless round-the-clock discussions on teaching, politics, and the essential relationship between the two. In fact it was on the basis of these discussions that the Party leaders intended to effect a profound transformation of the teaching. In-depth investigations were made into the way schools had functioned in the past and on the conduct of former administrators. Brochures and fliers multiplied thick and fast inside the schools and universities. The outside walls as well as the classroom walls were literally covered with posters sporting big-character slogans painted in a variety of colors. This characteristic backdrop of wall newspapers, of manuscript-posters juxtaposed, superimposed, like some vertical patchwork quilt, would spread throughout the coming months from the schools to the streets of every city and town, transforming the walls and sidewalks into a welter of many-sided, ebullient literature.

In the summer of 1966 an initial episode of the Cultural Revolution had occurred. There was nothing very extraordinary about it, except at the last, and virtually no one outside China had noticed it. And yet it had resulted in a considerable success for Mao Tse-tung. Not only had he managed to eliminate from power an initial but important faction of dissidents, he had also managed to arouse a national ideological movement based on the principle of mass participation. Of the population, only the young intelligentsia had moved into action, but that is normal for any revolution. In this regard, it is interesting to note the existence in China of a student controversy not unlike that—although the orientation is different—existing in various capitalist countries. It is also worth noting that in China too the liberal arts students were the most fiery.

3. The Episode of the Work Teams

The "Fifty Days"

A major event occurred between June 10, 1966, and the end of July. After the fall of 1965 and the winter of 1965–66, marked (but without any particular splash) by the attack on Wu Han's play, the spring of 1966 saw a quickening of the pace of the Cultural Revolution. After the elimination of the P'eng Chen–Lu Ting-yi faction, Mao Tse-tung and his partisans, not concerned with merely cleansing the Party apparatus, moved to arouse the population as a whole. Mao's strategy can be explained by the simple fact that he was convinced that it was what the people needed, and he was sure the masses would follow and support him. Well aware of his own enormous prestige, the Chairman of the Party counted on that support as constituting an extremely valuable arm with which to break the back of the opposition in certain sectors. But that was not his only goal, as I have earlier pointed out: he also wanted, in the course of this showdown, to politicize the population on a vast scale, through a mixture of ideological education and practical problems connected with this struggle.

The publicity given in the press and on the radio to the *ta-tzu-pao* of Nieh Yuan-tzu and her fellow students had given rise throughout the length and breadth of China to a massive expression of opinions. In various places people set to writing this kind of poster and using it as a point of departure for debate and discussion. These big-character posters flowering on the walls were written with brushes, using India ink diluted with water. Produced on big rectangular sheets of colored paper, they were often attractively presented: their titles and subtitles were emphasized by the unconventional way the characters were drawn.

Their authors tried to satirize graphically the names of persons under attack (quivering characters to suggest the creeping movement of someone considered especially base, horizontal to indicate an overpedantic person, upside-down to indicate the fate in store for entrenched bureaucrats), Chinese calligraphy aiding enormously in this venture. Anyone could pen a *ta-tzu-pao*, and all could read them. Throughout the Cultural Revolution paper and ink were furnished free to factories and schools, and given without conditions to workers and students alike. It is an efficient method which allows everyone to express himself, to formulate an opinion, and to dispute whatever he doesn't like. It helped to politicize the population on a mass scale, especially the young, among whom the literary fever was at a high pitch.

The *People's Daily* of June 20 concluded its editorial in this manner: "Let us mobilize the masses without reservation! Let them compose their *ta-tzu-pao* and, beneath the banner of Mao Tse-tung's great thought, let us carry forward to the end the Great Proletarian Cultural Revolution." Nonetheless, between the beginning of June and the beginning of August, this movement, which was still barely under way, was to encounter further obstacles. In fact, between the months of May and July 1966 we were to witness a complete metamorphosis: the effervescence of raging discussion gave way to a bureaucratic and repressive reaction.

Since June, a great many people had begun to criticize certain Party authorities whose conduct they deemed bureaucratic, not sufficiently revolutionary, or even counterrevolutionary. In many cases, young people, whether or not they were Party members or members of the Communist Youth League, often made lively posters in which they blamed this or that authority for his conduct in a particular situation, asked him to explain his actions, or simply denounced his daily work habits.

This practice was not completely without precedent in the history of the Communist movement. During the last years of his life, Lenin, extremely concerned over the danger of the regime's slipping into encrusted bureaucracy, had resorted to it in order to provoke what in Marxist terminology is called "rectification campaigns." These consisted of subjecting Party members to review by people who did not belong to the Party, in order to bring any excesses to light and subsequently correct them. The Chinese Cultural Revolution was based essentially on the same principle. Its difference lay in its scope, since it took place in every city and town, large and small, throughout China, and it went on all at once. Moreover, we should remember that its goal was not to subject all Party members to review, but only *those in positions of authority who had deviated from the revolutionary way*. On this point the Chinese vocabulary is extremely precise: the only people in question are "those persons in authority who have taken the capitalist road," and they are designated by the term *tso tze-pai*, "capitalist roaders."

The organization of any rectification campaign always runs afoul of an obstacle inherent in the principle that governs its evolution. The Party authorities are obliged to provoke a movement of which some of them stand a good chance of becoming victims. It is understandable, therefore, that at least those who suspect the worst can be counted on to give only lip service to the venture, or try to find convenient scapegoats. This tendency occurred during the Cultural Revolution. It was all the more evident because the people in question were limited to Party members in positions of authority. Those who felt themselves threatened were able to influence in large measure the organization and evolution of the critical movement. Some were thus able to pass the buck for their errors and shortcomings down to their deputies, without any great difficulty. The dispatch at this time of specialized groups referred to in China as "work teams," into various sectors where the Cultural Revolution was going on was in fact a maneuver of this kind, a large-scale maneuver which in actuality tended to brake the revolutionary movement and divert it from its real targets. We shall see in rapid succession what the origin of these groups was and how they operated.

The Origin of the Work Teams

The communiqué of June 3, 1966, announcing the reorganization of the leadership of the Peking Municipal Committee, indicated that the new Party committee was taking the leadership of the Cultural Revolution in hand. This same document announced for the first time the dispatch of a work team to Peking University, which was in a state of extreme agitation.

During the following days the dispatch of similar work groups to different institutions and various work sites throughout the capital became commonplace. This example was emulated by the authorities in several other cities of China, which in turn organized and sent off work groups to various local establishments.

Earlier, in 1964, work groups had been formed during the period of the Socialist Education Movement. Some of them, which had remained active, resumed their duties in 1966; elsewhere, new groups were formed. They were generally made up of about twenty people from the middle echelons of responsibility, who were Party

members and were named by the local authorities as both worthy
of their confidence and involved in the areas of their responsibility.
In some places the personnel of the group was embellished by the
presence of an adviser, who in some instances was a high-ranking
official. Vice-Premier and Minister Ho Lung[19] and former Minister
of Industry Po I-po both played this role upon occasion at Tsinghua
University, together with Wang Kuang-mei, Liu Shao-ch'i's wife.
The members of these work groups were almost always foreign to
the establishments where they were sent. Since some cities were
lacking in sufficient numbers of cadres, there were times when
people were brought in from outside provinces and were thus
unfamiliar not only with the specific establishment but even with
the province itself. Their task was to assume, for a fifty-day period,
the local leadership of the Cultural Revolution, in a way that was
to reveal itself as very controversial.

Mao Tse-tung's Principles

Here it should be recalled that since Maoism was the official
doctrine of the state and of the ruling Communist Party, the work
teams obviously ought to pattern their conduct on the principles of
Mao Tse-tung relative to the struggle against revisionism and the
repression of counterrevolutionaries. These two themes had been
the subject of articles by Mao during various periods of his life.
The most important of these date from 1957 and 1964, during the
polemic with the Russian Communist Party. According to Mao's
theses, in any socialist regime, and within the confines of the Party
itself, there are leaders whose views and political actions deviate
from the principles of Marxism. In so doing they are working, consciously or unconsciously, for the restoration of capitalism. One
must make a distinction between these *tso tze-pai*, who are to be
counted as conscious enemies bent on the destruction of socialism,
and the cadres who, though they may have committed errors, can be
recovered or, as they say in China, "reeducated." These cadres Mao
views as a contradiction *within* the people, therefore not antagonistic. Mao also emphasized that this was by far the most common
deviation, the Party and the regime being to his mind basically
revolutionary, therefore healthy. The revisionists, Mao has often

---

[19] Named a marshal of the People's Liberation Army in 1955, Ho Lung had also
been Minister of Physical Culture.

stated, are only a tiny minority; 95 percent of the cadres and the masses are truly revolutionary. These distinctions are indispensable if one is to fully understand the subsequent evolution of events.

The work teams were supposed to head a critical movement of the leaders of the former Municipal Committee of Peking, the faction of Mayor P'eng Chen, the Black Gang, and manifestations of its policy termed the "black line." Throughout the fifty days the work teams pretended to act in this sense, presumably applying the principles of Mao Tse-tung. In various schools and classrooms, and in a number of factories, these groups were supposed to explain the insidious and noxious character of certain measures taken by the Black Gang not only in cultural and pedagogical matters but also in economic affairs, and at the same time were to analyze and debate their local repercussions. In a number of provincial cities, where a similar line had been followed, other work teams were charged with much the same mission. Their other job was to investigate and ferret out, wherever they existed, other persons of authorities allied with the P'eng Chen–Lu Ting-yi faction who promulgated the black line. As for those who had simply fallen into bad habits and sloppy work methods, they were to be the subject of reeducation in an attempt to bring them back to a more militant and more revolutionary stance. If the work groups had acted in accordance with the Maoist principles set forth above, the first part of their mission would have involved only a handful of people, and the second a larger number which would have got increasingly smaller as the weeks went on.

The Performance of the Work Teams under the Direction of Liu Shao-ch'i and Teng Hsiao-p'ing

Mao Tse-tung was away from Peking, for fifty days, from early June to mid-July. Liu Shao-ch'i, chairman of the People's Republic, and Teng Hsiao-p'ing, general secretary of the Central Committee, administered the current affairs of the Central Committee during this interim period. They personally took charge of the work teams operating in Peking and closely followed the activities of those in the provinces.

The orientation they gave these groups differed from the political rules outlined above. Let me hasten to add that this contradiction did not appear so clearly at the time as it may in the account which follows, since that period was rife with confusion. The targets of the work groups were basically intellectuals, suspected of revisionist sentiments, who had suddenly become surprisingly numerous. On the other hand, in the cultural milieus, and especially in the universities, the work cadres acted as though the Party organizations had been profoundly affected by revisionism and had gone over in large numbers to P'eng Chen's faction. That led them to dismiss a great many persons of authority in these organizations and to undertake radical purges involving sections and in some cases whole cells. A case often cited as characteristic of this attitude was the activities of the work team at Tsinghua University, under the direction of Wang Kuang-mei, the wife of Liu Shao-ch'i. On several occasions she maintained that the sum total of the Party organizations was one vast "brotherhood of black liners."[20]

Rigorous self-criticisms were demanded from those who were the target of these attacks, and restrictive surveillance was imposed on them, generally meaning that they were not allowed to leave their rooms, which were placed under guard. The work groups' orientation was later severely criticized, for the battle was being fought not against a minority of high-echelon Party officials but against a broad spectrum of middle and lower cadres and grass-roots militants. In Chinese political slang the work-group heads called this "peeling the onion skin by skin." What was more, persecutions and pressures spread to people who were not Party members, and to teachers, students, and workers (who in China are generally considered part of the "masses," as opposed to the people in positions of authority).

In fact these emissaries had been specifically sent into areas where the excitement had been the greatest during May and the beginning of June. A goodly number of students and workers whose militant enthusiasm was running high because of the heady events of the preceding weeks were quick to denounce what they considered the outrageous attitude of some of these groups. It was revealed that at Tsinghua University this opposition to the work teams was discreetly encouraged by Ch'en Po-ta, Mao Tse-tung's former secretary, and Chiang Ch'ing, Mao's wife.

The work teams countered the attack, and in so doing did not

[20] One can get a pretty fair idea of how the work teams operated at another university in the capital from the article by Victor Nee and Don Layman, "The Cultural Revolution at Peking University," which appeared in *Monthly Review*, Vol. 21, No. 3, July-August 1969, p. 42. See also William Hinton's *The Hundred Day War: The Cultural Revolution at Tsinghua University*, Monthly Review Press, New York, 1972.

hesitate to falsely accuse those they were responding to as being part of the anti-Party "Black Gang." One of the slogans they used was the accusation that those opposing the work groups "used a leftist language to conceal their rightist tendencies." It was later reported that they had received the go-ahead directly from Liu Shao-ch'i himself, in the course of one of the periodic meetings where the groups received its directives. The work groups then issued various edicts aimed at limiting the people's freedom to express itself through posters. One of the edicts forbade anyone from revealing outside the university what was happening inside. This was later condemned as inimical to the spread of the Cultural Revolution and an effort to prevent the mobilization of the masses.

During this period of the Cultural Revolution, it was very common, in places where the work groups were operating, for constant meetings to go on, often far into the night. All the student body, or in the case of offices or factories, the employees, were gathered together so that they could hear the political or ideological indictment against the many people who had come under fire. We should bear in mind that the governing principle of the movement had been to have the masses evaluate and criticize the cadres; but under the present circumstances their participation was strictly a formality.

The Resistance

Since the methods and activities of the work teams had provoked a hostile response, a struggle took place in a number of places. Often the students or workers in a specific place split into two opposing groups, one favoring the work teams, the other against them.

These conflicts took various forms. Anti-work-team people made and put up posters denouncing them, which would soon be joined, or pasted over, by those in favor. Students and workers would congregate to read the posters, the former throughout the day, since there were no classes, the latter in the morning before work and during their lunch break. As was to be expected in such cases, the inevitable happened: quarrels broke out, people insulted one another, and there were instances of pushing and shoving. The work team leaders took steps to punish those who were critical of their efforts, branding them as counterrevolutionaries, and many a meeting in the schools and factories turned into a shouting match. The work teams often took even more serious steps against their opponents, confining them to a guarded wing of a dormitory where they were subjected to various forms of persecution. Those thus treated responded as they could, sometimes, as at Tsinghua University, by going on hunger strikes. If we've mentioned this institution more frequently than others, it is because it was there, it seems, that the resistance to the work teams was the strongest.

The dissenting workers and students, in an effort to collectively combat the work teams' methods, themselves banded together into relatively small groups, which were obliged to conceal their purpose or activities. In the high schools and universities these centers of resistance were the embryo of an organization which soon would become known throughout the world: the Red Guards. Other groups were formed to counter them, to respond to their posters, prevent them from speaking in meetings, to bad-mouth and slander them, and to exert various pressures upon them, both moral and physical.

Little by little, during the course of the period known in China as the "fifty days," an extremely confused situation developed, with the work teams encountering constant opposition. Later, the Party was to single out this opposition for high praise. From my own experience, and bearing in mind the limitations a single witness must impose on his judgments, I must say that this opposition, which was greater in the universities than in the factories, was nonetheless not very substantial, all in all. Those who disagreed with the work teams and wanted to resist their efforts were in a difficult situation. In fact, in the eyes of many people, most with no experience in this sort of thing, the work teams were the creation of the municipal authorities, had official status, and therefore had to be obeyed. This feeling was reinforced by the obvious fact that some of the highest authorities in the country were behind them. On the practical level, the upshot of the work teams' efforts was to cool the anti-bureaucratic ardor that had marked the month of May and replace it with a wave of repression and intimidation so strong that, ten months later, Vice-Premier and Minister Hsieh Fu-chih, chairman of the Revolutionary Committee of Peking, declared in a speech that at that time the Cultural Revolution in the capital had been on the verge of collapsing.

The Return of Mao Tse-tung

We should bear in mind that during this period not only was Mao Tse-tung absent from Peking, but most of his high-ranking followers were also invisible. On July 25 the *People's Daily* carried on its front page the news—capped by a full-page double-photo spread showing, on the left side, Mao and several Party officials swimming, and on the right a healthy, youthful-looking Mao in a swimming robe—that "Chairman Mao Joyously Swims the Yangtze." The news that Mao had performed what can only be called, especially considering his seventy-three years, a spectacular feat in swimming some ten miles in the Yangtze River, was generally greeted in the West with irony and disbelief. What Western journalists failed to grasp was the political meaning of the event. The wide publicity given Mao's feat was, purely and simply, a political tactic meant to dissipate certain rumors about Mao's declining health that had been circulating over the past several years, and to stimulate and give heart to those who saw him as their guide and inspiration for their revolutionary activity and who might have had doubts about his ability any longer to lead the struggle. More precisely, by turning the spotlight on Mao for the first time in several weeks,[21] the propaganda machine, which until now had been relatively discreet, gave the first sign of what in retrospect can be seen as a full-scale counteroffensive against Liu Shao-ch'i and the work teams.

The Chairman's swim in the Yangtze took place on July 16, at Wuhan. On the following day, July 17, Mao was back in Peking, where he received several Africans and Asians in the capital for a writers' conference.

There was no lack of problems facing Mao. The Americans had just bombed Hanoi and Haiphong, bringing the Vietnam War to the very borders of China, as the international situation took a dramatic turn for the worse.

In the Chinese capital the Cultural Revolution was in the state of crisis that we have just outlined. In all probability, Mao wasted no time, once he was back in Peking, looking into the aims and methods of the work teams. On August 1, all the work groups stopped what they were doing and left the places where they had been operating. Just what happened between July 17, when Mao returned to Peking, and August 1? It is difficult to know exactly,

[21] Actually Mao had been absent from public view since the fall of 1965. On November 26, he attended a series of receptions for foreign visitors, after which his presence was not mentioned in the national press until May of 1966, when he was reported as having received the Albanian delegation in his provincial retreat. The next news of him was the swim in the Yangtze, reported more than a week after his return to the capital.

since no decision was announced during that period, nothing spectacular happened, and the Party press carried nothing extraordinary except for the Yangtze feat. Nonetheless, one can speculate that a good deal of the Chinese leaders' time must have been spent during these two weeks discussing the problem of the Cultural Revolution during the "fifty days." At the same time it is safe to assume that busy preparations were under way in view of a forthcoming key event: the meeting of the Central Committee, scheduled for August 1–12, a meeting which in retrospect was highly significant in the history of the Cultural Revolution.

What Was the Real Strength of the Opposition to Mao Tse-tung?

Having witnessed the events just described, I was struck by the sudden change of political atmosphere in Peking during these two months. The first, tumultuous period, marked by the dynamism and spontaneity of the youth, gave way to a heavy climate of repression and denunciations of the most bureaucratic sort. The activities of the work teams were clearly far removed from the principles and strategy of Mao Tse-tung. This can be understood if one clearly defines the matter of the real targets of the Cultural Revolution. For Mao, it was a question of utilizing the combined force of the masses and the Party members faithful to him to counter the faction of high officials who disagreed with his policy. What strikes one as amazing is that during the relatively long period of fifty days a dissident current of such scope could have been maintained in the capital of the country. Those on whom the work teams set their sights —aided and abetted by Liu Shao-ch'i and Teng Hsiao-p'ing—were the rather broad spectrum of people that included the middle- and lower-echelon cadres of the Party, and the most vocal elements among the young people, students and workers alike. The dispatch of special teams, in the circumstances then prevailing, can probably be explained as the maneuver of certain leaders to subvert a movement they had every reason to fear. In Chinese political jargon, this is referred to as: "Striking out at a large number of people in order to save a handful." The work teams, in fact, were an extension of the P'eng Chen–Lu Ting-yi policies.

Here again certain Western commentators saw in these facts the clear indication that Mao had lost political control and sought refuge in his provincial retreat. There is, in my opinion, another explanation.

There is no question that opposition to the Party Chairman increased during the years that preceded the Cultural Revolution, and we have given a number of examples. But the fact remains that Mao was still able to guide the Party according to his views, for otherwise how can one explain the Socialist Education Movement of 1964 or the Cultural Revolution of 1966? What seems safe to assume is that the opposition, while still unable to impose its views, constituted a considerable force in 1966.

We have no hard facts to rely on in trying to assess the exact strength of this opposition to Mao. And yet there is one piece of extremely interesting information which allows us certain insights into the situation as it was then, one furnished by Mao himself. In a conversation he had in 1967, the gist of which was subsequently reproduced in posters and widely disseminated in the streets of Peking, Mao indicated that in August 1966—that is, immediately following the events we have just described—only a slim majority of Central Committee members adhered totally to his views.

This is not to imply that the totality of those who disagreed with Mao had made up their minds to join in a pitched battle against him. Mao, moreover, had taken precautions to make sure he would not have to confront these dissidents *en bloc*. Later, during the subsequent phases of the Cultural Revolution, we will see that this same policy of allowing some high officials, in spite of their errors, to retain their posts was often followed. What we can say with relative certainty is that both Liu Shao-ch'i and Teng Hsiao-p'ing represented the hard-line dissidents, firmly opposed to Mao's policy and in no mood to compromise.

These people may well have been few in number, but because of their high place in both the Government and the Party, it is obvious that their capacity to resist was great. We should note in passing that some of them headed the administration of certain provinces, a fact which helps explain the movement of flux and reflux that was later to occur in the course of the Cultural Revolution. These salient facts explain how it was that the work teams, initiated and encouraged by anti-Maoist forces, were able to operate effectively in both Peking and other cities.

Mao Against Mao

At this point I should like to try and define the limits of this opposition. To do so, we must mention a factor of prime importance to the subsequent development of the Cultural Revolution. Any profound analysis of political events in China must take into careful account the specificity of its social regime. It is characteristic of contemporary Chinese political life that *the opponents of Mao generally refrain from ever admitting their opposition to him*; on the contrary, they generally refer to him and repeat his slogans and watchwords, always ready however to deflect the targets and denature their content. It is what the Chinese call "waving the red flag to oppose the red flag." Thus both those who were for and those who were against the work teams proclaimed themselves partisans of Mao Tse-tung and adversaries of P'eng Chen's "Black Gang." Throughout the Cultural Revolution we shall see this same thing repeated, with different, opposing groups confronting one another, often violently, even though they claim to be representing the same man and the same doctrine.[22] *However disconcerting that may seem at first glance, there is no example, so far as we know, of anyone between 1966 and 1969 openly taking sides with P'eng chen or Liu Shao-ch'i against Mao Tse-tung.*

This fact obviously limits the parameters of any political opposition. There are those who will combat, deform, contract the activities and influence of the Chairman, but never openly. And at the end of any confrontation, the dissidents will never have deviated in principle from Maoist doctrine, nor will the regime as such have been challenged. In such cases it takes very careful and subtle analyses to determine precisely where the differences and points of opposition lie. The episode of the work groups offers a first example.

Another explanation lies in the fact that Mao's prestige is so exceptional that it has to be considered as a specific factor in the political life of China. There are no grounds for thinking that Mao Tse-tung exercises power in a rigid or despotic manner. On the contrary, there are numerous indications tending to show that he is meticulous about consulting his collaborators before making a decision, and that he subsequently makes a point of saying that it was a joint decision; there are even cases where he has not hesitated to stand aside and made no effort to impose his views over theirs. This

---

[22] There is nothing unusual about two tendencies claiming kinship with the same doctrine or the same man. Lenin and Kautsky both fought each other in the name ᶜ Marx, as did Stalin and Trotsky in the name of Lenin. What is unusual here is that different political forces confront each other, both in the name of Mao, during his lifetime.

personal prestige serves a useful political purpose in present-day China, namely to lend human support to abstract notions such as national unity, the state, and revolution. It evokes a moral rather than an absolute authority. The Chairman's prestige and reputation for perspicacity are such that, when the country is faced with a serious, complicated, or nagging problem, his opinion becomes vitally important. To understand the special position and veneration of Chairman Mao in China today, one has to remember the poverty-ridden conditions, which approximated slavery, the unbearable humiliations which were the lot of the average Chinese prior to 1949. The fact is that the regime of which Mao is the head liberated the Chinese from their servitude, and that in itself explains the sometimes naïve veneration which typifies the political life of the country.

This phenomenon tempts some commentators to compare Mao to Stalin. I should simply like to point out one of the consequences of this aspect of Chinese politics. In a regime where the masses as well as the members of the Communist Party are in the habit of associating whatever they do with the person, the doctrine, and the work of their Chairman—both because that is how they feel and because the propaganda machine is there to remind them—it is politically ineffective to say that one is anti-Mao. Therefore, those who oppose him do so indirectly. On the surface good Maoists, they carry on their dissidence through a kind of clandestine warfare.

What Mao managed during the Cultural Revolution was to create conditions that obliged this subterranean opposition to abandon at least certain of its subterfuges and surface, where it was easier to deal with. He created conditions such that, to apply the new policy he had launched with the Cultural Revolution, various and contradictory initiatives could develop. In ordinary times the members of the Communist Party and the population have an area defined by the political line laid down by the Party Center in which they operate freely. The Chinese Communists have the good sense to consult the masses before embarking on any major policy, but once that policy is determined, its application by each individual is guided by directives from the higher echelons of authority. But if the Party relaxes the discipline that it generally demands from its members and from the population, the area of freedom is considerably enlarged. If the possibility is also offered to dispute the decisions of the higher-echelon authorities, then the area of initiative becomes very broad indeed. The Cultural Revolution took place in accordance with these principles. What it did—and it was a veritable tour de force—was to give free rein to various currents and tendencies, many of which clashed, without ever challenging the regime of Mao himself.

To bring this off, what is required—and perhaps all that is required—is for the Central Committee, the Politburo, and the specialized organs which emanate from them—the Group in Charge of the Cultural Revolution, the Military Commission, etc.—to cease and desist, at least for a certain time, from giving direction and supplying detailed directives, to abstain from approving—or disapproving—the various decisions made by the middle- and upper-echelon authorities of the Communist Party. This was the case a number of times during the Cultural Revolution, particularly during the episode of the work teams. Although reduced politically and operationally, centralism remained powerful ideologically through the intense propaganda of the radio and press, which incited the people to unite and work for the Cultural Revolution. Deprived of the possibility of precise directives on which to rely, forced to interpret broadly based ideological documents, expected to take the initiative, each person had to react creatively to the situation, in as many ways as human conduct could devise, revealing in so doing his deep social and political tendencies.

The reduction of centralism explains why the decision to send out work teams was not the brain child of the central organisms but was decided on locally, by certain city governments and in some instances by various ministries (Industry, Agriculture, Foreign Affairs).[23]

I tend to believe that the Chairman's absence from the scene during the "fifty days" was voluntary. It can be seen as responding to the desire to make his absence from Peking—which abroad was judged as mysterious—point up the reduction of central power and give its consequences full play. Mao's opponents were thus given an opportunity to manipulate the work teams as they saw fit. What we have here is a situation roughly parallel to that created by the presence of P'eng Chen at the head of the Cultural Revolution in January and February 1966.

---

[23] Liu and Teng, however, made use of their positions on the Politburo and the Party Secretariat to disseminate certain reports about the work teams as though they emanated from the Central Committee.

This tactic tended to set the revolutionary dynamic in motion by spontaneously bringing to light any basic division between the conservative elements and others more in tune with that dynamic. By coming to the fore and assuming the leadership of the former group, Liu Shao-ch'i and Teng Hsiao-p'ing revealed their hostility to the masses.

CHAPTER TWO

· FROM THE MEETING ON AUGUST 1, 1966, ·
· TO OCTOBER 1, 1966 ·

*1. The Eleventh Central Committee Plenum of the
Chinese Communist Party, August 1–12, 1966*

Condemnation of the Work Teams' Activities

One constant of the Chinese Cultural Revolution is that times
of political and structural central control periodically give
way to times of strong, clear-cut leadership and direction. The work
team episode offers an instance of one of those periods of reduced
central control during which the opposition had a larger than normal latitude to operate in. The opposition used this time to try and
prevent the masses from also taking advantage of the enlarged
parameters of freedom; in the case of the work teams, the attempt
was made to nip in the bud the effervescence and initiative of the
students and workers that had exploded during the months of May
and June. The latters' resistance to this repressive effort led to a
conflict of tendencies.

The meeting of the Central Committee at the beginning of
August would offer it the opportunity to analyze the various and
conflicting currents and countercurrents, to condemn the activities
of the work groups, and to provide much clearer guidelines than it
had in the past concerning the future development and evolution of
the Cultural Revolution. The official Chinese press time and again
stressed that this meeting was held under the chairmanship of Mao
Tse-tung and that several of the documents subsequently published
had been written by him.

We know relatively little about what went on during this meeting,
as no minutes or résumés of the discussions were published. Not

even who attended the meeting was announced until the week after it was over. The importance of this meeting, however, becomes immediately clear on reading the two documents which it adopted.

One of the documents is the "Communiqué of the Eleventh Plenary Session of the Eighth Central Committee of the Communist Party of China." Relatively brief, and written in an especially vigorous style, the communiqué is in three parts.

The first deals with the domestic situation of the country. It takes note of the progress made in various areas, and the growth of the Chinese economy. But it also devotes an unusually large space to ideological problems. It recalls the progress already made in the sense of transforming more strongly and effectively revolutionary mores and ideas, and stresses the necessity to carry forward and develop "the revolutionary tradition of the mass line." The prose literally bristles with energy and purpose, and some of the text reads like a call-to-arms, or an admonishment:

> "Have faith in the masses, rely on them, boldly arouse them and respect their initiative."
> "Dare to make revolution, and be good at making revolution."
> "Don't be afraid of disturbances."
> "Oppose the taking of the bourgeois stand, the shielding of rightist, attacks on the Left, and repression of the Great Proletarian Cultural Revolution."

The last point is clearly aimed at undercutting and condemning the activities of the work teams and those who, either by bureaucratic reflex or conscious opposition to Mao's policies, had up to this time tried to restrain the mobilization of the masses.

All in all, this first part reminds the people of the stakes of the Cultural Revolution: consolidation of the dictatorship of the proletariat, prevention of a revisionist takeover of the leadership of the Party and the state and the restoration of capitalism, renewed adherence to the principle of proletarian internationalism, and the creation of conditions for the country's gradual transition to communism in the future.

The second part deals with the international situation and sets forth the complex of themes which have since become the basis for Chinese foreign policy.

The writing of the third part is even more vigorous than that of the first two. Entitled "Hold High the Great Banner of Mao Tse-tung's Thought," it underscores Mao's original contribution to Marxism-Leninism which, it says, "he has inherited, defended, and developed . . . with genius," and calls for the intensive study of Comrade Mao Tse-tung's works by the whole Party and the whole nation, and to make full use of them in the course of the Cultural Revolution.

Since 1965 it had become common to praise the Party Chairman, but generally in the context of eulogizing not his person but his doctrine. This is the first time that the highest officials not only express but emphasize, not the thought but the person of Mao. Taking into account the absence of such eulogies at an earlier period and their almost constant appearance in later texts, we can only deduce that this Eleventh Plenary Session unquestionably saw a strengthening of Mao's personal position on the Central Committee, and that the lines of the first part of the communiqué indicate disapproval of Liu Shao-ch'i and Teng Hsiao-p'ing, without however citing them by name.

The Sixteen-Point Decision

The second important document to issue from the Eleventh Plenum is the "Decision of the Central Committee of the Chinese Communist Party Concerning the Great Proletarian Cultural Revolution," known as the Sixteen-Point Decision.[1] This text condemns the activity of the work teams even more clearly. More, it is the basic, programmatic "charter" for the Cultural Revolution, detailing and evaluating the movement up to that point and setting forth principles and policies for its future evolution.

In order to understand the Cultural Revolution from this point forward, a relatively detailed analysis of the Decision is required.

The first point reestablishes clearly the targets of the Cultural Revolution, a matter that the work teams had managed to confuse. Those targets are persons in authority who are taking the capitalist road—the *cso tze-pai*—as well as certain academic and cultural authorities who continue to propagate bourgeois ideology. This in effect reversed the thrust of the movement whereby people not in the above categories—workers, students, middle- or lower-echelon Party authorities—had been the object of attacks.

Point two stresses that while certain revolutionaries can and do

[1] See Appendix 3.

make errors and show shortcomings, "*their general revolutionary orientation has been correct from the beginning.*" [Emphasis added.] The document reemphasizes its faith in the young people —whom it terms "pathbreakers"—who in the month of May showed their revolutionary zeal in debates and big-character posters, and condemns those who tried to discredit them as either ultraleftists or counterrevolutionaries. Point two also candidly admits that the resistance of those who would take the capitalist road is still "fairly strong and stubborn," and adds that the mobilization of the masses, under the Party's direction, is more necessary than ever before to surmount these obstacles.

Point three declares that the outcome of the Cultural Revolution will be determined by the ability of the leaders of the Party "*boldly to arouse the masses.*" [Emphasis added.]

Point four predicates that it is up to the masses to liberate themselves, "and any method of doing things in their stead must not be used." The masses must be trusted: "Rely on them and respect their initiative. Cast out fear. Don't be afraid of disturbances."

Point five condemns the attacks on the masses and on the broad numbers of cadres, and reasserts the strategic principle of the unity of "more than 95 percent of the cadres and more than 95 percent of the masses" against the rightists and revisionists. At the same time it calls upon the people to make a careful distinction between the anti-Party rightists and those who, while supporting the Party and socialism, have said or done something wrong.

Point six reaffirms the necessity to distinguish the contradictions that exist among the people, which are healthy and normal, and those which exist "between ourselves and the enemy," which are not. This point also indicates that reason, not physical violence, is the proper method to be used in this struggle. This is a condemnation of certain acts of violence committed in the early phases of the movement by pupils and students against their teachers and against some ex-bourgeois. But it is also aimed at the violence committed during the "fifty days" of recent memory against certain elements of the revolutionary left who were sometimes assaulted by people whom the work teams had convinced that they were dealing with anti-Party elements. Point six also stresses that it is normal for the masses to hold different views, and adds that those who are in the minority must not be coerced into adopting the majority views, for "sometimes the truth is with the minority." The full import of that point becomes apparent when one remembers that during the period of the work teams and of Liu's line this was the situation of those who opposed them.

Point seven wastes no time in dealing specifically with this problem: "In certain schools, units, and work teams of the Cultural Revolution, some of the persons in charge have organized counterattacks against the masses who put up big-character posters criticizing them." And it adds: "These people have even advanced such slogans as: opposition to the leaders of a unit or a work team means opposition to the Central Committee of the Party, means opposition to the Party and socialism, means counterrevolution." Which is clear condemnation of the line imposed by the work groups. "No measures should be taken against students at universities, colleges, middle schools and primary schools because of problems that arise in the movement," except where "there is clear evidence of crimes such as murder, arson, poisoning, sabotage or theft of state secrets, which should be handled in accordance with the law." The implication here is that any other disturbance except those specifically cited will be tolerated, and since the spectrum of such possible disorders is rather large it is easy to understand that the subsequent disorders and disturbances were sometimes intense.

Point eight stipulates that there are four categories of cadres: the first and second, which constitute the vast majority, consists of those who are "good" and "comparatively good"; the third category is made up of those who have made serious mistakes but have not become anti-Party or antisocialist rightists; the fourth and final category is comprised of the small number of anti-Party, antisocialist rightists. This last classification is very important, for it had to be applied to all cadres, and as we shall see long debates will be required to determine just who, in the various Party branches, falls into it.

Such are the salient points of the Central Committee's Decision. Its publication marks a complete reversal of the direction taken by the movement in its preceding phase; it is the beginning of an entirely new phase.

From this point onward the principle of full and complete mobilization of the masses is an accomplished fact and will be further stimulated. The problem that must still be settled properly is that of hitting the true targets of the Cultural Revolution, as this document so clearly points out.

In neither of the two texts is Liu Shao-ch'i or Teng Hsiao-p'ing mentioned by name. Nor did the official party press single them

out as opposing Mao Tse-tung. The parallel press of the Red
Guards, which was just beginning to appear, and the big-character posters were conspicuous by their silence about these two
leaders. As anyone familiar with Chinese political practices and
customs will realize, what this meant was that at this stage the
nature of their errors had not yet been clearly defined and they had
not yet been classified in the category of anti-Party leaders who
should be relieved of their functions and dismissed.

2.   The Consequences of the Eleventh Central Committee
Plenum

The Appearance of the Red Guards

One of the first consequences of the Eleventh Plenary Session of
the Central Committee was the open appearance of the Red
Guards. This was a mass organization made up of high-school and
university students and teachers. It was not born all of a sudden. Its
existence, as we have already noted, went back to the beginning of
the upheaval in the schools and universities. At that time certain
students and teachers had banded together into cells of varying
sizes whose purpose was to focus their activities and criticize bourgeois teaching methods as well as those who practiced them. During
the period of the work teams these revolutionary cells were frequently reduced to operating semiclandestinely, for they were the
target of scathing attacks. It is probable that upon his return to
Peking in mid-July Mao Tse-tung took pains to establish contact
with these groups and encourage them to persevere. The official
communiqué of the Eleventh Plenum indicated in any case that
their representatives were present at the meeting which put a stop
to the line advocated by Liu Shao-ch'i and Teng Hsiao-p'ing.[2]
Immediately after August 12 these groups were organized not only
in Peking but throughout China. They existed in every teaching
establishment in the country.

One of the principal reproaches made against teaching methods
prior to the Cultural Revolution was that it disadvantaged the students with peasant and working-class backgrounds. For understandable reasons these students had little help from their family
background in studies whose purely intellectual, impractical aspects

---

[2] The official texts use the term "were present," which may mean that they were
simply there as observers, without the right to vote.

were strong. The sons of ex-bourgeois, on the contrary, had considerably less trouble assimilating a curriculum that differed only slightly from traditional methods. That doubtless explains not only the fact that there were a disproportionate number of the latter in the universities but also the accusation leveled against the leaders of some teaching establishments that they discriminated against and were hostile to, at least in their attitudes, the children of peasants and workers. Only these last named were authorized to enter the Red Guards, thus turning the tables and instituting a reverse discrimination.[3]

These young people, both boys and girls, who were sometimes referred to as "little generals," soon appeared in large numbers both in the schools and in the streets. They could be recognized by their red cotton armbands on which could be discerned three large characters: *Hong Wei Bing* (Red Guard); other, smaller characters along the edge indicated their detachment and the name of their school. These designations were reproduced on the big red flags they carried when they paraded to meetings. Usually they wore khaki, but there was no general rule, and some members of the Red Guard wore blue or gray cotton. Since in China you don't have to be a soldier to wear khaki, their real distinguishing mark was the armband. In age they varied from twelve to thirty, with the high-school students, whose ages ranged from twelve to seventeen, in the majority. There were similar groups in some offices and factories, but these were relatively few and were mainly in apprentice schools. They were organized into sections, with several sections forming a detachment, and they set up progressive headquarters at the provincial and municipal levels. The use of this terminology should not lead the reader to conclude that we are dealing with a military or paramilitary organization, although a number of poorly informed journalists have jumped to this conclusion. These groups freely elected their leaders, who were constantly subject to recall by those who had elected them. There was nothing very military about either the discipline or the sense of organization of the Red Guards, and in fact these were often missing, which is not really all that astonishing considering their youth and inexperience. What is more, we should bear in mind that the Red Guards were never granted authorization to bear arms.

[3] There were exceptions, for it was stipulated that anyone who had proved his revolutionary ardor or political awareness, even though he was not of peasant or working-class background, could join.

The Role of the Red Guards

The Red Guards' activities had two goals: one was psychological, the other political. And both, ultimately, were intended to increase the number of people participating in the Cultural Revolution.

In August 1966 the Cultural Revolution was in a state of uneven development. It had aroused enthusiasm and wild debates in the schools and universities, but was felt less in the factories and offices; further, Peking above all, and to some extent Canton and Shanghai, were where the action was. Therefore the situation had to be changed.

What was needed was some sort of spectacular indication that the class struggle between the proletariat and the bourgeoisie was far from ended, and to impress that fact strongly on the minds of the people through some palpable proof. Once this "climate" had been created, it would be far easier to involve the population as a whole in the movement. Therefore, suddenly and swiftly, the full power of the Party propaganda machine was focused on the Red Guards of Peking who, emerging from their schools, streamed out into the city. One of their first efforts was to debaptize the names of streets and store signs which either derived from or evoked memory of Imperial China, and to paint over with white paint the mandarin images on the wooden porches of the Summer Palace. The purpose of this initial enterprise was to point up, through a very simple yet graphic example, the persistence of feudal influences in the life of the socialist regime. These acts resulted in the Western press' exaggerated reports that the Red Guards were "fanatic iconoclasts." The truth is, vandalism and destruction were rare indeed, and this may have been due in part to the fact that the authorities took precautions to close the museums and protect the monuments from the very first days of the Cultural Revolution.[4]

The second act of the Red Guards was to conduct searches among former capitalists and landed proprietors. There they proceeded to

---

[4] It has been reported that the Red Guards burned books; I can only say that I never personally saw it happen. Still, there were excesses. In one part of Peking the Red Guards smashed some stone lions, and elsewhere a bas-relief sculpture. In one cemetery gravestones were desecrated. The leaders of the Cultural Revolution strongly condemned these acts, which at no time became generalized. Nor was there any basis for writing, as one Western newspaper did, that the treasures of old China were being destroyed "by fire and sword." The death of the writer Lao She (Lau Shaw) occurred under circumstances that remain obscure, but to attribute it to the Red Guards or make them responsible is pure speculation, for there is nothing in the facts to warrant any such allegation.

confiscate gold, jewelry, opium pipes, and opium stores that these latter had managed to keep, as well as any weapons they found and the deeds to their former property. This was broadcast by the Chinese press, and exhibitions of the confiscated material were held as proof positive that the bourgeoisie still existed and was waiting in the wings for better times. These acts on the part of the Red Guards were at times accompanied by useless acts of violence, which in large measure accounted for the highly unflattering picture that the Western press painted of them, but the truth is that this picture was greatly distorted.

Using articles in the newspapers and magazines, films, and radio programs of various kinds, the Communist leaders soon familiarized all the Chinese people with the activities of these young people whom one met in swarms in the streets of the capital. The press did not stop singing the praises of these Red Guards who were hostile to any idea that smacked of conservatism, whose aspirations were generous and pure. It thus prepared public opinion for the second phase of their operations, which began very rapidly and lasted for several months, whereas the first phase, just described, lasted only three weeks.

The objective of this new phase was more complex: to bear the torch of the Cultural Revolution to the entire Chinese society. These young students and high-school pupils whose task it was to bear the torch had not been caught up in the strain of professional or other routines, nor had their sense of initiative or critical acuity been dulled by bureaucratic vexations. They were less inhibited than their elders, and little inclined to respect any discipline. True, they lacked experience, but that had its positive aspect, too, for their ideals had not been tarnished by disappointments and afflictions. Thus they constituted a kind of ideal catalyst for a society which seemed threatened with hardening of the revolutionary arteries through lack of internal controversies. It was through the influence of the Red Guards that the population learned to discuss, dispute, to talk loudly and freely. What Mao and his followers managed so skillfully was to calculate how to use this force within the framework of their strategy without ruining its spontaneity, all the while orienting it constantly toward the preservation and reinforcement of the revolutionary ideal and not toward the sterile discussion of its goals.

The goal of the Red Guards, then, was to carry their ideas, their enthusiasm, and their critical sense to those centers where the movement had made but little progress, and to stimulate the discovery and criticism of the "capitalist roaders," of the rightists, and of the "Black-Gang" faction of P'eng Chen.

This implied that there should be Red Guards everywhere. Shanghai, another avant-garde city, had its share, as did Canton and several other major Chinese cities. But it also meant that the Red Guards were free to go out into the countryside, to those places—which were then far from few—where the revolutionary movement had not really taken very deep root. Point three of the August 8 Decision had emphasized that "in many units, the persons in charge have a very poor understanding of the task of leadership in this great struggle," and that "their leadership is far from being conscientious and effective."

The leadership of the Communist Party, therefore, encouraged the Red Guards to travel the length and breadth of China in order to have *"chuan lien"*—exchanges of revolutionary experiences. Special measures were taken so that most of the Red Guards had a chance to come to Peking and see for themselves what had taken place, profit from the example of the revolutionaries in the capital, and take the good word back with them to their native towns and cities. Meanwhile, the Red Guards from Peking also fanned out into the provinces to tell about their experiences and urge the local population to take a careful look at the Party cadres in their area, in an attempt to ferret out those who might be followers of the black line. They further urged the local people to make full use of big-character posters and to organize to resist the possible abuses and bureaucratic methods of certain leaders. Finally, they disseminated as widely as possible the Party directives and the Party Decision, the "Sixteen Points." Indeed, it was a question of mobilizing literally millions of people, and in various places far removed news often traveled slowly or poorly. In certain cases, old or relatively old people did not know how to read or had little practice at it. Besides, at times some cadres of the Party dragged their feet in disseminating news from the capital. This was why that oral propaganda was so necessary. Free transportation was provided the travelers, while others set out on foot, thus renewing the traditions of the Chinese Communist Army.

Some Red Guards traveled considerable distances. Several detachments undertook "long marches" of more than 600 miles, stopping along the way in factories and communes. They participated in manual labor and handed out copies of Mao's sayings, which they sometimes printed on small portable presses that became one of their trademarks. They distributed copies of Mao's *Little Red Book* everywhere they went (till then it had been generally distributed only in the army), and it too became part of their outfit at the same time it became part of history.

After the Eleventh Plenum the Central Committee decided to reprint Mao Tse-tung's works in massive quantities, as well as the famous *Little Red Book*. These quotations, which the Chinese brandished so freely and widely in meetings during the Cultural Revolution, were assembled in 1964 for the soldiers of the People's Liberation Army. They offered in brief Mao's fundamental views on a number of problems: the class struggle, the Communist Party, war and peace, literature and art, the relationships between the army and the people, etc. Starting in August, 1966, hundreds of millions of copies of the *Little Red Book* were printed; it was an ingenious way of acquainting the Chinese masses with the basic elements of Marxism.

In Peking the visiting Red Guards were taken care of with remarkable organization by the military: they were housed, fed, and transported in such a way that over a four-month period Peking had a supplementary, transient population of a million extra people without any apparent strain on the food supply or the transportation system. There was a new look in the city streets: young, booted Mongolians dressed in long belted tunics strode side by side with Uigurs from faraway Sinkiang, with their bright, shimmering provincial costumes. Among the Red Guards from the western region of China, which for centuries has been the crossroads of various migrations, one could see, next to local types, close to the Turks ethnically, a smattering of blue-eyed blonds. There were also slight Tibetans, their faces tanned by the mountain winds, wrapped in their multicolored coats and wearing broad-brimmed felt hats similar to those worn by the Indians of Peru. Stores and buses, gardens and restaurants resounded with various accents and dialects. All of China was in Peking, in all its prodigious, manifold variety.

Mao Tse-tung Receives the Red Guards

The arrival of the Red Guards from the provinces led to a number of spectacular rallies in the capital. Every two weeks huge rallies, comprising over a million people each, were organized on T'ien-an-Men Square, where high-ranking Party members gave important speeches to guide and direct the Red Guards' activities.

The first of these gigantic rallies was held on August 18, 1966, in the course of which Mao Tse-tung donned a Red Guard arm-band, thereby publicly demonstrating his support of the movement. This gathering, like those that followed it, was an extraordinary spectacle, a mass meeting but also a kind of youth rally held in an atmosphere of indescribable enthusiasm.

The Party press reports on this meeting furnish us with a number of basic clues. This rally confirmed the increased importance of the role henceforth played by the Defense Minister and from that point on Vice-Chairman of the Central Committee, Lin Piao, who appeared as Mao's "close comrade-in-arms" and eventual successor. Those familiar with political customs of socialist countries know that official press reports of any public meeting or rally are accom-panied by the list of personalities present, who are not named in any haphazard order but in the order of their rank in the hierarchy. Thus in the reports of August 19 it is interesting to note that Liu Shao-ch'i and Teng Hsiao-p'ing were listed seventh and eleventh respectively, instead of in their former positions, which were second and sixth—a sure sign of their semidisgrace. On the same list one could also note the change in rank of Ch'en Po-ta, Mao's former secretary in Yenan, who jumped from twenty-third to fifth and became head of the Group in Charge of the Cultural Revolution, responsible directly to the Central Committee. This Group, which had been in existence for only a few weeks and about which little had been heard, was destined to play a major role in subsequent events. Bear in mind that it was not made up exclusively of mem-bers of the Central Committee, but that it included as well members of certain local cadres of the Party which the Group had recruited. For the sake of simplicity I shall refer to this group as GCCR.

Another person to rise in the hierarchy at this time was K'ang Sheng, who jumped to sixth position below Mao and was named an adviser to the above group. K'ang Sheng had long been close to Mao Tse-tung, especially at Yenan, and had had the responsibility for relationships with Communist parties in other countries. Finally, another person to rise noticeably in rank was T'ao Chu, who moved from ninety-fifth to fourth position in the Politburo. Since 1949 he had been a leading Party secretary in South China.

Aside from these details—which were certainly important—the official press remained silent about Liu Shao-ch'i, still chairman of the People's Republic, and Teng Hsiao-p'ing, still secretary of the Central Committee. Aside from what was stated in the Sixteen-

Point Decision, no allusion was made to their past activities, to those of the work teams, or to the necessity of attempting a critical evaluation of the one or the other. The press, on the other hand, scathingly attacked the "Black Gang" and analyzed their misdeeds at great length, suggesting at various times that those leaders who had opted for the capitalist road should be ousted, thus implying that others were involved, even though they were not named nor was it specified in just what areas they were operating. The leaders who were about to be criticized by the masses at this time were therefore going to be assimilated by the masses as members of the "Black Gang."

During the first meeting between Mao and the Red Guards, on that morning of August 18, two speeches were given; one by Lin Piao and the other by Chou En-lai. Mao himself did not speak, nor was he to at any of the subsequent rallies.[5] The Minister of Defense expressed his support and that of the Central Committee for the activities of the Red Guard. He declared once again, without going into precise details, that the leaders still following the capitalist road —the *tso tze-pai*—must be ousted, the "monarchists" had to be fought, and the masses had to be mobilized. The Sixteen-Point Party Decision, he said, must be rigorously followed; at the end of his speech he suggested that the Cultural Revolution would last a long time and pass through many complicated and varied phases. Premier Chou En-lai, who had been absent during the "fifty days" on diplomatic missions to Rumania and Albania, made a shorter speech on more or less the same themes.

Popular mobilization was encouraged on every front, and continued to develop stage by stage.

The Extension of the Cultural Revolution

By inviting the population to voice its opinions freely on the activities of the local Party cadres, the central organs of the capital

---

[5] Mao Tse-tung had not spoken in public for many years. Nor had he given any radio speeches for a very long time. There are two possible explanations for this which complement each other, though neither is really satisfactory. One is that his position as arbiter for the Chinese State obliged him to maintain a certain reserve vis-à-vis immediate internal conflicts, and that rather than pronounce himself on any such subject he preferred to allow a certain margin for development. This reserve on his part was voluntary, and authorized the various conflicting factions to confront one another, even though each might claim to be following the Maoist line. The other specific explanation sometimes given is that Mao's provincial accent, in a country where the number of dialects poses a considerable problem, makes him difficult to understand.

were hoping to accomplish two things: first, to bring to light any possible bureaucratic abuses, and second, to expose those who opposed the Party line. The local organizations of the Party were obliged to accept the criticisms, sum them up and correct any errors, and at the same time place the blame on those leaders responsible for these errors, either dismissing them from their functions or asking them to mend their ways.

The mass movement was meant to act as kind of "detector," revealing who the cadres were in whom the population had confidence, and whom they rejected. Mao Tse-tung was well aware of the fact, after the experiences of the Socialist Education Movement and the work teams, that the opposition inside the Party ranks would do its best to check the undertaking and limit the criticisms of the Party from elements outside the Party ranks. He also knew that the encrusted bureaucracy and red tape would also act in the same direction. The mass movement, however, could also reveal these restraining efforts wherever they appeared, which was exactly what the Party leadership was hoping for. Once they had been forced to surface, an effort would have to be made to separate the real opposition from simple bureaucratic abuse.

It is always difficult to rouse any population and incite it to participate in political activities. Not only do the goals have to be clearly explained, but leaders have to be found to guide the people and arouse their enthusiasm. This generalized phenomenon was made all the more complicated in China by the sheer weight of the Party apparatus and the presence within its ranks of people opposed to the undertaking. It was obviously to surmount these built-in difficulties that the decision was made to press into service the high-school and university youth, and to send them on revolutionary-exchange missions throughout the country. The Party was betting on the youth's spontaneity and spirit of contradiction to bring others into the movement, and the calculation worked.

Little by little, in every province, Red Guards who returned from their trek to Peking became organized. They proved to be extremely active and effective, making good use of big-character posters, informing the local population what had happened in the capital, and urging everyone to examine, in the light of the Sixteen-Point Party Decision, certain local cadres whose conduct struck them as being less than acceptable. One could see Red Guards streaming through the streets of the cities and, in trucks on which loudspeakers were mounted, driving along provincial roads. Wherever they went they revealed the kinds of criticisms being leveled at some cadres. Bouquets of handbills and mimeographed brochures were distributed, in which detailed explanations were given of the problems the people were facing both in their own provinces and elsewhere, especially in Peking.

The Red Guards tried very hard to make close contacts wherever they went with the entire population, and in particular with the workers, who were meant to play a prime role. After the departure of the Red Guards a growing number of people got involved in the movement of criticizing certain municipal and provincial leaders of the Party who might be associated with the "Black Gang" led by P'eng Chen and Lu Ting-yi. And little by little, with the help of the press which did not let a day go by without mention of the movement, it took root and the population began to mobilize itself. Following the example of the Red Guards, mass organizations began to appear in offices and factories alike.

The Cultural Revolution Reaches the Factories

By asking the workers to emulate the Red Guards and proceed to question and evaluate their cadres, the central authorities were taking a risk of impeding production. It was obviously impossible to stop the factories from functioning as classes had been suspended. The initial arrivals of the Red Guards at the factories did in fact disrupt production: they came at any hour, moved right into the work sections, made on-the-spot proclamations, and improvised meetings then and there.

When the first groups of workers were organized they also began criticizing and evaluating and using big-character posters. They held discussion meetings which did tend to disrupt the normal work flow. To counter this, one began to see and hear a theme that was very often repeated: the freedom to meet and discuss on the part of the masses should not lead to neglect of their work. This theme was taken up and a slogan was coined out of point fourteen of the Sixteen-Point Decision, which had already foreseen this eventuality: "Grasp the revolution and promote production," a theme that Chou En-lai was to reiterate on September 15, 1966, during the third rally of the Red Guards.

From this point on the leaders of the Cultural Revolution would make periodic recommendations both to the Red Guards and to the nascent workers' groups to guide their activities and organization.

The first recommendation was to respect, in all factories, the measures that had been taken at the time of the "four clean-ups," a component part of the Socialist Education Movement. These measures were aimed at keeping material and equipment in good working order, at organizing production teams and rotating them, and at maintaining proper stocks and sales.

The second was to make the revolution in the place where you work. Since the Red Guards were not workers, they should carry on their revolutionary activities outside the factories. Workers and Red Guards should establish their political contacts outside of working hours and away from the factories.

The third recommendation, which derived from the second, was to refrain from going into production areas other than your own, and to organize political groups in conformance with the administrative subdivisions of your factory. In other words, workers in one shop ought to confine their criticisms to their own shop and not attempt to criticize neighboring shops whose problems they knew but imperfectly. However, when it came to evaluating higher echelons of authority, all workers were free to join in that endeavor.

This structure is the one the mass organizations would follow as they developed: detachments at the shop level; regiments at the factory level; headquarters at the municipal or provincial level. This same basic structure prevailed in the offices and universities: detachments at the departmental level and regiments at the university level, or, in the case of offices, detachments for any given office, and regiments at the departmental level. This tendency on the part of the Chinese to use military terminology is therefore not by any means confined to students, but appears to be general.

As more and more people and units began to follow the example of the Red Guards, and as the national press and radio multiplied their appeals to mobilize the masses, the number of these organizations increased: they formed, joined into larger units, and took on a recognizable structure.

Let us remember that, even though their members wore red armbands on which was emblazoned the name of their regiment, they should not be thought of as "Red Guards," a name applicable only to high-school and university students. The workers and office employees involved in the mass organizations were "rebels" or "proletarian revolutionaries." In this respect the Chinese vocabulary is very precise, and the term "Red Guard" cannot be applied indiscriminately to anyone involved in the Cultural Revolution.

It was not long before there was a veritable flowering of these organizations concerned specifically with the ideological front, for there were no restrictions on the formation of such groups, and ultimately the Chinese were few and far between who had not participated in some way in the Cultural Revolution, through their shop, their office, their department. As with the Red Guards, their leaders were elected and were subject to dismissal at any time. The paper and ink required to compose the big-character posters were made available in all work areas at no cost. Vehicles, whether motorcycles, cars, or trucks, which were assigned to various sectors or offices, were put at the disposal of the "rebels." The cost of printing leaflets, installing loudspeakers, and arranging meetings was also covered by the various local offices and factories. Both organically and materially the possibility of assessing and evaluating Party policies at all levels, and the conduct of the cadres, was turned into a reality.

Workers-Students: The Same Struggle

The publication of the Sixteen-Point Decision and the condemnation of the work teams obviously did not put a stop to the activities of the opposition. Where this opposition now decided to turn its attention was to preventing the workers' movement and the student movement from joining forces, especially in those areas where for one reason or another the Cultural Revolution had been slow to take hold.

From Mao's point of view, the activities of the students were not in themselves enough to be decisive. The students, having had the initial awareness, could play the role of catalyst, but only the working class, once it had been mobilized to enforce his policies, was in a position to shift the balance of power and crush the opposition by a thrust of revolutionary fervor. At least we can be sure that such was Mao's wager. In the West, a number of fanciful speculations about Chinese communism tend to make one think that Chairman Mao's sole concern has been the political role of the peasants. The following statement by Mao, made in July 1967, several months after the stage of the Cultural Revolution that we have been discussing, is revealing:

> The revolutionary intellectuals and the young students were the first to achieve consciousness, which is in accord with the laws of revolutionary development. . . . The devel-

> opment of the movement showed that the workers and peas-
> ants are always the main force—the soldiers are only workers
> and peasants in uniform. . . . Only when the broad masses
> of workers and peasants arose was all that bourgeois stuff
> thoroughly smashed; while the revolutionary intellectuals and
> young students had to fall back into a subsidiary place.

The decisive role of the workers made their mobilization manda-
tory. The Red Guards therefore made every effort to make contact
with them in the factories, and as we have seen this resulted in the
creation of massive worker organizations analogous to those of the
Red Guards. These worker and student organizations were to constitute centers of joint leadership on the urban and provincial level
which, subsequently, would play a predominant role.

It is necessary to add that this melding took a certain time, and
in some cases the contacts between workers and the Red Guards
were not without some friction. Mao's opponents on the Central
Committee were almost all high-ranking provincial leaders. Aside
from those who had been compromised and associated with the
P'eng Chen–Lu Ting-yi faction, the others—even more numerous—
were still in office. In the provinces or cities where they held sway
they maneuvered, often furiously, to keep the students away from
the factories.[6]

Reading the big-character posters that lined the walls of Peking,
and hearing the accounts by countless Red Guards of their adven-
tures during this period shows that in many places Party leaders put
as many obstacles in their path as possible.

It was easy enough for certain provincial leaders to take advantage of the difficulties that intellectuals had in establishing relationships with the workers. There were differences of customs and
mentalities: a tendency on the part of the students toward abstract
theories, counterbalanced on the part of the workers by a practical
sense and a certain sensitivity, which at times led to misunderstand-
ings and hurt feelings. What is more, at times the Red Guards
tended to be heavy-handed. The nascent resentment thus caused
was upon occasion fanned, by devious and secret methods, into
real hostility. Frictions arose because the Red Guards, as they criss-

---

[6] One cannot help but be struck by the similarity between the Chinese situation
and what was to happen in France two years later. In May 1968 one saw the
French Communist unions doing their best to keep the students and workers apart.
The similarity is all the more remarkable when one realizes that what happened in
France was not based on any effort by the French to emulate the Chinese. In fact
the Cultural Revolution was virtually unknown in France in 1968.

crossed the country, would land in localities with which they were completely unfamiliar and, instead of proceeding to talk with the local inhabitants and exchange information, would become involved with the criticisms in progress. Being poorly informed, they sometimes committed errors. Certain hardened bureaucrats took advantage of the situation to incite workers and peasants to attack, sometimes physically, the Red Guards. Reminding the local people of what the Party had done for them in the area since Liberation, recalling how much their living standards had been raised, ticking off the list of living quarters and factories that had been built, these local leaders implied that any attack on them was an attack on all these advances. Resorting to the methods of the work teams, they portrayed the Red Guards as counterrevolutionaries.

Hoodwinking one part of the people this way, they went on to set it against another part which, in the wake of the Red Guards, was becoming involved in the trend toward criticism. The opposition, realizing that it was impossible to stop the mobilization of the masses, did their best from this point forward to limit its effects by splitting it up.

On September 15, Lin Piao, speaking from the rostrum at T'ien-an-Men Square, alluded to these events and warned:

> Some people are now going against Chairman Mao's instructions and the sixteen-point decision. By exploiting the profound class feelings of the masses of workers and peasants for the Party and Chairman Mao, they are creating antagonism between the masses of workers and peasants and the revolutionary students and are inciting the former to struggle against the latter. Under no circumstances must we let them hoodwink us![7]

From then on the central organs of the Party multiplied their appeals and warnings: the *tso-tze-pai* constitute a minority, but they can fool and confuse well-intentioned people. Thus the people must remain constantly on their guard and not allow themselves to be led in any direction without giving each proposal careful thought. That differences of opinion exist is not abnormal; on the contrary, there should be differences. The important point to remember is to resolve the problems that arise with these differences. Above all, differences should be dealt with through discussion and not through violence,

[7] See *Peking Review*, No. 39, September 23, 1966.

for as Chairman Mao has noted, internal disputes should not be treated in the same way as disputes with the enemy.

The Sixteen-Point Party Decision, the press recalled, had noted: "In the course of normal and full debate, the masses will affirm what is right, correct what is wrong and gradually reach unanimity." Such assertions may well seem highly optimistic; and yet it is undeniable that they provided the inspiration for the conduct of the Cultural Revolution at least during its first two years. They stem from Mao's conviction that one has to have faith in the masses. For him, the confrontation of various opinions is not only inevitable but desirable and beneficent. As for the possible disturbances that might result from such confrontations, Mao is ready and willing to take that risk, for as he says, the revolution is "not a dinner party." The Party Chairman seems to have been convinced that the overall leadership of the Cultural Revolution by the GCCR, the activities of the revolutionary cadres of the Party, and the dynamism of the youth would prove sufficient to keep the struggle right on course. The vicissitudes, the contradictions, the debates, even the clashes or the rash or abortive efforts, are part and parcel of any revolution and should not be cause for concern. Nonetheless, the Party press, referring to the Sixteen Points, stressed that the people should assure the triumph of right over wrong through peaceful means. Opposing groups should not, they said, fight or allow themselves to call one another names that ought to be reserved for true enemies, but in the spirit of the Party Decision try to convince one another of the soundness of their position.

The Question of Disorders

At this stage a few words should be said regarding the disturbances which marked the Cultural Revolution. During the period that we have just discussed, for example, there were incipient disturbances and clashes, but they constituted only a minor aspect of the situation, the most important of which was the extension of the movement to the people throughout the whole of China, at the instigation of the Red Guards and in particular by their making contact with the factories. This was the major goal of the period, and it was reached.

The Chinese leaders seemed to feel that under the circumstances a certain amount of disturbance and violence was normal. Some fifteen years ago Mao Tse-tung had written: "In a big country like ours, one should not be upset by the disturbances caused by a hand-ful of people." Several times in the course of the Cultural Revolu-tion Mao went even further and stated in declarations that were not reproduced in the official Party press: "We must not be afraid of rows. The bigger they are the better it is."[8]

It is obvious that the immensity of China attenuates the effects and scope of any disturbances, which tend to remain localized. General-ized disorders are virtually a practical impossibility in China. In that same declaration of July 1967 Mao went on to say:

> In the cataclysmic changes that have developed over the past year there has naturally been chaos everywhere. There is no connection between the chaos in one place and that in another. Even violent struggle is very good, because once contradictions are exposed they are easily resolved.

An understanding of such ideas casts a whole new light on the upheavals that occurred in China during the Cultural Revolution. Foreign papers often explained them as being symptomatic of the difficulties Mao Tse-tung was running into in applying his policies, and to a certain extent this is true. The fact is, most of the disturb-ances stemmed from those opposed to the official line. But what was often omitted was that not only were these disturbances toler-ated but it was as if they were actually desired, at least in the initial stages of the movement. The scarcely concealed pleasure with which some anti-China hands commented on the events that occurred on the mainland—I am thinking especially of the Soviet commentators —can only be understood by their total lack of knowledge of this aspect of the matter.

It is impossible to conceive of any revolution without the massive involvement of the people. The Chinese Cultural Revolution is no exception to that rule. And no mass movement is possible simply by state fiat dictating that it operate within strictly defined limits. For the Cultural Revolution to take place, the Chinese state was, by its own initiative, obliged to restrict its control over the life of the people. With the regime of the proletarain dictatorship withering away, certain forms of popular democracy had to be allowed full scope. Therefore, in accordance with this principle of diminished

[8] See Appendix 4, "Mao Tse-tung Analyzes the Cultural Revolution."

central control, the police, the army, and the government that controlled them had to limit their involvement during the Cultural Revolution and not only allow the differences that existed to surface but also allow the people to settle their own problems. The Sixteen-Point Decision had foreseen this possibility and had clearly stated: "Put daring above everything else" and "Don't be afraid of disturbances." Ultimately, these disturbances were even necessary, if one wanted the population, and especially the youth who had never seen the revolution, to educate themselves in the course of the struggle.

Here again, the Sixteen-Point Decision had clearly traced the evolution the struggle was to take: "Because the resistance is fairly strong, there will be reversals and even repeated reversals in this struggle. There is no harm in this. It tempers the proletariat and other working people, and especially the younger generation, teaches them lessons and gives them experience, and helps them to understand that the revolutionary road zigzags and does not run smoothly." However, to pretend that Mao was unconcerned about the violence, or that he actively encouraged it at all times, would be a gross exaggeration. Soon afterward, in the spring and summer of 1967, all the Chinese leaders were to become deeply concerned about the chaos and confusion. Some of their previous statements would then appear far too sanguine.

New Brakes, New Struggles

Throughout this period from the beginning of August to October 1966, the Cultural Revolution spread out to include the whole of China, but there was no noticeable increase in its scope.

What was especially noteworthy was that the episode of the work teams, with all the burning questions it had raised, was virtually passed over in silence. Aside from the allusions to them contained in the Sixteen Points, and the demotions of Liu Shao-ch'i and Teng Hsiao-p'ing, there were few signs that the problem had even been discussed. Yet there can be no doubt whatever that the Eleventh Plenum had indeed debated the matter. What appears to be the case is that no final conclusion was reached. No open criticism had been leveled at the general secretary of the Central Committee or the head of the government. The work teams had been withdrawn and no more was heard about them. One might have concluded that the incident was closed.

Mao Tse-tung and his followers did not seem to want to enlarge the scope of the Cultural Revolution. Was it because the opposition was still strong enough to prevent them from going any further? That seems far from certain. What seems more likely was that the Maoists were proceeding in accordance with preconceived, progressive plans and preferred to wait, meanwhile furbishing new weapons. During the summer Mao and his followers were focusing their efforts, with some degree of success, on speeding up the mobilization of the masses. Using the Red Guards as their detonator, they spread far and wide throughout China the habit of questioning, and promoted the creation of mass organizations, thus setting up the apparatus which would allow them to move to the next phase. The objectives, meanwhile, remained rather vague: those promulgated—fight against old, entrenched habits, unmask any new aspects of the "black line"—were really short-range goals. Looking back, one gets the impression that the summer of the Red Guards, in spite of all the publicity it received abroad, remains an important but nonetheless fairly unclear episode. One had the constant feeling of watching battle preparations rather than the battle itself. Mao Tse-tung is mobilizing his troops, but it is an armed vigil for a battle to be fought in the fall.

Within the Central Committee this situation corresponded to a sort of temporary and unstable equilibrium. The Maoists had put an end to the work teams and, through the creation of the Red Guards, had stimulated the mass movement. But the damage had been slight, and the opposition had not been dealt any real, clean-cut blows. Liu and Teng in particular still held positions of relatively high rank, even though they had been demoted.

In principle, everyone was agreed that an attack against the "Black Gang" ought to be continued—even though it had been rendered inoffensive—but every faction was preparing for new confrontations. For as we have seen, the opposition was far from inactive. Mao is reported to have said, at the close of the Eleventh Plenum, and referring to the Sixteen Points: "Don't think that whatever is written in a resolution will be automatically applied by all the Party committees!"

The fact is, in places where the mobilization of the masses was impeded, and where during the "fifty days" the revolutionaries were attacked, there was little change in the overall picture. The August 8 Decision was followed only with reluctance.

T'ao Chu, the Man of the Hour

At Peking, after the departure of the work teams, we saw the arrival of the "liaison agents." These people, who were few in number, were theoretically in charge of coordinating the political activities within the framework of the Cultural Revolution in the schools, universities, and factories. They were in contact with the leaders of the movement, the GCCR among others, and especially with the man whose star was in the ascendant at that time: T'ao Chu.

T'ao Chu was a veteran cadre of the Chinese Communist Party, having been a member since about 1927. After 1949 he was a leading Party secretary in South China. Fairly tall and with sharp features topped by a gray mop of hair, he was about sixty, although he looked younger. After the Eleventh Plenum, as we have seen, he rocketed from the middle ranks of the hierarchy to fourth position, behind Chou En-lai and ahead of Liu and Teng.

Foreign observers considered T'ao Chu a dyed-in-the-wool Maoist whose promotion could be traced to Mao's confidence in him. His subsequent dismissal therefore appeared incomprehensible. In fact, in China appearances are deceiving—this is a rule one can never repeat often enough—and from outside appearances are often all one perceives.

As adviser to the GCCR, T'ao soon emerged as that body's most influential member. All the other members of the GCCR were lower than he in rank, and for all practical purposes he became the top man in that organization, ahead of his nominal chief Ch'en Po-ta. It was he who was to enforce and apply the middle line which emerged from the Eleventh Plenary Session: pursuit of the Cultural Revolution by focusing the attack on the P'eng Chen–Liu Ting-yi faction while sparing Liu Shao-ch'i and Teng Hsiao-p'ing. T'ao Chu had championed this policy during the Eleventh Plenum. Mao Tse-tung was well aware that that was a way of protecting his enemies, and one more obstacle to be overcome. He overcame it with a tactical subtlety that can only be described as consummate. He cleverly allowed this orientation, which T'ao Chu had been charged with implementing, to develop, thus enabling its anti-revolutionary aspect to be clearly revealed.

With T'ao Chu leading the way, therefore, the movement against the "Black Gang" proceeded, and he made a number of declarations against them in Peking to various representatives of the Red

Guards. It was his idea to send liaison agents into the universities, and he chose them carefully among those in whom he had full confidence. The main one among them was Wang Jen-chung, a member of the Central Committee and an important Party leader at Wuhan, who coordinated the activities of the liaison agents and took directly under his wing the justly famous Tsinghua University. The liaison agents were quite efficient in preventing the criticisms from moving off target, that is, away from P'eng Chen and Lu Ting-yi. What this meant in effect was that, either directly or indirectly, any attempt to reexamine the "fifty days" was repressed. In the case of Tsinghua University, where such repression was difficult given the smoldering resentment among the students about the way the work teams had acted, Wang Jen-chung resorted to the most underhanded methods to keep Liu Shao-ch'i and his wife Wang Kuang-mei from being profoundly criticized. Since the victims of those work teams were in no mood to be repressed, the problem of protecting Liu and his wife from their attacks became increasingly difficult. In other places where persons victimized by the work teams requested their rehabilitation, the liaison agents opposed them in the same way, so as not to be compelled to reopen the files of the "fifty days."

Out of this developed the famous "black documents" quarrel. In China there are ideological files on citizens who have committed serious political errors or counterrevolutionary acts, and these files are kept in local Party Committee headquarters. The people who had been attacked by the work groups requested that the files on them which the work teams had compiled be destroyed. Many of the files on these people contained serious allegations of counterrevolutionary activities. The people with such files wanted them burned because they judged that to keep them was tantamount to maintaining means of possible bureaucratic and police pressure against revolutionaries. Their demands were not met, for T'ao Chu's tactic was to avoid doing anything that might embarrass Liu Shao-ch'i. Thus the files remained hermetically sealed, and the "black documents" remained part of their subjects' records. The tensions that were born during the "fifty days" were thus prolonged; the most disputatious elements, whose activities had been restrained and opposed by the work teams, little by little began to resist T'ao Chu's liaison agents. As had happened in July, their resistance earned them the epithets of "anti-Party" and "antisocialist."

One aspect of T'ao Chu's policy, locally enforced by the liaison agents, was to help form committees for the Cultural Revolution. Point nine of the Sixteen-Point Decision had called for the creation of such committees in the schools, in local and central administrations, and in the factories. In theory, they were to be formed through a system of general elections, after the manner of the Paris Commune, after ample discussion and consultation; further, if any elected members proved inadequate or incompetent, they could be recalled and replaced.

In fact, under the prevailing circumstances, the opposition of Mao, incarnated henceforth by T'ao Chu, continued strong, as the policies and tactics employed by the work groups were still enforced, at times by the intermediary of the liaison agents, at others by those sectors of the Party apparatus that the opposition still controlled. Through both these channels, the formation of local committees was influenced.

In some key places, especially in the Peking universities, where the disputes had raged hot and furious, and where opposition to the work teams had been fairly strong, the intervention of the masses, which was required by the Sixteen Points, was still blocked. By maneuvers both direct and indirect, both the liaison agents and the Party committees under the influence of the opposition—aided and abetted by the personal intervention of T'ao Chu, who visited several schools himself—managed to keep those avant-garde elements who had shown where they stood in June and July by their unrelenting opposition to Liu Shao-ch'i, away from the leadership of the committees. Basically, these committees were manned either by persons intent on compromise or by openly conservative members who refused on the one hand to reconsider the files on the victims of the "fifty days" and on the other directed the movement solely against the "Black Gang" of P'eng Chen and Lu Ting-yi.

Later on, some Red Guard publications blamed T'ao Chu and his liaison agents for having prevented the development of revolutionary exchanges, that is, keeping the students from traveling freely and widely in the provinces. On this point we have too little to go on to make any proper assessment. All we can say is that if indeed they tried to stem the student movement, they apparently did a rather poor job of it.

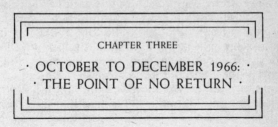

CHAPTER THREE

· OCTOBER TO DECEMBER 1966: ·
· THE POINT OF NO RETURN ·

1.   Red Flag *Number 13*

The Rubicon Is Crossed

Reading the editorial that appeared in *Red Flag* on October 3, 1966, many Chinese understood that the Cultural Revolution was about to take a new tack. So far there had been that strange episode of June and July when the work teams had been suddenly dispatched and then just as suddenly withdrawn—not without leaving their share of bitter memories behind—after which the attention had focused on something else, on the "Black Gang" again and its misdeeds, on the struggle against tradition and the bourgeoisie. And then there were those Red Guards with their constant coming and going, making a lot of sound and fury. There was no longer any mention of the work teams now, and yet their presence in the universities had raised many problems, to judge by the polemics and clashes which they had provoked and which, according to rumor, were still going on. And what to make of the fact that Liu Shao-ch'i and Teng Hsiao-p'ing were no longer mentioned and photographed with Chairman Mao? Some people claimed that they had committed serious errors at the time the work teams were rampant. Wasn't it possible that these two things were linked?

Red Flag No. 13, 1966, which appeared shortly after the national holiday—this year characterized not by processions of flower-bedecked tanks or artistic exhibitions but by an immense parade of more than two million Red Guards and "rebels" which lasted for some seven hours—explained the situation more precisely.

91

In factories, schools, offices—everywhere—collective readings of this editorial were held. It was thus confirmed officially that in certain places repression continued to be exercised against the revolutionaries, that those who had been falsely accused had not always been properly rehabilitated, and that certain leaders, with malice aforethought, were still trying to pit students against each other.

For the first time, the readers and listeners of this *Red Flag* editorial noted, new terms appeared. Mention had been made of a "struggle between two lines within the Party." The implication was obviously that since the start of the Cultural Revolution there had been in the Party midst a truly reactionary current opposed to Mao's line, followed by certain leaders.

The Chinese, with a long experience of political battles since Liberation, remembered the Kao Kang affair in 1952,[1] and the campaign against "rightists" in 1957. They knew that they were in for more of the same kind of struggle, but in all likelihood they had no idea that the battle looming would dwarf those that had gone before. What they could gather, however, from reading words such as "If those who have committed errors persist in their attitude and thereby render them more heinous, these contradictions can become antagonistic," was that men of high rank who till this point had been spared public disgrace were possibly in for a hard time.

The citizens of Peking had this feeling confirmed a few days later when they found at several intersections posters which reproduced a text by Mao that had been written two months earlier during the Eleventh Plenum. In essence it said that during the "fifty days" when the work teams had been active, "some leaders" had adopted a reactionary position and had tried to choke off the Cultural Revolution. "They have stood facts on their head and juggled black and white . . . suppressed revolutionaries . . . imposed a white terror," proclaimed the posters.[2] These were serious accusations, and doubtless announced important events to come.

P'eng Chen, Lu Ting-yi, and their close collaborators had been stripped of their functions in May, and since that time had been in no position to play any political role. Who were the leaders Mao was alluding to without specifically naming them? The answer had to be: Liu Shao-ch'i and Teng Hsiao-p'ing.

---

[1] Kao Kang was the target of a Party purge in 1954, accused of "splitism." Dismissed in disgrace, he committed suicide.

[2] See *Peking Review*, No. 33, August 11, 1967. The Party Chairman titled his article "Bombard the Headquarters—My *Ta-tzu-pao*."

In the days that followed rumors spread throughout Peking that posters attacking the two by name had been placed at both Peita—Peking University—and Tsinghua University.

Other posters violently attacking Li Hsueh-feng, the new leader of the Peking municipality whose role in the dispatch of the work teams we have already noted, simultaneously appeared in the streets in the center of the city.

From this point on events moved thick and fast. At the end of October further posters in the city announced that on October 23 Liu Shao-ch'i had made a self-criticism before the Central Committee. Extracts of what he had said were cited. The posters also indicated that this self-criticism had not been satisfactory and had not settled the problems.

In the course of a sixth meeting with the Red Guards on T'ien-an-Men Square on November 3, Lin Piao clearly suggested the existence of and struggle between two lines within the Party. Gradually the nature of the conflict and the context of the Cultural Revolution were becoming apparent.

A policy struggle in the highest echelons of government was going on, and the elimination of the P'eng Chen faction had in no way ended it. Above and beyond this struggle was another one that pitted Mao against some of the highest-ranking Party leaders, whose positions had till then, with good reason, seemed much more solid than that of P'eng Chen.

A Few Specifics about Political Habits in China and the Treatment of Political Opponents

After the episode of the work teams and the Eleventh Plenum, Mao Tse-tung had marked a point against his opponents by having their political orientation scored and by downgrading them in the Party hierarchy. Nevertheless, in Communist China it is rare that an opponent in the Party apparatus is immediately considered an enemy to be expelled from the Party and stripped of his functions, as was—and still is—the case in the Soviet Union, for example. And, in China such people are not threatened with physical liquidation.

Generally the opponent finds himself placed in the following situation: The press and the official Party organs carefully refrain from making any definitive judgment on him, or even naming him, nor is he tagged with any of the familiar epithets applied to those in disgrace. However, he is asked to explain his viewpoint or conduct before the members of the Party organism to which he belongs. In the case of Liu Shao-ch'i it must have been either an expanded meeting of the Secretariat of the Party or the Politburo. Aside from this, he may be accused by name, but only in a nonofficial way, as was the case with the Peking posters. During the Cultural Revolution the numerous posters which attacked and criticized the Party leaders remained the responsibility of their authors only, and we shall see that the central organs of the Party were far from officially backing the stands taken.

At the end of a relatively long period, then, some official action is taken concerning an opponent's case. If it is judged that he has modified his position, he can resume his function and everything that was written on the posters in the streets is "forgotten." If on the contrary he is deemed to have persisted in his errors, then he can be relieved of his responsibilities and even expelled from the Party; it is then and only then that his name appears in the official Party press and he is pointed out as an enemy of the Party.

This system allows for a continually escalated attack against an opponent. The case of Liu Shao-ch'i offers a concrete example. At the Eleventh Plenum there was talk of the errors of the work teams, of counterattacks against revolutionaries, but no mention was made of Liu. However, in the official listing he was downgraded in the hierarchy, an initial sign that he was in trouble. In October the posters quoting Mao took a harder line, alluding to bourgeois, reactionary tendencies, but still not naming him. At the same time the press, likewise not referring to Liu by name, was filled with innuendos regarding a bourgeois, reactionary line and contradictions which, while not antagonistic, might become so.

Finally, a new step: students are encouraged and authorized to put up posters attacking the head of state by name. All this may appear extremely complicated to Westerners, but the Chinese understand perfectly each successive stage of this progression, and in every instance give it the significance it deserves.

While this system may be tortuous, it is not absurd. It has the merit of leaving the exit door ajar as long as possible for anyone in the opposition. During this period any adversary has ample time to give up his ideas and correct his ways. If he does, he helps dry up the opposition's spring and will sometimes be allowed to retain his responsibilities.

The complement of criticism is self-criticism or self-evaluation, to which Liu Shao-ch'i subjected himself in October 1966. In the highly individualistic Western societies self-criticism is looked upon with disfavor. In China, where individualism has been downgraded, it is widespread and no one seems overconcerned about it.

Self-criticism is the balance sheet drawn up by a person in response to the accusations leveled against him by others, generally his co-workers. It takes a certain amount of time for the object of outside criticism to receive and analyze the allegations, and if they are justified take measures to adopt them. Sessions involving criticism and self-criticism are therefore fairly common.

When a political opponent is involved, self-criticism had a more subtle objective. It allows for the efficient reduction of a flow of ideas. The more self-criticisms there are, the more the opposition is reduced and its influence contracts, for those who remain faithful to any political conviction have fewer chances of holding onto it if the leaders give it up. But in both cases it derives essentially from the same principle.

It is not a punishment. It is based on this formula enunciated by Mao: "Treat the illness to save the patient." It is not a question of repression but of reeducation. The mind and spirit of the person being criticized must be touched, to allow him to reach the ideological root of his errors, which is always a matter of individualism. The self-criticism, then, leads to a reversal of values and, through a kind of victory over oneself, results in the subject's rediscovering the true path of revolution.

To be valid, such a self-criticism cannot be a mere formality, nor can it be extracted by physical constraint. On this point, Mao declared, "We must turn our attention to those accused of being counterrevolutionaries or those who have committed errors. The target of the attack must be limited. We must help and educate. The accent must be upon valid proof, inquiries, and study. It is absolutely impermissible to extract confessions by force or to make use of any such confessions. Those who have committed errors must receive our help and be reeducated."

This attitude virtually does away with the need for imprisoning or executing one's adversaries, with all the inexpiable hate and rancor that follow in its wake. One can only regret that the Soviet Union and some of the Eastern European countries did not have the foresight to avoid this sort of error, which today weighs so heavily upon the conscience of the whole European Communist movement.

In order not to be formalistic, self-criticisms must also truly touch the root of the conflict in order to effect reconciliation. Although it is rare in China for anyone accused of political recalcitrance to refuse to offer his self-criticism, all self-criticisms are not automatically accepted. During the Cultural Revolution, Liu Shao-ch'i's, for one, was not. Which brings us back to our account of the events.

The Major Turning Point

For the Cultural Revolution, the fall of 1966 was a period of growing complexity and dissensions. The new offensive launched against the bourgeois reactionary line brought with it a certain number of consequences, not the least of which was the stiffening resistance it provoked. Indeed, the opposition marshaled its forces both to defend itself and to launch a counterattack.

We have already mentioned this invisible, imperceptible opposition which refused openly to declare itself. The elimination of the P'eng Chen faction had cast some light upon it, but only weakly. The activities of the work teams had further clarified both who and what that opposition was before the Eleventh Plenum condemned them. Liu Shao-ch'i and Teng Hsiao-p'ing had been attacked, but no sanctions had been levied against them, and they still held their posts. The targets of the movement were still limited. Officially, only P'eng Chen's "black" faction was under attack. But there was no assurance that the movement would remain so restricted. The Liu–Teng file might be reopened at any time, and that threat hung like Damocles' sword over the heads of the anti-Maoists.

During the August Plenum some people hoped that that matter would be settled without further ado. But their desires were frustrated, and a middle-ground policy was adopted.

T'ao Chu personally wanted the attack to confine itself to denouncing P'eng Chen. His presence in the leadership of the GCCR guaranteed that the middle-ground policy would be followed. Liu Shao-ch'i and Teng Hsiao-p'ing, according to him, were "old revolutionaries who had encountered new problems." What had to be resolved in their case was a "problem of conscience." They had misunderstood the new conditions of the struggle: they had prepared themselves poorly for it. T'ao Chu minimized the case, and during the entire summer one might have thought that his position prevailed.

But things were worsening for the opposition. The Red Guards had inculcated far and wide the habit of writing big-character posters denouncing bureaucratism and attacking the cadres. From this point on these practices were no longer the prerogatives of the schools and universities, but were widespread, especially in the factories. Faced with this highly volatile situation and the unusual methods the masses were using, the opposition felt nervous. Weren't Mao and his followers preparing some new offensive against them?

Weren't there rumors that, at Tsinghua University, the young hotheads, always the same, not content with attacking the liaison agents and the new committees for the Cultural Revolution, had gone so far as to attack by name both Liu Shao-ch'i and his wife and call them traitors?

Even more disquieting to the opposition was the *Red Flag* editorial of October 3. On all fronts, things were growing more serious, for now the attacks were not directed solely against the P'eng Chen faction but also against Liu and Teng. Their concern grew even deeper when they saw that, while posters hostile to the two above-named leaders were being raised in the city by the students, the GCCR, which till then had followed T'ao Chu's line, was taking no measures to stop them. The crucial end game was about to get under way, and the opposition, now aware that T'ao Chu's conciliatory middle-of-the-road policy had been thrust aside, was prepared to fight with renewed vigor.

The Opposition's Weapons

This opposition consisted of some members of the Central Committee, and various local leaders under their influence. The already widespread habit of middle cadres disputing their superiors' decisions to a large extent deprived the latter of their major asset, that is, the powerful responsibilities that enabled them to maneuver major sectors of the Party apparatus. It no longer became a simple matter of issuing cleverly phrased directives to prevent the masses from mobilizing, but in the course of this mobilization and mass organization there was a great deal of confusion and differing opinions on various concrete problems. Since everyone claimed Mao Tse-tung as his authority for speaking or acting, it became possible to intrigue with a certain amount of efficiency.

There was considerable dissension among the population. We have seen that the Cultural Revolution had not developed and expanded at the same rate throughout China. After the summer of the Red Guards the movement had indeed spread throughout the country, but on the work sites and in factories and offices where there were debates and discussions the personnel were often divided.

In any human society there are conservatives, progressives, and people in between. There are those who become more quickly aware than others, and more naturally prone to rebellion, while others get more easily bogged down in routine and tend to be passive. In Chinese factories there were also deeper differences separating certain workers who were better paid, more privileged, and less activist than some of their less well-paid co-workers. Moreover, the work teams had often withdrawn from various schools and factories leaving behind them an atmosphere of division and contradiction. The upshot of all this was that in each individual work unit or school the concepts of what the bourgeois reactionary line and the proletarian revolutionary line really were was often quite different.

Everyone said that the former had to be attacked and the latter supported, but that did not prevent differences, and this quickly led to a very thorny problem. The judgment the masses were supposed to make on the Party cadres became a source of conflict and contradiction and would remain so during a substantial part of the Cultural Revolution. One may recall that during the time of the work teams the cadres had found themselves in a most uncomfortable position: they were the target of the work teams' attacks, and therefore victims. Later they were involved with the suppression of the left and therefore themselves repressors. How could anyone involved on either side look upon these cadres without strong feelings because of this recent past?

This led to the emergence of various mass organizations which either defended or attacked the cadres, and got into heated discussions among themselves. Throughout the many phases of the Cultural Revolution what we find, therefore, is this kind of political equation: faction A attacks X and defends Y; faction B defends X and attacks Y; etc.

In each organization the stands taken reflected the great variety of human conduct: some were moderate, intent on conciliation; others were openly conservative; others were dynamic, leading the way, but at the same time muddle-headed. The Party leaders opposed to Mao Tse-tung obviously reveled in these unsettled conditions, which offered them a marvelous opportunity for maneuver. They soon learned how to make use of every conservative tendency, whether openly or secretly, directly or indirectly, to counter any revolutionary tendencies. Utilizing differences of opinion about the cadres that existed virtually everywhere, they tried with varying degrees of success to divert the main thrust of the attacks away from them and their assistants and colleagues in lower echelons of responsibility. The result was a tangle of tendencies. Those conflicting tendencies that existed within the leadership of the Party were refracted into a multitude of heated controversies in the factories and schools. Mao's opponents used the situation to protect themselves from the attacks of the avant-garde; they also made every effort to fan the flames of conflict and turn them into violent confrontations whenever possible, to keep the masses divided and the nascent mass organizations, whose birth they had not been able to prevent, from growing.

2. The Opposition's Counteroffensive

T'ao Chu's Role

In Peking this divisive process was especially acute. Earlier, during the month of August, two general headquarters for the Red Guards' organizations had been set up in the capital to coordinate their activities. Conflicts appeared in these centers in the course of the summer. Should a profound analysis and criticism of the line applied during the time of the work teams be undertaken, or should that be taken merely as a momentary deviation of the movement, which ought to revert to the bases of the month of June, namely the attack against P'eng Chen? How the work-team episode was judged, and how those Party leaders who at that time had erred in their conduct were to be considered, depended in large measure on their own attitude. If they benefited from the fact that a door was left open to them and mended their ways in the light of the Sixteen Points, automatically the criticisms leveled at them would be modified. But if they persisted the consequences could be more serious. In fact it soon became apparent that the Sixteen Points were not always being applied properly or universally, and that opposition to the growth of the Cultural Revolution was still strong. Since the committees of the Cultural Revolution were sometimes rather timid, there was never any lack of young revolutionaries ready and willing to stimulate the movement of criticism and to extend it. Within a very short time they judged the attitude of the two Red Guard headquarters to be conservative.

This opposition between conservative and revolutionary elements among the Red Guards reflected a diversity of analogous currents within the leadership of the Communist Party itself. During the Eleventh Plenum two tendencies had confronted each other head-on among the leaders: one group wanted to pursue the attacks against Liu Shao-ch'i, the other wanted to protect him. The result was the middle-ground tactic applied by T'ao Chu, and during August and September he was virtually in charge of the Cultural Revolution. Perhaps he should have been on his guard, for his two predecessors were P'eng Chen and Liu Shao-ch'i, and both had been later stripped of their functions and disgraced.

During these two months T'ao Chu was in a position to influence considerably the course of the Cultural Revolution. Having replaced Lu Ting-yi as director of the propaganda bureau, he held a key post, and as adviser to the Group in Charge of the Cultural Revolution he often had the opportunity to see and talk to both high-school and university students. It was he who gave the two Red Guard headquarters their conservative bent. It was on the basis of his advice that during the months of August and September they refrained from attacking Liu and Teng in the universities, or reopening the case of the work teams.

The Third Headquarters of the Red Guard

In the beginning of September some Red Guard groups—and especially those from Tsinghua University, the Aeronautical Institute, and the Geological Institute—fed up with the inhibitions and lack of revolutionary fervor on the part of the two existing Red Guard headquarters, decided to establish a third. From the very beginning this third headquarters launched an attack against both Liu Shao-ch'i and Teng Hsiao-p'ing and sought to criticize the line the work teams had followed during the "fifty days." There is reason to believe that Mao Tse-tung, probably with Ch'en Po-ta as intermediary, was discreetly responsible for the establishment of the Red Guards' Third Headquarters. The nucleus of this new center was made up of students who during June and July had resisted the efforts of the work teams (often with the encouragement of this same Ch'en Po-ta) and who, ever since, had kept on asking not only to be rehabilitated but also that the work teams be tried, a position that had led them progressively to oppose T'ao Chu's liaison agents. When on October 3 the attack against the bourgeois reactionary line personified by Liu and Teng was officially launched, it could only be taken as a repudiation of T'ao Chu's policies, and those who had resisted them took heart.

The new offensive of the Maoist line immediately ran into renewed resistance, which was soon to become violent. At the end of October and beginning of November some members of the Red Guard escalated their differences with the Third Headquarters to the level of pitched battle, with the backing and encouragement of T'ao Chu. Up to now T'ao Chu had managed to play the role of the moderate, but starting with October the wind changed. It was doubtless in order to make people forget his initial moderation, and to parry an expected offensive from the Maoists, that T'ao Chu assumed the stance of a fanatic ultraleftist. It was this public "hardline" image that tended to pull the wool over the eyes of foreign observers.

When he visited the universities, or when students paid him visits, he was full of revolutionary fire and brimstone. Since everyone was now taking an anti-Liu–Teng line, he too found himself obliged to condemn and castigate them, but he managed to do so in such a way that he simply included them among other anti-Maoists. What he was doing, really, was emulating Liu's tactics with respect to the work teams: attack a broad spectrum of people in order to protect a handful. What he implied was that those following the capitalist line were legion and were everywhere. Therefore, according to T'ao Chu, these leaders should be roundly attacked, no matter how exalted their position. "Aside from Mao and Lin Piao," he was reported to have said, "every leader is open to criticism." This opened the way to attacks against Ch'en Po-ta and Chiang Ch'ing, which were led by all those who supported Liu Shao-ch'i or who, for one reason or another, found themselves following a conservative line. One of the prime targets of this same attack was the Red Guards' Third Headquarters.

And once again this conservative current, which involved not only part of the Party leadership but also a portion of the Chinese people, called itself Maoist, revolutionary, and proletarian. More than ever, as the Cultural Revolution progressed, there were people and factions fighting against Mao in the name of Mao. What was happening was a showdown between one current which was really trying to preserve Maoist ideals and strengthen the revolutionary characteristics of the regime, and another, opposite current whose source lay in their levels of Chinese society which could fairly be termed privileged or relatively privileged.

The Lien Tung

The fall of 1966 made the existence of these two basic and opposite currents increasingly obvious. The signs were clear both among
the students and the workers.

The new offensive of the Maoist trend, whose spectacular debut
was the flowering of posters attacking Liu and Teng which
appeared in the center of Peking in October, used the Red Guards'
Third Headquarters as its spearhead. On September 25, Chou
En-lai had received the leaders of this group and given them the
go-ahead.

As October ran its course, a new kind of poster began to appear
in the streets of Peking. These posters were printed, and on them
you saw enlarged photographs of wounded people, some with their
heads bandaged, others in hospital beds with their wounds or
bruises clearly evident. The new posters accused certain organizations of having failed to follow the Sixteen Points' enjoinders of
peaceful debate, and accused them of various acts of violence. Often
those accused of these acts could be seen putting up posters of their
own accusing their accusers of similar acts of violence, or blaming
them for having started the escalation. Since every organization
filled its posters with big-character imprecations and epithets, calling one another "revisionists" and "anti-Maoists," it is understandable that many foreign correspondents cited them as ample evidence
of the trouble which, in their opinion, the Maoists were having. If
one had taken these posters literally, one would have thought that
those attacking were counterrevolutionaries, while those being
attacked were always the defenders of Mao.

In the midst of all this, posters signed by the Central Committee
appeared in the streets of Peking calling for peaceful confrontations,
asking the people not to fight, to kidnap, or to make illegal searches
of anyone's premises. With the arrival of November and the onset
of winter, the Cultural Revolution moved into its most implacable
phase. In spite of the warnings by the Central Committee, the acts
of violence were slated to continue.

During the second half of November there were violent incidents
among the students of the Aeronautical Institute in Peking, and
frequent incidents between Red Guards belonging to the Third
Headquarters and those from the first and second.

The Red Guards counted among their members not only children
of workers and peasants but also the children of the Party cadres.

Some of these had been previously enrolled in special schools, which in some cases had been created especially for them; they were better housed, better equipped, and better staffed than the average school. These schools, whose existence went back to the time of the free zones, had been transformed by Lu Ting-yi and Liu Shao-ch'i into a nursery for a Communist neomandarin class. Today these schools have been done away with, but at the beginning of the Cultural Revolution they still existed and the students who went to them engaged in politics like everyone else. They were privileged, and well aware of it. Thus it was that the students of these schools entered the Cultural Revolution with the following slogan on their lips, revealing where they stood both socially and politically: "From a revolutionary father, a worthy son; from a reactionary father, a vile son!"[3] In other words, as sons of revolutionary leaders, they considered themselves revolutionary by birth. This incredible pretension was tantamount to disinterring the concept of "lineage" and clearly showed that feudal, bourgeois ideas were still alive and well in a socialist society.

These Red Guards joined forces in Peking under the aegis of a United Action Committee (in Chinese, *Lienhe Hsingtung Weiyuanhui*) which wasted no time launching an attack against the Red Guards' Third Headquarters. Themselves convinced, or having been persuaded by persons who had discreetly infiltrated their ranks, that the members of the Third Headquarters were sons of bourgeois or of landowners, and were reactionary, they went after them with a vengeance.

It is hard to know how many victims there were as a result of the United Action Committee's activities. Some murders were reported, although fortunately they seem to have been few and far between. But in all probability there were a great many cases of brutality, assault, kidnaping, and false imprisonment.

The GCCR, which reported directly to the Central Committee, with Ch'en Po-ta and Chiang Ch'ing leading the way, wasted no

[3] At this point the name of Tan Li-fu, a student at Peking University, should be mentioned. Tan Li-fu was the son of an associate state's attorney in the highest people's court. On August 20, 1966, he published a text which was widely circulated in which he elaborated on the theory of lineage. He was one of the leaders of the United Action Committee. During the Cultural Revolution the terms "lineage theory" and "Tan's theory" were synonymous.

The Trotskyist historian, P. Broué, searching hard for some leftist Chinese opposed to Mao, finally thought he had found his man (see *La Verité*, No. 551, March 1971, p. 61). The choice was unfortunate. Tan Li-fu was a pure product and defender of that bureaucracy the Trotskyists everywhere want to tear apart.

time in coming to the support of the Third Headquarters. That did not stop the *Lien Tung*, which simply added the GCCR to its list of targets! And as usual, the conservative *Lien Tung* attacked its opponents in the name of Mao Tse-tung! In particular, the *Lien Tung* accused the GCCR of not following the Sixteen Points and opposing the mobilization of the masses. Once more we see a phenomenon of the Cultural Revolution, in which the right accuses the left of its own shortcomings.

Slogans appeared, especially in the Forestry School, calling for the dissolution of the GCCR. Some of these slogans suggested that since October 3 a false orientation had taken root. That date should come as no surprise when we recall that it was on October 3 that the *Red Flag* editorial had marked the point of departure of a new struggle against Liu Shao-ch'i.

We can see, therefore, that beyond the deceitful slogans and abusive ideological references that this group of Red Guards might make concerning Mao Tse-tung, its deep-rooted policy was to subvert the new policy put into effect by the Maoists since the month of October. This was going to appear all the more clearly in December when the *Lien Tung*, without going so far as to attack Mao himself[4] —which would have been unthinkable in China—did attack Lin Piao by name and call him a "conspirator."[5]

Photostats of documents later revealed that the *Lien Tung* had been the recipient of considerable sums of money from high-ranking officials. What is certain is that this organization had quite important resources at its disposal. Its members traveled widely, generally in motorized vehicles, which are very expensive and hard to come by in China. You could tell them in the street by the fact that they always traveled in fairly large groups and wore a red silk armband with big black characters: *Hong Wei Bing*, the same characters that were to be found on their flags.[6] Specialists in wielding iron bars and bicycle chains, they soon acquired a sinister reputation based on their savage nocturnal forays. Many a wary

---

[4] Still, some Peking University students wrote articles in which they openly denied that Mao could be considered as a Marxist theoretician comparable to Marx, Engels, Lenin, or Stalin.

[5] When Radio Moscow learned of these posters it gave them a big play. What the Russians forgot to mention, though, was the fact that the *Lien Tung* was accusing Lin Piao of being a "new Khrushchev"!—a further proof that Mao's opponents cannot escape the Maoist ideological framework.

[6] All Red Guards wore red armbands with "Red Guard" on them, but the characters were generally yellow or white.

citizen of the capital saw them venturing forth by night on their way to one school or another whose students were their designated victims.

The Red Worker's Army

During this time mass organizations grew by leaps and bounds in the working class. We have seen how, in spite of obstacles, the example of the Red Guards did spread to the working class and led to the latter's participation in the Cultural Revolution. But this "working class" is itself far from unified: it contains a number of layers whose trends are sometimes different. This is true of any working class the world over, and China's is no exception.

The reactionary bourgeois counteroffensive in the fall of 1966 also found a certain support among certain workers' organizations. Thus in October an organization known as the Red Workers' Army was created (principally among the workers of Metallurgical Factory no. 1) which also launched attacks on the Red Guards' Third Headquarters, and on the GCCR. We have little information on this organization, but it would appear that it was made up basically of a number of industrial workers who had benefited from the bonuses and material stimulants that had been instituted during the preceding years by Po I-po when he was Minister of Finance. It also appears that some ranking union leaders (Liu Shao-ch'i had in the past tried to organize the Chinese unions along the lines of their Soviet counterparts, and still had good friends there) either belonged to this organization or gave it their support. In all probability this is the basis for the unfortunate and inaccurate reputation which had Liu as "the workers' man," whereas Mao was sometimes referred to as "the peasants' man." These judgments were based on very flimsy evidence, but carried an aura of authenticity from being repeated so often, and were sometimes taken as gospel truth in the West. In fact, Mao has carried as much weight and authority among the workers as among the peasants.

3.   The Backlash—T'ao Chu's Last Policy

Editorial No. 15

November 1966, then, was a month of tension marked by occasional violence. With the arrival of December, the organs of the

Party which, as was their custom, had remained in the background and allowed the various trends to develop for a few weeks, re-emerged and asserted themselves.

In a speech delivered to representatives of all the mass organizations of Peking, Chou En-lai, in an obvious retort to the *Lien Tung*, declared: "Chairman Mao and Vice-Chairman Lin Piao have full confidence in the Group in Charge of the Cultural Revolution." On December 13 *Red Flag* No. 15 printed a very important editorial, "Seize New Victories,"[7] which called for a counteroffensive to crush the reactionary bourgeois line. Now that the central authorities had condemned their activities, the conservative organizations saw their members desert them en masse. The police tried to disarm them, but without dissolving them.

On December 16 and 17 the Red Guards of the Third Headquarters, whose numbers had swelled considerably over the preceding few weeks, held two giant rallies at the Workers and Peasants' Stadium in Peking, to denounce and counter the Liu Shao-ch'i line. Ch'en Po-ta, Chiang Ch'ing, and K'ang Sheng were present for the first meeting, and Chou En-lai for the second, together with all the members of the GCCR. Some 100,000 people filled the stadium for these rallies, during which the *Lien Tung*'s activities were condemned, as were the different reactionary trends that had been revealed in the attack on the Third Headquarters. This latter organization now pulled out all the stops. On December 17 it launched an attack on an important personality: Wang Jen-chung, the man in charge of coordinating the activities of the liaison agents, the "moving force," if one can use that term, of the Cultural Revolution at Tsinghua University, and a close collaborator of T'ao Chu. At this point T'ao Chu must have felt himself in a very tenuous position.

The offensive against the Third Headquarters had been conducted beneath the cover of T'ao Chu's slogan: "Everyone is open to criticism except Mao and Lin." Mao's opponents use various tactics depending on the particular circumstances: the conservatives willingly employ repressive measures on occasion, either direct or indirect; the "radicals" (who are often the same people in different guise) tend to enlarge the targets and sow confusion on all fronts, thus covering their tracks. T'ao Chu resorted to the first tactic during the summer when he made several speeches which tended to

---

[7] See *Peking Review*, No. 51, December 16, 1966.

make the Liu Shao-ch'i problem seem less grievous, and to the second in the fall when he tried to confuse the meaning of the offensive announced in *Red Flag* No. 13. The accusation against his right arm, Wang Jen-chung, on December 17 was followed soon after by an attack against T'ao Chu himself. About that time posters appeared announcing that he had offered his self-criticism, which had been refused. About two weeks later a *ta-tzu-pao* campaign without precedent in the capital initiated a vilification effort aimed at Liu Shao-ch'i and Teng Hsiao-p'ing; shortly afterward T'ao Chu became part of the same target. For months the streets of Chinese cities rang with shouts of "Down with Liu-Teng-T'ao!"

It was at this time that the foreign observers erred in their assessment of T'ao Chu's role. Since they had concluded from his public utterances that he was an advocate of a "tough-line" policy—an image his dizzying ascent in the ranks helped to foster, and his violent speeches during the preceding few weeks had reinforced—when he was accused by the posters they figured that the accused-accuser was the victim of an anti-Maoist counterattack.

The New Situation

During the icy month of December loudspeakers at every intersection of Peking blared forth the accusations against Liu Shao-ch'i and Teng Hsiao-p'ing. The walls were covered with an avalanche of posters and caricatures vilifying them; thousands of issues of Red Guard newspapers did the same. And yet the official press, although its full force was directed against the reactionary bourgeois line, had not once cited them by name, nor had the official radio. On November 11 and again on November 26, at the time of the two final Red Guard rallies, they had appeared on the rostrum at T'ien-am-Men. Officially, therefore, their fate had not yet been decided. Were they enemies? Or were they comrades who had erred but who could still be saved and rehabilitated? Were the contradictions reparable or irreparable? Although these questions were still officially open, all evidence pointed to the fact that their position had deteriorated. The attacks against them had escalated, and at this juncture all China knew that they had been classified as "uncertain elements."

What about their personal situation? It is impossible to know for sure. What we do know is they did not reappear at any official function after November 27. It is probable that they, like other Chinese leaders who have fallen from grace but whose cases have not been

ultimately decided, were under house arrest and restricted in their
movements except to report for sessions of criticism and self-criticism. We who were in China at the time also recall reading in the
papers that newly assigned ambassadors presented their credentials
not to Liu Shao-ch'i, the head of state, as in the past, but to Soong
Ching Ling.[8]

How can we explain then, given the above circumstances, that
these men who had been deprived of any political influence, or even
any possibility of becoming involved with state affairs, were later
held responsible for subsequent events, and that the vilification
campaign grew even more intense? It may appear illogical but it can
be explained simply by the fact that, even though they had been
rendered politically impotent, the policies they had advocated continued, and their banners were picked up by other men. The subsequent vicissitudes of the struggle between the two lines owed
nothing whatsoever to either Liu or Teng, but in China as elsewhere
any political idea or concept needs a human embodiment. If Mao
was the incarnation of political power, revolutionary line, and
Marxist ideology, Liu Shao-ch'i would henceforth become the per-
sonification of the reactionary, revisionist trend.

The *Red Flag* editorial of December 13 gave an overview of the
movement and began a new phase. While the revolutionary trend
had made progress, it noted, the advocates of the bourgeois reactionary line and the leaders who had opted for the capitalist route
had not been disarmed. Distorting the battle cries of the true revolutionary line, they had sown confusion and insidiously turned some
segments of the population against the proletarian revolutionaries.
"Because the revolutionary masses are firmly opposed to the bourgeois reactionary line," said the editorial, "certain persons with
ulterior motives make use of the slogan of 'opposing the bourgeois
reactionary line' to deceive and confuse the people . . . they continue
to organize those of the masses whom they have hoodwinked to
attack the revolutionary left."[9] This editorial alluded to the fact that
some workers and peasants had been misled into attacking the
revolutionary Red Guards. It also noted that the reactionary line
had been applied not only in places where the work teams had been
sent but in other places as well. The Party Committees had therefore based their attitude on that of the work teams and persecuted

---

[8] The widow of Sun Yat-sen and Vice-Chairman of the People's Republic.
[9] See *Peking Review*, No. 51, December 16, 1966.

real revolutionaries. The leaders in places where this had happened could not reply to the accusations henceforth made against them by pretending that since there had been no work teams in their areas there could be no such problem there. The method employed by some leaders in their opposition to the people and to the revolutionaries consisted of defending themselves against all accusations by the specious argument that the accusations were aimed at the representatives of the proletariat. In case that seems confusing, let me explain by saying that since the October publication of Mao's own *ta-tzu-pao*, "Bombard the Headquarters," it had been generally agreed that the Liu–Teng headquarters, considered bourgeois, should be destroyed and the proletarian headquarters of Mao protected. Some leaders, T'ao Chu among them, tried to defend themselves by claiming that they belonged to the proletarian headquarters. "This," noted the *Red Flag* editorial, "is a typical manifestation of the bourgeois reactionary line."

Alluding to the *Lien Tung* and those who controlled it, including T'ao Chu, the editorial went on: "At the present time, one of the characteristics of the handful of persons within the party who are in authority and are taking the capitalist road, as well as stubbornly clinging to the reactionary bourgeois reactionary line, is that they act behind the scenes—manipulating those mass organizations of students and workers hoodwinked by them, sowing discord, creating factions, provoking conflicts in which force or coercion is used and even resorting to various kinds of illegal means against the revolutionary masses." The editorial emphasized once again the necessity to refrain from using force, congratulated the people on the many successes already achieved, and concluded with a ringing appeal to the proletarian revolutionaries to "do still better . . . seize new victories and fulfill the great historic task entrusted to us by Chairman Mao."

Postscript 1973

With the recent reopening of China to the outside world, and the arrival of a number of foreign journalists and various foreign delegations, a greater flow of information has been made possible, with the result that we have a much clearer view than before of at least some of the events of the Cultural Revolution. With this change, fuller analyses of the meaning and impact of the Cultural Revolution are possible, whereas when I wrote this book it barely finished;

some of its facets were unclear, and most interpretations open to question.

In Chapter 2 I dispute the allegation that the vandalism of the Red Guards was widespread, as was commonly believed in the West. Since then Jacques Guillermaz, in a recent work, has provided a detailed list of monuments desecrated. I have to say, at the risk of being repetitious, that I am reporting in the present volume what I saw and know to be true. Obviously excesses may well have been committed to which I was not a witness. It is nonetheless absurd to maintain or insinuate that these excesses were part of the overall intent of those who planned and promoted the Cultural Revolution.

In this same section I note that the Red Guards had searched the premises of ex-bourgeois, where they had discovered and confiscated weapons and old deeds. I should have also said that counterrevolutionaries and ex-landowners are kept under close surveillance by the masses and are subject to stringent police control. Thus it was to their places of work and residences that the Red Guards repaired, after receiving the lists of names and addresses from the local police stations.

The passage relative to the Chinese leaders in the same chapter needs clarification. Today the world has been informed that Lin Piao died in an airplane accident in Mongolia, on September 13, 1971. According to Peking news releases in July 1972, Lin was fleeing to Russia after having plotted to assassinate Mao. The stories of the conflicts within the top-level of the Chinese hierarchy are often confusing and imprecise; too often they emanate from Taipeh, and are therefore suspect. What we do know, however, is that Lin was already "disgraced" as far back as the fall of 1970, as a result of conflicts having to do with the relationships between the Party and the army, and of differences over foreign policy.

Nonetheless, even with the benefit of hindsight, there is little I need modify or qualify in this work concerning Lin's role in the Cultural Revolution. The fact is, he appears but seldom, for indeed he seemed to play a secondary role, especially compared to that played by Chou En-lai during the same period. There can be little doubt that part of the good opinion earned by the army up to 1969 was due to his leadership. But he nonetheless indulged in oversimplification and was involved in caricatural excesses, in the impoverishment of the context of ideological work and revolutionary theory, with its inevitable corollaries of spontaneism and ultra-leftism.

It is highly probable that Lin and Chou were at odds during the Cultural Revolution. Today we know that Mao, to defeat Liu Shao-ch'i, used a coalition of forces part of which were represented by Lin and part by Chou. But it was not an unshakable coalition. For a long time Mao played the role of arbiter, maintaining a delicate balance among the conflicting tendencies. Later, circumstances compelled him to make choices which were doubtlessly painful in many cases. The speeches both men gave at T'ien-an-Men to welcome the Red Guards were different enough in tone to suggest underlying conflicts. Mao's silence on these occasions fully confirms his role as arbiter.

As for Teng Hsiao-p'ing, whose name is often associated in the same derogatory sense with the counterrevolutionary activities of Liu, we know today that he has been exonerated of that accusation, according to what Chou told Edgar Snow in 1970. Teng remained a member of the Party at the specific request of Mao himself, and he has regained an important post in the government.

Everything I say about T'ao Chu in Part I of the present volume has been solidly confirmed. Nonetheless, his is an especially complex case, the ramifications of which have no place here; to explain it fully, in fact, would require access to the Chinese Communist Party archives, which at present is out of the question. Suffice it to say, however, that his slogan, "Everyone can be overthrown except Mao and Lin," did not fall on deaf ears. Indeed, the resistance of certain Party committees to the Sixteen-Point Decision had resulted in the rejection of all authority. In the eyes of his peers, T'ao Chu thus became the promoter of an anti-Party line which was later to help bring about the collapse of a fairly large number of Party committees. All of this was to make itself felt in the events that followed, especially during the months of February and March.

What I say in the section A Few Specifics about Political Habits in China and the Treatment of Political Opponents in Chapter 3 also calls for further comment.

While it is true that executions in China have been few and far between during the past eighteen years, there were, starting in October 1967, some executions of persons convicted of murder, espionage for Taiwan, and child rape.

As for the matter of self-criticism, I should like to say that I know first-hand, from having lived in China and talked to a number of people who had made their self-criticisms, that it is a long and painful experience. I also know that these practices have often been branded in the West, and especially in the United States, as "brainwashing." This problem is not limited to the time of the Cultural Revolution, and for those interested in the question I refer them to Part Four of Edgar Snow's *Red China Today*.[10]

[10] Random House, New York, 1970.

II

JANUARY 1967
TO APRIL 1967

THE HEART OF THE MATTER

CHAPTER FOUR

· THE JANUARY REVOLUTION
IN SHANGHAI ·

1. The Sharpening Contradictions

The Displacement of the Center of Gravity

We have seen that the Cultural Revolution evolved along two parallel lines, passing from the literary-artistic to the political realm on the one hand, and from the Party apparatus to the universities and factories on the other.

Born on November 10, 1965,[1] the Cultural Revolution revealed its true objective on October 3, 1966,[2] when the open battle against the Liu Shao-ch'i faction began. Prepared by the activities of the Red Guards, this new phase could be led to a successful conclusion only with the assistance of a social force which till that time had not been fully mobilized: the working class.

Throughout the fall of 1966 the role played by the Chinese working class grew in both scope and solidity. As it grew, the role of the students, so important in the beginning, correspondingly declined. This explains why we witnessed at this time a displacement of the center of gravity of the revolutionary movement from the intellectual and administrative center of the country, Peking, to the industrial regions of Heilungkiang (formerly Manchuria) and Shanghai.

[1] Date of the publication of Yao Wen-yuan's article "On the New Historical Play *Hai Jui Dismissed from Office*."
[2] The date on which the editorial appeared in *Red Flag* No. 13.

Shanghai especially would, from this time on, find itself in the vanguard of the Cultural Revolution. From November 1966 forward, the events that occurred in Shanghai follow a fairly typical pattern of the way the Cultural Revolution evolved in the provinces. It should simply be kept in mind that although many regions experienced conflicts similar to those taking place in Shanghai, the time required to resolve them varied, depending on the specific local conditions.

The revolutionary situation in Shanghai stabilized fairly quickly in early 1967, doubtless thanks to the relatively high degree of political awareness among the population. The same was generally true for Heilungkiang, Shansi, and Kweichow. Elsewhere, however, especially in the center and south of the country, the evolution proved to be considerably slower.

The Events of Summer 1966 in Shanghai

If it was in November of 1966 that the events occurring in Shanghai brought that city into the limelight—notably when the powerful workers' organizations accused the mayor and his right-hand man of applying the Liu Shao-ch'i line—a quick look at the events leading up to that confrontation are necessary.

The Municipal Party Committee of Shanghai, having been responsible for firing the first salvos of the Cultural Revolution with its attack on Wu Han, thus enjoyed considerable prestige. Shanghai appeared to be a solidly pro-Maoist bastion, and the remarkable achievements which since 1949 had turned the city into a flourishing industrial capital made the city leaders extremely popular there. Two members of the Municipal Committee had been especially responsible for the explosive events of November 10: Yao Wen-yuan and Chang Ch'un-ch'iao.[3]

At the beginning of the summer of 1966 these two men were summoned to Peking to join the ranks of the GCCR. Ch'en Pei-hsien, first secretary of the East China Bureau Party Committee, and Tsao Ti-ch'iu, the mayor of Shanghai, then became the sole guides of the Cultural Revolution in this great seaport of eastern central China. The political line they applied revealed itself as more and more questionable.

---

[3] The latter was named a permanent member of the Politburo at the Ninth Party Congress, in 1969.

In July work teams appeared in some schools and factories of Shanghai, acting in concert with the Peking work teams. Various pressures were exerted against the students and workers, and some were persecuted. After the Eleventh Plenum had condemned this trend, the Municipal Committee adopted a policy similar to that of T'ao Chu: the episode of the work teams was buried and those revolutionaries who had suffered injustices at their hands were simply not rehabilitated. As in Peking, the "quarrel of the black documents" occurred in Shanghai, with the revolutionaries requesting that they be destroyed and the local Party committees refusing to do so.

At the time when the Red Guards were beginning to fan out throughout the country, Shanghai did not exactly greet those who arrived from Peking with open arms. It is reasonable to assume that the Municipal Party Secretariat was not ecstatic at the sight of these unruly youths streaming into town. They must have been afraid that they would stir up trouble that might well end up focusing on the question of their responsibilities during the work team episode. In many and varied ways, therefore, they tried to prevent the Peking Red Guards from making contact with their Shanghai counterparts, as well as with the workers. This attempt to thwart the Red Guards resulted in an incident that occurred on August 31. Several groups of Peking Red Guards, together with some Red Guards from Shanghai (with whom, in spite of everything, they had managed to make contact), formed a delegation and went to the city hall to request a meeting. The municipal authorities refused to see them. In protest the Red Guards decided to occupy the approaches to the building. The occupation went on until September 4, and caused a furor in the city. Ch'en Pei-hsien and Tsao Ti-ch'iu were furious, and made up their minds to react. Taking advantage of their prestige among their colleagues in the city administration, they called for the Municipal Committee to be defended against the strikers, whom they described as antisocialist troublemakers. A counterdemonstration was organized to try to drive the Red Guards from their positions, and the results, predictably, were violent.

Under the influence of T'ao Chu's middle-of-the-road policy, in Shanghai the Cultural Revolution had remained dull and routine during the months of August and September. Ch'en Pei-hsien and Tsao Ti-ch'iu were of a mind to control the movement as tightly as possible and keep it within limits they considered acceptable. A few members of the "Black Gang" came under attack, but the Municipal Committee of the Party was careful to prevent the scope of the attack from broadening, and was especially careful to prevent the reopening of the work-team files. Thus the Cultural Revolution slipped into the rut of bureaucratism. All sorts of administrative orders and instructions kept the posting of *ta-tzu-pao* and open debates to a minimum. "We must make a distinction," said Ch'en and Tsao, "between the exterior and interior." In the name of this principle it became impossible to know what was going on inside any particular school or enterprise. Attacks against certain members of the Communist Party were perforce kept a secret, and those who were not Party members were not allowed to take part in them.

After the clashes of September 4, however, the Red Guards took matters into their own hands and ignored these municipal prohibitions; they paraded through the streets of Shanghai calling for the perpetrators of the violence to be unmasked. These posters strongly emphasized the fact that opposition to the Red Guards was a direct violation of the Sixteen Points. The Peking Red Guards, together with the elements of the Shanghai Red Guards that had rallied to their position, began a relentless campaign against the bureaucratic restrictions that Ch'en and Tsao had imposed. The Party Decision of August 8 had insisted on the necessity of mobilizing the masses and encouraging both free exchange of opinions and attacks on abuses. To make a distinction between "internal" and "external," the young people asserted, is merely a ploy, a sophism, whose purpose is to intimidate the masses and dissuade them from freely debating the problems and acting upon them. The Red Guards invoked, like a leitmotif, those passages from the Sixteen Points which said: "Put daring above everything else, "Don't be afraid of disturbances," The only method is for the masses to liberate and any method of doing things in their stead must not be used. To do otherwise was to oppose the Central Committee's line, to apply the reactionary bourgeois line.

In spite of the difficulties put in their path, the Red Guards did manage to make contact with the workers who had been persecuted by the work teams and were fighting for their rehabilitation and the destruction of the "black documents." Their tenacious denunciation of the violation of the Party Decision slowly spread until an increasing number of Shanghai citizens began to feel that a real problem did exist. In the evolving circumstances it became impossible for the authorities to completely control or restrain the Red Guards.

What further complicated and compromised the position of the local authorities was the fact that at the same time they were trying to repress the Red Guards, the central press and radio were praising them to the skies. The "little generals" knew full well how to take advantage of this maneuvering room.

2.   The Revolt

The Reversal of the Situation

The editorial in *Red Flag* No. 13 signaled a new escalation in the revolutionary struggle, with widespread repercussions. In a few weeks it would cast a new light on the conflict taking place in Shanghai. By attacking the past episode of the work teams, by condemning the bureaucratic pressures being exerted on the revolutionaries, including the refusal to rehabilitate them and destroy the "black documents," by vigorously denouncing the continuing restraints placed on efforts to mobilize the masses, the October 3 editorial in effect castigated the policy and position of the Shanghai Municipal Committee and the East China Bureau, and of all those who, throughout the length and breadth of China, were following a similar trend. The editorial strongly backed the actions of the Red Guards, which had the immediate effect of making it easier for them to act.

We should again emphasize the overwhelming role that official propaganda plays in Chinese political life. Editorials are disseminated by the millions and are picked up and used by local dailies and radio stations; later they reappear in pamphlets and are read collectively, and the themes reappear as well in newly written articles. Conceived to be read and understood by the least cultivated readers, these simply written articles always exercise an enormous influence.

In October a further article in *Red Flag* underscored the fact that leaders who opposed or resisted the students and pupils by referring to them as ultraleftists, or even as counterrevolutionaries, were applying the reactionary bourgeois line. The fact was, in Shanghai these were precisely the epithets the leaders had been applying to the Red Guards.

At the same time a parallel campaign had been started by the Party press urging the workers to participate with increasing vigor in the criticism movement, and exhorting them not to be deceived by the maneuvers of some Party leaders. The result was a decided upsurge in interest in the Cultural Revolution in the factories: the posting of *ta-tzu-pao* multiplied, and more and more workers began to demand that certain Party cadres account for their actions during the time of the work teams.

In Shanghai, where there is a high-density population of workers, this movement mushroomed. Workers' organizations appeared, multiplied their contacts with the Red Guards, and began to support their activities. This effort had been supported from Peking by the GCCR, which had dispatched two militant Maoists from the capital to Shanghai to speed up the movement. The two militants sent were Nieh Yuan-tzu, who had written the first Marxist-Leninist *ta-tzu-pao*, and K'uai Ta-fu, a student of Tsinghua University famous for having resisted the work team headed by Wang Kuang-mei, the wife of Liu Shao-ch'i. Both these envoys went from factory to factory in Shanghai explaining what had happened in Peking and urging the workers to do the same locally.

In November the Shanghai Workers Revolutionary Headquarters was established. It was made up of various factory organizations in Shanghai determined to fight Ch'en Pei-hsien and Tsao Ti-ch'iu. Thereafter this organization was to work hand-in-glove with the Red Guards and to play a key role in the evolution of events. It began a campaign attacking the two local leaders, whom it accused of having been delinquent at the time of the work teams and also of having tried to subvert the activities of the Red Guards during August and September. Hostile posters began to appear in the streets of Shanghai. From this point on, Ch'en and Tsao were on the defensive. The wind had shifted.

The Anching Incident

The General Headquarters of the "Revolutionary Workers" did not include the entire Shanghai working class. The prestige of the Municipal Committee was still great enough so that it had the confidence of part of the workers. Thus two factions developed in the factories, one pro-Ch'en and Tsao, the other against, and at times they clashed violently.

The two contradictory currents among the working class in Shanghai—based on both natural human differences and economic ones—resulted in the formation of two major organizations which opposed each other: one is the Headquarters already mentioned, which contested the trend of the local authorities; the other was called the Detachment of the Red Defense of Mao Tse-tung, a conservative organization set up by the authorities with the help and backing of some union leaders. Knowing what we know about China now, it will come as no surprise that both organizations claimed to be following the precepts and policies of Mao, and each condemned the other for following the reactionary bourgeois line of Liu Shao-ch'i.

In early November the Workers Revolutionary Headquarters asked Ch'en Pei-hsien and Tsao Ti-ch'iu to appear before them to offer their self-criticisms. Both refused, claiming that while they supported the revolt against the bourgeoisie, they could not condone any revolt against themselves, who represented the proletariat. Needless to say, the upshot was a plethora of disputes and debates among opposing groups throughout the city.

At this point the Headquarters decided to send a delegation to Peking to report to the Central Party organs on the state of affairs in Shanghai and to denounce before them both the mayor and the head of the East China Bureau. With the knowledge and complicity of other Party leaders in East China, Ch'en and Tsao arranged for the train carrying these emissaries to be blocked by demonstrators who had been misled into believing that the train was carrying reactionaries. This incident occurred on November 9, 1966, at Anching, a small station north of Shanghai.

First Intervention of Peking

Since the situation in Shanghai was fairly typical of what was going on in a number of provinces, this seems an appropriate place to attempt to tell how the leaders in Peking were reacting to such events. It is too facile and simplistic to say that the opposition to the Cultural Revolution in certain local branches of Party government was a sign of dissidence, which was often the analysis and conclusion of a number of foreign correspondents. The strength of certain conservative currents in no way meant that these currents were questioning or contesting the continuity of the administration or the political or ideological loyalty of the Communist Party and its leaders, at least superficially. Actually, the fact that this loyalty or continuity was not questioned explains the force of these policy struggles, for everyone thought he was acting in the interest of socialism and according to Mao Tse-tung's doctrine—with the obvious exception, among the conservatives, of certain instigators who were concealing their real objectives. Therefore the Party leaders in Peking refrained in such cases from taking any precipitous action.

Because of their lack of experience, the initiatives undertaken by the Red Guards and "rebel" workers who joined the Cultural Revolution were marked by confusion and a fair share of errors. This might explain why they received the cold shoulder from certain local branches of the Party. When these Party leaders adopted certain measures to limit the activities of the Red Guards or their allies, one had to wait for a while to allow the regional organizations to adjust to a new or unusual situation and to overcome their bureaucratic tendencies. It was therefore not simply a question of blithely condemning as opponents local leaders whom the Cultural Revolution had "taken by surprise." Here again Mao's concern not to over-enlarge the target of revolutionary attacks, which is mentioned again and again in his writings, showed through. Gradually and moderately the Maoist leadership indicated, through written and oral propaganda, the direction to follow, constantly stressing the necessity to mobilize the masses.

It was only after a relatively long period of time that a local Party committee's real persuasions and policies could be fairly determined. If it adapted to the situation and succeeded in guiding the masses toward an increasing involvement in politics, one could forgive and forget. If in spite of repeated directives obstacles were still put in the way of their mobilization and initiatives, then one had to conclude that it was no longer simply a case of entrenched bureaucracy but a sign of open opposition. It was at this point that the Central Party organs stepped in.

This explains why, after the Anching incident in November, the GCCR dispatched its number-two leader, Chang Ch'un-ch'iao, to Shanghai, his native city. He was sent by Peking on a sort of "warning mission." He had orders to have the people who had been arrested at Anching released, and he also came armed with a warning to the two local leaders that they should forthwith abandon their efforts to discourage criticism by the masses on the one hand and to try to divide them into vying—and therefore inefficacious—factions on the other. It was a clear invitation to mend their ways and give up the political line they had been following up to now.

While the *People's Daily* and *Red Flag* were exalting the slogan "To rebel is justified,"[4] which the taboos of authority and the notion of total discipline with respect to one's superiors had tended to erode, it became intolerable for local leaders to brand as reactionaries those who criticized them, and to try to impute antisocialist motives to those who proved to be most outspoken. Since the appearance of the editorial in *Red Flag* No. 13, launching the initial attacks on the work teams, and with the extension of the critical movement throughout the entire country, those who persisted in these maneuvers were coming very close to open opposition to the Party.

The Conflicts Continue

Chang Ch'un-ch'iao singled out for special blame the fact that Ch'en and Tsao had secretly maneuvered some of the mass organizations into a position of opposition toward the Workers Revolutionary Headquarters and had incited them to violence. Perhaps, as he left Shanghai, he still had hopes that they would come around. If such were his thoughts, they were rudely jolted when his Shanghai residence was sacked by members of the Detachment of the Red Defense. The situation in the city had not improved and in fact had even worsened, with a renewal of violence. It was at this critical juncture that Peking openly stepped in.

Those opposed to Mao made liberal use, in their struggle against him, of the tendency on the part of their subordinates to apply bureaucratically any and every directive they received. The fact was, it took a good deal of time for these subordinates to detach themselves from an organizational discipline which was not directed toward revolutionary ends. First of all, it took considerable lucidity on their part: the "rebels" claimed they were acting in the name of Mao, but then so did the Party officials they were criticizing. Each vied with the other in adopting Party slogans and utilizing Marxist terminology. Under these admittedly confusing circumstances, how could one easily tell what was truly revolutionary and what was not? It also took courage to break with one's superiors. Communist discipline is rigorous: to deviate from it can cause all kinds of difficulties, including dismissal. How can anyone justify an act of in-

---

[4] "Marxism comprises a multitude of principles, all of which come down to the single phrase: "To rebel is justified!" That phrase is from Mao's writings. The Red Guards made it their motto.

subordination in the name of the highest interests of the Party if the recognized officials of that same Party condemn you for it? It is understandable that, faced with this problem, many hesitated, all the more so because the freedom to dispute one's superiors in keeping with the slogan "To rebel is justified" was unusual in China, and in fact throughout the entire international Communist movement.

Nonetheless, as soon as the cadres of any given branch of the Party apparatus realized clearly the pernicious role played by some of their leaders, they did break with them. As a result, the leaders found themselves isolated and stripped of their most efficient weapon: the blind obedience of their subordinates. At this point, their opposition to the official line was effectively neutralized.

In December Chang Ch'un-ch'iao returned to Shanghai to try and speed up this process of isolating and neutralizing the opposition, and to keep the momentum of bureaucracy from working in its favor. He made it widely known that the GCCR reproved the conduct of Ch'en and Tsao, and he made a concerted effort to woo the cadres of the Shanghai Municipal Committee away from their influence and control. Chang was well known among the Shanghai cadres, and by December 18 he had succeeded in his plan: a goodly number of the Committee members posted *ta-tzu-pao* disaffiliating themselves from the two secretaries.

That, plus the fact that the Workers Revolutionary Headquarters and the various Red Guard groups had considerably increased their numbers during the preceding few weeks, created conditions favorable for a broad-based coalition against the two leaders and thereby isolated them. The policy of Ch'en and Tsao was verging on defeat.

Sensing the increasing vulnerability of their position, Ch'en and Tsao made one last counterattack. Such was the origin of the "economist" wave which began in the waning days of December.

3. The "Economist" Counteroffensive and the January Revolution

Economism

The Shanghai workers, at this point fully mobilized, formed the vanguard of the Chinese proletariat whose role in the Chinese Cultural Revolution became decisive. They provided the movement with an unprecedented élan. At this stage, the only effective counterattack possible for the opposition was to try and disorganize the workers' ranks. In such cases one of the most widely used weapons is "economism." This term is open to a number of meanings. In Marxist terminology, though, it means diverting the working class from its political goals and channeling it toward purely material demands. This is a tactic often used when the working class is joining battle. It is characteristic that at the dawn of the proletarian battles in Russia, Lenin found himself faced with this problem. Other, similar examples of it exist historically in many countries.

Thus, at the time when the revolution in China was moving out of the schools, universities, and offices, away from the various cultural milieus into the factories, the neobourgeois forces opposed to the Maoist line resorted to economism as well.

Claiming that economic losses could be tolerated as long as they were compensated by political advantages, Ch'en and Tsao tried to mislead the masses by the concession of material advantages. It would appear that the measures taken were not from some well-defined overall plan. They were many and at times contradictory. They seemed intended above all to create a climate of chaos and confusion.

It is unlikely that the decisions taken with a view toward giving impetus to the economist wave—payment of bonuses, withdrawal of funds put at the disposal of various enterprises in banks, etc.—came from the Municipal Committee, given the fact that by this time the committee was split into rival factions. It does not appear that Ch'en and Tsao used their official seals.[5] It is fairly safe to assume that these arrangements were made after consultations between the two leaders and some Shanghai factory heads whose political orientation was more or less the same as theirs. Some of these were simply misled, while others were fully aware of what they were doing; whatever the case, a number of them continued to accept the municipal leadership. Thus economist measures came into effect in various branches of industry.

Ch'en and Tsao were counting on using material incentives to consolidate their hold on that portion of the workers, which was constantly diminishing, with whom they still had influence. In some

---

[5] After the arrival of Chang Ch'un-ch'iao and the support he had brought for the Headquarters, Ch'en and Tsao were more careful. They even sometimes tried to strike a stance as neutral parties between the rival factions. That stance fooled a number of observers, who were misled into believing that a subsequent strike was directed against the Municipal Committee. In fact, Ch'en and Tsao remained linked to the very end to the conservatives. The Detachment of the Red Defense had its headquarters on the top floor of the city hall.

sectors salary increases were granted effective retroactively, and in others many promotions were made. Other measures seemed to aim at creating a divisive and disruptive atmosphere in the factories. Some students, for instance, who had been sent by the Party to work in factories during the Cultural Revolution, were suddenly and inexplicably given substantial raises. The goal was obvious: to arouse the jealousy of the regular workers. The decision to offer larger bonuses meant the creation of an ever greater diversification of salary classifications, which tended to disrupt the unity of the workers.

As soon as material advantages of whatever nature were granted in some sectors, others began to press for the same treatment. It was not long before an "economist" climate had been created. Workers in industry who were employed on a temporary basis wanted a contract. Workers in the same category or profession—taxi drivers, for example—joined forces and made demands applicable to their type of work.

The fact that the Shanghai workers wanted to reform the salary system was not a departure from the revolutionary line. Salary inequalities did exist, and they gave rise to discontent in some areas. During the years before the Cultural Revolution a close relationship had been established between pay and productivity, which had increased the intensity and difficulty of the work. These arrangements had been made under the aegis of Minister of Finance Po I-po. During the Cultural Revolution these policies came under heavy fire, not only among the people but in the official Party press. The major reproach was that this system fostered the rise of a workers' aristocracy and the division of workers by giving them different interests. Certain administrative structures, and some planning and management methods which had been closely copied from the Soviet model, stemmed from a similar tendency. Thus, the Chinese worker felt, drastic changes had to be made in the system.

It is not improbable, nonetheless, to think that these problems were tackled in quite another spirit by the two Shanghai leaders. If one could, relatively quickly, modify certain management methods based on the workers' suggestions or criticisms, the general transformation of the salary system and planning methods could only be done on a national scale in accordance with some overall plan and appropriate measures relating thereto. There obviously is a difference between such a reform undertaken with a view toward making the administrative superstructure more democratic, and the exploitation of salary problems by local bureaucrats with a view toward thwarting the political character of a struggle.[6]

If I have gone to such lengths to explain these points, it is because many Western newspapers, from the far left to the far right, completely misinterpreted the events in Shanghai at this time. They generally interpreted the rise of "economism" as proof of the antagonism between the workers and the Red Guards. They saw the workers with their material demands opposing the visionary dreams of the Maoist Red Guards, with their cries of "politics in command." Such interpretations not only betray a complete misunderstanding of the social and political life in China, but also woefully underrate the political role of the proletariat. Since these Western reports were repeated so long and so often without being refuted, they gained credence with many people; and yet they are based on erroneous speculations. The basis for the wrong assumption is the oft-repeated notion that Mao is the "peasant leader."

One indication that the maneuvers of Ch'en and Tsao were aimed solely at sowing confusion in the city is that they were often contradictory: in some places they raised productivity bonuses, which tended to stimulate production, while in others they encouraged work stoppages. As had been the case in Peking, they profited from the support of some union leaders who had risen to prominence under Liu Shao-ch'i, who helped to implement their policies.

Using the time-proven method of accusing the left of being the right, the Detachment of the Red Defense accused the Workers Revolutionary Headquarters and the various mass organizations which supported them of representing the reactionary bourgeois line, whose influence, it was claimed, was growing daily. On this false basis the Detachment incited the dockers and train workers to call a protest strike. The strike was only partly effective, but other workers were pulled from their posts and, under the guise of "revolutionary exchanges," given authorization to travel to Peking to "protest" against the activities of the Shanghai "reactionaries." These people were given not only travel money, but also expenses out of all proportion. Armed with these fat purses, they would go into the city stores and purchase all manner of merchandise—

[6] Subsequently the Central Committee stated, without further elaboration, that strictly economic questions would be dealt with in the final stage of the Cultural Revolution.

bicycles, transitor radios, cameras, watches—to such a degree that they threatened to create shortages in some areas and disrupt the normal flow of commerce in the city.

The "Rebels" Retort

These early days of 1967 in Shanghai were solemn and fraught with danger. Something had to be done, and done quickly. It was basically a task which befell the workers and their Workers Revolutionary Headquarters. Ten other mass organizations in the city stood behind them. On January 5 these eleven organizations addressed a "Message to the Entire Population of Shanghai," which was published in *Wen Hui Pao*, now controlled by the revolutionaries. The "Message" was really a cry of alarm to the people, denouncing the economist counteroffensive. It pointed out the disruptions that had occurred in various services, and the heavy losses they could entail for the national economy. It appealed fervently to those workers who had remained on the job to redouble their efforts, and it called upon those who had let themselves be led astray to realize the error of their ways and resume their jobs. Further, the "Message" forcefully insisted on the necessity to respect the Sixteen-Point Party Decision and the basic principles put forth by the Central Committee which stated that the revolution should be carried out and at the same time production increased. To the workers who had been misled into striking the "Message" said: "We warmly welcome your return so that together we can carry out the revolution and jointly help meet our production goals."

On January 6 the "rebels" assumed control of another major Shanghai newspaper, *Liberation Daily*. Their takeover of the paper was not entirely smooth, for some opposing organizations tried to prevent it. Once again clashes occurred. Now in control of the two major Shanghai papers, the revolutionaries published, on January 20, a ten-point "Urgent Notice."[7] This text, which is considered a key document in the Cultural Revolution, again called on the striking workers to return to their posts. The propaganda services of the city were now in the hands of the revolutionaries and, with all the power of which these organs are capable in China, they immediately began a vast campaign, with the backing of "rebel" organizations, denouncing economism. Thousands of multicolored posters were

---

[7] See *Peking Review* No. 4, January 20, 1967.

put up in the streets showing the workers breaking the resistance of the bureaucrats, who were pictured behind barricades made up of sacks of gold. They were accompanied by big-character posters which also asked those who had left their posts to return to work. There was also a new wave of caricature-posters. One very famous one, which was reproduced later far and wide, depicted Liu Shao-ch'i and Teng Hsiao-p'ing feverishly trying to derail the Revolution Train by blocking the tracks with fat bundles of banknotes.

In Peking too the streets were filled with posters asking the Shanghai visitors to return home and resume work. In both cities stores specializing in the sale of bicycles, radios, and other costly objects were closed and all dispatch of goods to these retail outlets was cut off to stop the wave of economism. All travel authorizations were rescinded, factory funds were frozen, and any salary increases forbidden. It was announced that anyone responsible for acts of sabotage would be dealt with appropriately. The mass organizations of Shanghai, together with the security forces, were given the job of carrying out these measures.

The Central Organs Intervene

One cannot help but remark how widespread the antirevolutionary current was in the events just related. A number of Western observers concluded that it showed how powerful the opposition to Mao's line was. This interpretation is not entirely false, but to be meaningful must take into account the specific political context of the situation. First of all, it must be stressed that the opposition was able to persuade part of the masses to follow it by falsely claiming to be representing the precepts and policies of Mao Tse-tung, and by usurping his watchwords and slogans. Ch'en and Tsao also claimed to be representing the proletariat and accused the "rebels" of being anti-Maoist and of following the reactionary bourgeois line. That considerably limits the scope of the opposition's maneuvers.

I have earlier indicated that the central authorities sometimes refrained from getting involved in local disputes in order to allow a confrontation between regional Party organizations and their administrators to develop, the better to judge the situation. The degree to which some of the opposition's activities were allowed to develop can only be explained—as in the case of the work teams—by the fact that the leaders of the Cultural Revolution allowed them to. Hadn't the Sixteen-Point Decision asserted that people should not

be afraid of these policy disputes, or of the heightened social and
political contradictions that would result? The disturbances, and the
increasing intensity of the confrontations, can only be understood
by assuming that it was a conscious, calculated risk on the part of
the Party leaders, and perhaps was even desired.[8] This method con-
forms to Mao's deep-seated desire to educate the people politically.
Let us not forget that the ultimate goal of the Cultural Revolution
was to transform people's way of thinking. This could not be accomplished simply by issuing directives; people had to experience the
revolution if Maoist ideology was truly to be implanted in their
minds. The Chinese people had to learn through hard, personal
experience how to distinguish what was revolutionary from what
was not. That implied debates, arguments, exchange of ideas and
opinions, dialectics, the struggle between opposing trends and
policies, and even violent confrontations, all of which the Cultural
Revolution nourished, and from which it in turn derived suste-
nance. Moreover, thanks to them, one saw a whole society become
aware of and participate in the struggle between two lines existing
within the Party. It was like seeing an enlarged photograph, and
on that enlargement being able to see more clearly the social roots
of the opposition, and thus more easily stamp them out.

To this end, periods of Party Center involvement would give way
to other times, some relatively long, of noninterference. This alternation marks each of the major phases of the Cultural Revolution.

In January 1967 the Party Center was to intervene again in
Shanghai, since the contradictions had by then evolved to a point
approximating antagonism.

On January 11 the Central Committee, the State Council, the
Military Commission of the Central Committee, and the GCCR
sent a message to the previously mentioned organizations in
Shanghai backing their "Urgent Notice."

This "Message of Greetings to Revolutionary Rebel Organizations in Shanghai" and the "Urgent Notice" were broadcast by radio

---

[8] Typical is the following declaration made by Chou En-lai to a delegation of
workers who had come from Szechuan to consult him, which was later reproduced
in poster form in the streets of Peking, on December 23, 1966:

"Chairman Mao has authorized me to tell you that we will most certainly be
experiencing rather widespread disturbances in the Southwest. You should not be
afraid of them. Problems mature through disturbances.

"You have asked that Li Ching-chuan and Li Ti-chang [first secretary of Szechuan
province and his lieutenant] be recalled to Peking. The Central Committee has
reached no final conclusion on this matter. You can deal with it as you see fit,
the Central Committee will not interfere."

throughout the country, while the various propaganda arms made favorable comments about them and held them up as an example, all of which immediately created a new climate extremely favorable to the rebels. The support of the Central Committee provided them with the decisive factor they needed to make their struggle finally successful. It also eroded that part of the opposition which had been fighting the rebels because, in all good faith, it had thought they were following a wrong line. It also pulled the rug out from under Ch'en and Tsao, and those mass organizations which till then had been backing them were deeply shaken. Party editorials made a point of reminding the people to welcome back with open arms those who had been led astray, and many, recognizing their errors, joined forces with those against whom they had hitherto been fighting.

On January 12 an article that appeared jointly in both *People's Daily* and *Red Flag* declared: "We must diligently carry out our political and ideological endeavors with the people who have been led astray. We must realize that the overwhelming majority of these masses want the Revolution. Once the facts are brought to light, they can distinguish true from false and return to the revolutionary, proletarian line of Chairman Mao."

Of course, even though there were widespread returns to the fold, the bitterness that had been engendered, and the opposition, did not disappear as if by magic overnight. It took time for the divisions to heal, but the intervention of the central organs facilitated this process, at least in Shanghai, where few subsequent problems developed. Within a relatively short period of time the economist wave was stopped short, work was resumed, and a normal situation restored.

One crucial phase of the Cultural Revolution had just occurred in Shanghai. The scope of the struggle, the massive appearance on the political scene of the working class, the important role it played as well as the violent counteroffensive launched by the opposition, showed that the decisive phases of the struggle were at hand.

The Lessons of the Movement

The previous seven months of the Cultural Revolution had provided Mao Tse-tung and his followers with a great deal of valuable information. In their eyes, of course, it was the proletariat which was running China, but in the very structure of its power there were contradictions. And, in some sectors men who were ruling in the name of the people had lost their revolutionary qualities.

All in all, as Mao Tse-tung had so often declared, the Party was healthy. Hadn't most of the cadres been forged in action and, for eighteen years, hadn't the Party successfully directed the development of the country? And yet a progressively insidious problem was lurking: the loss of revolutionary vitality. Wherever the cadres had ceased to be the servants of the people and become bureaucrats, corruption and decline threatened. Some leaders had even opted for the road of revisionism; a minority, to be sure, but determined, and in some cases in positions of power, which lent them added strength. The Party and state machinery offered these leaders favorable positions wherein they could entrench themselves and clandestinely carry out their plans.

It was doubtless for these reasons that Mao Tse-tung decided that, to stop this process, the cadres should be stripped of this kind of power, which would be passed on to the revolutionaries.

But that was not in itself enough. A simple redistribution of responsibilities was not tantamount to a blood transfusion. Since the change in certain areas of power stemmed basically from a break between this power and the masses, it needed to be recast in such a way that it would be henceforth exercised under a heightened control by the people. One form of this control was the possibility offered to all to criticize and evaluate the activities of the Party cadres at every level. But new structures were needed to institutionalize this control. As for the altered forms of power, they had to be broken.

At a certain stage of their struggle, the "rebel" mass organizations therefore had to dismiss the Party leaders to whom they were opposed. Then they had to name their own leaders to replace them, it being clearly understood that they retained the right of expressing their opinions and evaluating the cadres, including those newly named.

The Transfer of Power

Red Flag No. 2, which appeared during the last two weeks of January 1967, justified the transfer of power in the following terms: "Proletarian revolutionaries have united to seize power from the handful of people within the Party who are in authority and taking the capitalist road, thus taking the political, economic and cultural power of the Shanghai municipality firmly into their own hands."[9] It was because they held these positions, the article explained, that those who opposed the revolutionary line were able to hold out so stubbornly, had been able to create so many obstacles to the movement of criticism. It was because of the power they held that they could make use of the factions within the Party, take advantage of any bureaucratic tendencies, encourage blind obedience on the part of those who served under them. They had used their administrative prerogatives to fire those who criticized them, and in some instances had had such people imprisoned. On the financial front, they had misused their positions to unleash a wave of economism. It was this power captured by bourgeois, revisionist, or counterrevolutionary forces, that the proletariat had resolutely to seize from them and exercise itself.

On January 22 a major editorial in *People's Daily* again dwelt on this subject.[10] Its opening lines left no doubt that Mao Tse-tung and the Central Committee were completely behind the effort to seize power from the revisionist leaders.

> Power of every sort controlled by the representatives of the bourgeoisie must be seized. . . . Reversals and twists and turns over the past several months, and the repeated hurricanes of stormy class struggle gave the masses of revolutionary rebels profound lessons. They are seeing ever more clearly that the reason why the revolution suffered setbacks is due precisely to the fact that they did not seize in their own hands the seals of power.

This transfer first took place in Shanghai. After the "rebel" offensive, the economist counteroffensive, and the vigorous response that followed, the Shanghai Municipal Committee had found itself extremely isolated, for the Central Committee of the Party had thrown its support to its opponents. The committee leaders had lost credibility, and most of their troops had abandoned them. Thus the stage was set for these men to be dismissed and for the takeover by the "proletarian revolutionary rebels." On February 5 this became reality with the formation of the Shanghai Commune, which later took the name Revolutionary Committee of the Municipality of

[9] See "Proletarian Revolutionaries, Unite," in *Peking Review*, No. 4, January 20, 1967.

[10] See "Proletarian Revolutionaries, Form a Great Alliance to Seize Power from Those in Authority Who Are Taking the Capitalist Road!" in *Peking Review*, No. 5, January 27, 1967.

Shanghai. All these heady, tumultuous events in China were given the name: January Revolution.

Shanghai was not the only place in China where economism had been rampant. The same phenomenon occurred in many cities and provinces where the situation was similar: Tientsin, Wuhan, Shenyang, and Sian, among others. It was less pronounced in Peking, where the municipality was no longer in the hands of the opposition.

What we have described of the events in Shanghai, then, is applicable in large measure to many parts of China. The repercussions of the January tempest were going to resound throughout the country, adding a new page to the history of China.

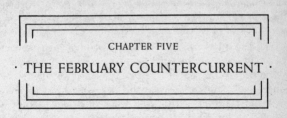

CHAPTER FIVE

· THE FEBRUARY COUNTERCURRENT ·

In February 1967 the Chinese streets offered an extraordinary
spectacle: the walls, the shop windows, even the sidewalks were
covered with posters, big-character slogans, and caricatures. The
last-named, which were usually done in a series and were remarkable for their subtlety and humor, depicted various episodes of the
battle being fought. The most common targets were Liu Shao-ch'i,
his wife Wang Kuang-mei, Teng Hsiao-p'ing, and T'ao Chu, but
other high functionaries were also sometimes singled out. By their
number, their bright colors, and the satirical talents of their authors,
they made the city streets of China look as though they had suddenly been transformed into so many pages out of some enlarged
picture magazine. One series of caricatures showed Lui Shao-ch'i
being given an X-ray examination which revealed his "black" heart
—black in China symbolizing every evil under the sun, including
revisionism, which is the worst sin of all. In another one T'ao Chu
was shown opening an insurance office specializing in protecting
revisionists; in still another Ho Lung was portrayed in the costume
and with the characteristics which in the old Peking opera had
indicated a militarist of feudal China.

In the beginning art students had been responsible for most or all
of the drawings, but later everybody—workers, anonymous students—got into the act: a new art form was born literally overnight,
and, looking back, one can only regret that the Chinese authorities

did not think to give proper publicity abroad to this astonishing
burst of creativity. To my mind this flowering of caricatures was a
far more interesting and meaningful form of popular art than the
relatively few examples of graphic art later so highly touted by the
press.

Peking, like all of China, seemed in a state of high excitement.
All day long processions wound their way through the streets. Students and workers, on foot or in trucks, came and went in a welter of
meetings, and everywhere they went they bore a sea of unfurled
banners and flags and portraits of Mao, and wore distinguishing
armbands. At the main intersections, along the main thorough-
fares and in the immense T'ien-an-Men Square, knots of people
formed and re-formed; crowds gathered, made contact, exchanged
information, and went on their way or joined another crowd.
Never had so many handbills been given out; never had so many
worker-organization and Red Guard newspapers been sold. In
Peking some 200 such papers were sold regularly, by students
and workers, who hawked them at every major intersection. While
the official Party organs tended to be reticent and selective about
what was going on in the course of the Cultural Revolution, these
parallel publications offered a much more lively picture of its
specific debates, quarrels, and phases. This unofficial press enabled all the Chinese to follow the day-by-day developments, but
they were also aware that the charges and accusations it contained
were indeed unofficial. Liu, Teng, and T'ao, for instance, were accused by name hundreds of times in this "parallel press," while the
official press still did not name them.

The GCCR had set up a reception center near T'ien-an-Men
which was a focal point for all visiting organizations from the capital
or the provinces. It was here they left and picked up messages,
reports, questionnaires, and it was to this center they came for
information. Loudspeakers blared constantly, not only from the tops
of trucks that were parked at busy intersections, but also in schools
and offices, factories and work sites: the latest news was given, any
new declarations made were passed on, and the speakers were not
above indulging in a diatribe now and then, all of which produced a
tremendous cacophony.

It was fairly common to see people parading through the streets
to the sound of gongs and drums, carrying two-sided posters with
the double sign of happiness on one side and a flower-framed por-

trait of Mao on the other, to celebrate publicly the transfer of power they had just effected where they worked. In such cases the students or workers affixed on both sides of the door to their school, university, or place of work red wood panels with gilded lettering announcing the formation of a revolutionary committee there. They also adorned the façade with a wide strip of pleated red cloth covered with many-colored flowers, and then hung purple paper lanterns—which are symbols of festive occasions—in their entranceways. And far into the night, one could hear the constant noise of firecrackers exploding—another traditional merrymaking method.

1. Problems in the Transfer of Power

A Complex Situation

At the end of January and the beginning of February one could begin to see the initial signs that the Maoists were gaining the upper hand. After the transfer of power was effected in Shanghai, other transfers took place shortly afterward in Tsingtao, in Shantung. On the provincial level, power was successively transferred in Shanshi, Heilungkiang, and Kweichow. A considerable number of anti-Maoists were thus eliminated, and at the same time the young militants of the Cultural Revolution arrived on the scene of government with their dynamism intact. That was a notable success, but its scope was limited by various problems which we shall describe.

The geographical progression of the transfers of power did not spread beyond those places already mentioned. The vastness of China, the diversity and disparity of local conditions, made it impossible for the rhythm of the Cultural Revolution to be the same throughout the country; therefore Mao's opponents retained enough power in some areas so that they could still maneuver. In Szechuan, Kiangsi, Shensi, Yunnan, and Mongolia, for example, there was a slow but sure movement toward the transfer of power, but the struggle was still going on, sometimes bitterly.

What we saw, then, was an overlapping situation. In some areas the provincial power was still in the hands of Mao's opponents, while some cities in that same province had already effected their transfer of power; the reverse situation also obtained, where the provincial transfer had already occurred but some municipal governments were still held by those opposing Mao. The relationship between "rebels" and "conservatives" varied, therefore, not only from province to province, but also from city to city.

Into this complex, confusing situation, a new element arrived to make it even more complicated.

An Unforeseen Circumstance

The transfer of power that had been effected in Shanghai, and shortly afterward in Heilungkiang, was constantly touted by the Party press, which urged others to follow their example. But, this same press was quick to add, transfers should be carried out only where they were indispensable. It did not seem necessary, in the eyes of the high Party authorities, that transfers of power be effected at other levels, that is, within the substructures of schools and factories. While it was not entirely ruled out, it was suggested that if and when it did occur it would not be on any large scale. A close study of the editorials of the period, in *Red Flag* and *People's Daily*, clearly shows that the leaders were working on the assumption that the middle- and lower-echelon cadres had already been won to their side, if indeed, as had been the case for a relatively few, they had ever strayed from it in the course of the difficult times through which they were passing.

However, during the last two weeks of January and in early February we saw transfers of power in several regions at the lower echelons of the administration and the Party apparatus. It looked as though the masses were spontaneously going much further than the leaders had anticipated.

The consequences of that phenomenon were double. First, opposition appeared as well in these administrative echelons of authority; although considered few in number, opponents often proved capable of considerable obstructionist maneuvering. This involved a further fracturing of power; in regions where transfers of power had been made on both the provincial and municipal levels, they had not occurred in all the schools, universities, and places of work. This was either because there was no need to, that is, the Party committee was functioning properly, or because the opponents of the revolutionary line had managed to hold out against the "rebels." Thus the power situation varied not only from province to province and city to city but also from school to school and factory to factory. As in 1966, the struggle between two opposing lines continued to splinter into a multitude of watered-down conflicts on all levels of Chinese society. The second consequence of that wave of spontaneous power transfers, which were often carried out swiftly and without proper preparation, was that it created problems that were to weigh heavily on the course of future events.

The Problem of the Cadres

The first and most compelling of these problems was that of the cadres. The transfer of power was accompanied on every level by the creation of new organs called revolutionary committees, in which new leaders of the "rebel" organizations took over. Those cadres who were not considered revisionists (a group which the Party Decision had called a tiny minority) had to participate in these new organisms of leadership. Their experience, their political maturity, their capacity for organization were the fruits of decades of revolutionary effort and constituted a precious, indispensable asset, without which the new structures could not grow and flourish.

And yet we have seen what difficulties the cadres had had to face during the preceding phase of the Cultural Revolution. The work teams, and certain Party committees under the influence of Liu Shao-ch'i, had used the cadres to combat and persecute revolutionary elements among the masses. Earlier, the cadres had been cited almost lock, stock and barrel by the masses as being objects of spite and scorn, at least in some places: at times the victims of the Liuist line, at others proponents of it, caught between the authority of their superiors and the pressures of the people, they found themselves between the devil and the deep blue sea. And when, because of the pressures besetting them, they hesitated, they were judged by some to have an ambiguous attitude. Some cadres had committed errors, grave or minor. Therefore some of the young revolutionaries harbored a grudge against them, or distrusted them. What was more, the material privileges some of them enjoyed—however modest they were in reality but, in a society with strong egalitarian sentiments, seemingly impressive—further militated against them in the eyes of certain workers.

Fairly frequently, these workers, carried away by their enthusiasm and the feverish excitement of the times, failed to judge the cadres properly. What they did was to mistake an error which was no more than bureaucratism for a counterrevolutionary act. But that was taking a simplistic view of things: To a militant revolutionary, a pen-pushing bureaucrat has to seem less than an ideal militant, but nonetheless it is not fair to tax him with revisionism or treason just because he pushes a pen. There were, unfortunately, an excessive number of cadres thrown out of their jobs. In fact, there were some workers and students whose attitude was to throw them all out. What happened was that in many cases the young, inexperienced revolutionaries who took over were simply not up to the administrative tasks that befell them.

Here I should like to open a brief parenthesis about the cadres who were dismissed, for several Western papers have reported incorrectly on the subject. Employing terms like "purge," sometimes interpreting wrongly or maliciously a clumsy Chinese expression, some articles tended to convey the impression that a real massacre of the opposition was going on. The Chinese tendency to use military terms such as "Bombard the headquarters of the bourgeoisie!" or "Storm the strongholds of revisionism!" was interpreted, even in some cases by serious journalists, as so many indications of the bloody battle in progress. As a result of a mistranslation of the figurative Chinese expression, "Open critical fire on the bourgeois reactionary line!" one foreign press agency reported that Mao's opponents were being thrown into the fire by his followers!

Actually, when a cadre—even one accused of revisionism—was ousted from his post, he was not arrested, much less executed. The ousted cadres still reported for work every day at the same places where they had formerly served. They continued to receive their normal salaries. The only thing they did not have now was the special "privileges" which were formerly required by their work, such as the use of a factory car. Part of their time now was spent doing simple manual work. They carried coal, or kept the furnaces in good repair, or worked in the kitchen. This kind of work usually took place in the morning; in the afternoon there were study, evaluation, and self-evaluation sessions.

The dismissal of a cadre did not put an end to his evaluation process, for the Chinese are convinced—and Mao has contributed greatly to this conviction—that man is always capable of change. As long as one does not kill or imprison one's opponents, the only recourse is to try and change his ideas. Evaluation and self-evaluation therefore appear to be part of a process of reeducation of the person involved. The evaluation of the ousted cadres' past activities was meant to go on for some time, in fact, in order to analyze what needed changing in the factory or school.

During the month of February 1967, when an excessive number of cadres had been dismissed, it was not unusual to see compact groups of former leaders leaving together for their work sites in the morning, and in the afternoon to see them in close ranks in assembly halls for criticism sessions.

One of the results of all this upheaval, during the early part of February, was a slow-down of work in the offices and factories. Some cadres were simply distressed by the violence of the criticisms leveled at them. Public opinion was divided, and many people hesitated and wondered whether things weren't going too far. And yet in school after school, and office after office, long lines of cadres would be stood up before workers convened to criticize them; and they were criticized harshly, often on the basis of scanty evidence. The Chinese are given to verbal violence, which added to the feeling of tension in the air.

The outcasts were made to wear dunce caps, a traditional sign of political infamy in China, until Mao stepped in and forbade the practice. Even more shocking was the sight of some cadres with glorious pasts being roughed up and maligned by the youth. No one, in this frenzy of criticism, seemed exempt from attack. Marshal Chu Teh was attacked by schoolboy Red Guards, in posters calling him "a doddering old idiot," although he had been one of the artisans of Liberation side by side with Mao, and one began to hear murmurs of disapproval from some of the population. The "rebels" and "little generals," it was said, were being overzealous.

The Tendency Toward Schism and the Sense of Cliquishness

The lack of preparation which accompanied some transfers of power resulted not only in lack of unity between the "rebels" and the Party cadres, but sometimes also within the rebel organizations themselves. In fact, students and workers often split up into a vast number of mass organizations, all agreed that they were against the Liu Shao-ch'i line but each with its own viewpoint or plan of attack. These various organizations also had differing views with respect to the Party cadres, the transfer of power, and the creation of revolutionary committees. Sometimes one rebel group would announce a transfer of power beneficial to itself simply to outdo or spite a rival group. These "minority maneuvers" seldom made any real effort to garner the support of the students or workers of the place in question.

Other organizations, which had been united at the time of the transfer of power, quarreled and split later. Either they were divided over who should be named to leadership, or in some cases split over the question of proportional as opposed to egalitarian representation.

Some groups claimed temporal priority: "We were the earliest committee," they would claim. "Our role was the most important. Therefore the other organizations ought to dissolve and join us." To which those so addressed would reply: "No way; in the revolution, everyone is equal." It was like the deaf talking to the deaf, and often the dialogues would be broadcast over loudspeakers in factory or university courtyards.

To further complicate matters, rebel unity was also affected by the fact that various organizations were responsible to different, and sometimes rival, headquarters. Thus you saw people who knew one another and worked in the same office and factory unable to meet because their leaders, at the municipal or multifactory level, disagreed. This vertical structure was hardly conducive to furthering the movement: the unity of people working together was in effect dependent on agreements that had to be made by a "summit" leadership that threatened to cut itself off from the masses. In an effort to overcome this problem, the Party press later suggested that alliances be formed according to work division or level involved. It cited the successful application of this method which had occurred in a textile mill in Kweiyang. The leaders of the Cultural Revolution were obviously trying to avoid conflicts among the organizations' leadership by encouraging unity at the grass roots. But that effort bore little fruit.

Schisms and divisions still persisted in a number of places, while the "small-group mentality" grew. Some revolutionary committees which had appeared in the factories and universities without any real backing from the workers and students were hardly representative and enjoyed only a tenuous authority. Moreover, the absence among them of experienced cadres limited their ability to operate effectively. For these reasons, relatively few of these committees received any official endorsement by the Maoist leaders in the early phases of their existence.

Together with all the other problems existing at this time, then, was added the proliferation of cliques, which tended to undermine the rebel forces.

2.   The February Countercurrent

The Chinese Cultural Revolution appears as a contradictory alternation of left and right currents. Basically, the mass mobilization and the transfer of power seemed to be a leftist offensive to counter a rightist trend which consisted of utilizing part of the Party apparatus for its own ends. This leftist offensive engendered some excesses, which called for a rectification which some anti-Maoist forces tried to influence in a rightist direction. All this occurred toward the end of February 1967, and is referred to in the history of the Cultural Revolution as the "February Countercurrent."

The Social and Political Context

At this point in its evolution the Cultural Revolution was in a state of effervescence, with feverish activity at all levels by the masses: it was a heady, tumultuous time. Chinese society was plunging headlong into a great, powerful whirlwind. It was normal that confusion and nervousness were part and parcel of this welter of political lyricism which, had they witnessed it, would have given much food for thought to many Western libertarians.[1]

This violent blow was necessary in order to cast off the heavy yoke of bureaucratic and revisionist tendencies which were threatening the revolutionary future of China. In accordance with what Mao had said the previous May, one had to begin by destroying; the construction would come later. But the risk was always present that destruction would feed on itself and its own logic and that, by its own momentum and acceleration, it would engender a kind of semianarchy. Some negative phenomena did materialize: certain Party committees could not adapt to the evolving situation and ceased to function, whereas the new organs of leadership, the revolutionary committees, were sometimes slow to take hold. The taboo of authority had been so shaken by the criticism of the cadres that, here and there, collective discipline tended to relax and work organization was affected. All this spilled over into daily life. There were

---

[1] Never did any revolution have a more profound content. Never did any regime in history seem to fear disorder so little and have such confidence in the people, allowing them to name their own leaders and dismiss, if necessary by force, those they did not want. All of this was unprecedented. It is especially important to remind the Western reader of this vital aspect of the Cultural Revolution, for it has too often been presented in the West as either unimportant or the struggle between two bureaucratic trends, and has even been described as a false revolution in which the masses were maneuvered, and even repressed, if they went too far.

times when I saw policemen who could not cope with the bicycle traffic, simply because too many citizens, remembering Mao's words that "To rebel is justified," refused to abide by traffic rules. In the parks the young people took to skating on the frozen lakes, in spite of the clearly marked signs forbidding the practice. Work was too often neglected while people spent all their time in politics. The trains were still filled with revolutionaries spreading out into the provinces, but although the time of free fares for them was past, many passengers refused to pay for tickets.

If the situation intensified, there was the chance of a political vacuum; there was even the possibility that the middle-echelon organizational structures might begin to crumble, opening the floodgates to the opposition, which was only waiting to take advantage of the opportunity.

Centralism and Spontaneism

All Marxists believe that in any revolution the masses must be led and directed by one class alone, the proletariat, which is considered the most revolutionary. This leadership must be exercised by the most aware and determined elements of the proletariat, organized into a Communist Party. Lenin devoted many pages to proving this thesis, which today is held to be one of the basic tenets of Marxism. Mao Tse-tung judges it to be a just and proper precept, and during the Cultural Revolution he guided his actions in accordance with its principles.

Communist leadership of the masses does not preclude the possibility of people expressing themselves, taking initiatives, and acting, all of which is the essence of democracy. But since the people are divided into classes, they have different tendencies, as they have varying capacities for carrying on the revolutionary struggle. Communist leadership must therefore attempt to act as a focal point for ideas and stress those initiatives it deems to be correct, evolving its policies on this basis, within the framework of Marxism. This is the "democratic centralism" which Mao describes as a unity of opposites. A delicate balance has to be maintained between these two elements. The Cultural Revolution and the mass mobilization which followed must be thought of, from the Marxist viewpoint, as an attempt to compensate for an excess of centralism by an increase in mass democracy. In February 1967, when this mass democracy reached a stage where it had given rise to "spontaneism"—muddle-headed initiatives that fell outside the framework of a clearly defined political orientation—this had in turn to be corrected by an infusion of centralism.

Rectification and Press Campaigns

Centralism could not be applied in any tough or repressive way, for that would have put an end to the mass mobilization and consequently the Cultural Revolution itself would have been compromised. Centralism had to be administered, then, but in careful, measured doses.

A huge press campaign was started in an effort to get the mass organizations to put their mistakes to right. The press campaign, which was an attempt on the ideological front to compensate for the fact that the dismissal of a great many Party cadres had weakened it in some places, evolved around two main themes. The first consisted of attacking the tendency to splinter into little units, the "small group" mentality. The Party papers went on at great length about the example of Tsingtao, where the rebels were already involved in correcting their errors. They also cited the example of the rectification effort under way in Shanghai by the "Lu Hsun Corps."[2]

The rectification movement which now began in various places consisted of holding meetings of all the members of any group and asking them to evaluate the leaders they had elected and their policies. The Party press advised that all such meetings should be completely open, not only to the members themselves but to members of other groups, who could offer their own evaluations.

The Party press also stressed the necessity for the people to bend their efforts toward the formation of the Great Alliance, by which it meant the desired combination of 95 percent of the workers and Party cadres which, it said, formed the pro-Maoist majority in any given school or enterprise. What it was also saying, in effect, was that the revisionists formed no more than 5 percent of the population. Sectarian and divisive tendencies should therefore be rejected forthwith.

The second prong of the press campaign focused on the crucial problem of the cadres. During the second half of February *Red Flag* No. 4 published an editorial entitled: "The Question of the

[2] See *Peking Review*, No. 10, March 3, 1967.

Cadres Must Be Accurately Handled." It pointed out that the number of antirevolutionary enemies who had managed to infiltrate the cadres was small and that the battle to weed them out had to be waged intelligently. "To mistakenly enlarge the front of attack," said the article, "to focus the attack on the mass of cadres, comes down to not making any distinction between the enemy and ourselves, and that is very dangerous." What was needed, therefore, was a close scrutiny of the cadres' activities at every level, in order to find out which fell into the classifications of "good" or "comparatively good" as outlined in the Sixteen-Point Decision. As for those who had committed errors, they should, after they had been evaluated and apprized of their wrongs, be given the opportunity to return to the fold: "They should be criticized in the spirit of helping them, and having done that, we should be generous and make use of their services," the article said.

Only a tiny portion of the cadres, then, ought to be dismissed, those who were either taking the capitalist road or who showed themselves to be incapable of mending their ways. The Party made a point of featuring successful examples of this, especially in the Heilungkiang province. The propaganda department of the Central Committee put posters up throughout the country bearing extracts from Mao's *Quotations* dealing with the question of the cadres. One quotation was especially prominent at this time: "We must know how to judge cadres. We must not confine our judgment to a short period or a single incident in a cadre's life, but should consider his life and work as a whole." This was a clear admonition to protect those cadres with a militant, glorious past, who had until now in some cases been ill treated. These quotations were often set to music and sung over the radio, something fairly frequent in China and which the Chinese language, by its very nature, helps facilitate.

The danger inherent in calling upon the people to reinstitute the cadres who had been dismissed was that some revisionists would be reinstated. There was also another: by emphasizing the errors of the "rebels" they could be discredited in the eyes of the people. In either case, the opposition, which was diminished but not dead, could take advantage of the situation to marshal its forces. Centralism, in its effort to curb the excesses of leftism and spontaneism, could give rise to the opposite, to rightist excesses. This is in fact what happened, thus marking the start of the "The Rightist February Countercurrent."

The Appearance of the Countercurrent

This is one of the most important but also one of the least known phases of the Cultural Revolution. At a time when the wall posters provided an impressive amount of information about events as they occurred, the precise steps leading up to the countercurrent remained cloaked in mystery. Contrary to what had happened earlier, the controversies within the top echelons of Party leadership for the most part remained secret. I am not in any position to clarify every facet of the picture. What I relate here corresponds simply to what a person in the streets of China at the time was able to see and learn.

It would appear that some Party leaders were extremely upset by the wave of massive dismissals of cadres which marked the transfers of power. It would further appear that some leaders chose this occasion to dissociate themselves from the political tendency followed since the Eleventh Plenum which called for the unqualified mobilization of the masses. In fact, their position apparently was very close to that of the Liu faction, and these leaders advocated a more moderate line that bordered on compromising with the Liu line. Later, the Central Committee condemned this trend as a new manifestation of the bourgeois reactionary line. Among the advocates of this countercurrent, the only name that can be cited is that of T'an Chen-lin, Minister of Agriculture and a member of the Politburo. His stand subsequently caused him to be classed among those opposed to the Maoist line. Other names were mentioned at various times, but the sources are uncertain. Since the persons named were retained in their posts, one must conclude that their responsibility for the countercurrent was, if not dubious, at least secondary. T'an Chen-lin purportedly declared that if a rather large number of cadres had followed the bourgeois reactionary line with respect to the masses, the "rebels," for their part, had applied the same bourgeois reactionary line with respect to the cadres. In the context of the times it was extremely serious to accuse an individual or a group of committing an error of line. I cannot say under what circumstances the Minister uttered these words: was it in public before the mass organizations, or behind closed doors in meetings involving the Party leaders? We don't really know. But at the time many declarations and watchwords were widely disseminated via the parallel channels of information, that is, the wall posters, the mass-organization newspapers, and the various brochures and handbills these organizations produced. T'an Chen-lin's words were picked up and published by these sources, and they gave the opposition a certain number of arguments to go on.

Within the Ministry of Agriculture, T'an Chen-lin reinstated on his own a goodly number of functionaries who had been dismissed,[3] and he was later blamed for having taken the opportunity to restore revisionists to their posts. Similar measures were taken in another important ministry. The Maoists watched these developments with considerable concern, for if they were to grow and spread they could undo all that they had won up to now. Some of the followers of Liu Shao-ch'i and P'eng Chen began to show up in the positions of central authority that they had earlier lost. This rightist trend at the highest levels of the Party administration constitutes the first phase of the February countercurrent.

T'an Chen-lin's allegation that the "rebels" had applied the bourgeois reactionary line against the cadres also led to another movement fraught with danger, which occurred not at the higher levels but in the factories and universities.

A Supplementary Contradiction

The rebel groups were in the main made up of members of the Party and nonmembers who had joined forces in a spirit of inquiry into the trends and policies of a certain number of leaders who, it was thought, were not following the line of Mao Tse-tung. The excesses of the preceding period, the unfair treatment accorded too many cadres, and the efforts of T'an Chen-lin to discredit the revolutionaries led to a tendency on the part of some members of the Party[4] and the Communist Youth League to withdraw from the "rebel" organizations. In the teeming atmosphere of discord and splits which we were then living through, "rebel" groups broke up and others were formed in which impressive numbers of Party and Youth League members began to criticize their former comrades-in-arms.

A basic contradiction separated the "rebel" mass organizations, which were playing an avant-garde role in the promulgation of Maoist policy, and the organizations influenced by the opposition. A new contradiction was added at this juncture, born of the division

---

[3] T'an Chen-lin personally organized bogus takeovers of power in the units dependent on his ministry.

[4] The term "Party member" here applies to persons who belong to the Party without holding any positions of authority, and are thus to be distinguished from the cadres.

in the "rebel" organizations themselves. That a cleavage tended to exist between Party and non-Party members was a rather serious development. Mao's strategic principle that 95 percent of the masses and Party members were united in an effort to find, and then weed out, the tiny minority—"handful" was the term used—of revisionists, had been not only emphasized in the Party Decision of August 8, 1966, but had been reiterated time and time again in the official propaganda. Now, it would seem, in certain areas the Cultural Revolution had deviated from this principle and, if the phenomenon spread, might well be imperiled.

As a good Marxist, Mao Tse-tung believed that a mass struggle could take place only if it operated under the leadership of a Communist Party. The principle of unity between the cadres and the masses reflected his concern that the activities of the latter should be backed up by the former. What was actually taking shape was the direct opposite.

This reverse tendency created two obstacles to the spread of the revolution: on the one hand, it splintered the ranks of the "rebels" by emphasizing the proliferation of existing organizations and their differences; on the other, it further rooted the trends toward sectarianism and the small-group mentality. It was not possible for the representatives of any single revolutionary organization to exercise power; power could be exercised only by all of them working together. These various organizations had to unite, and that was becoming more and more difficult.

If the trend toward grouping together into a number of different organizations continued, the members of the Party and the Communist Youth League might end up fighting not against Liu and his followers but against other revolutionaries. This of course would only work to the advantage of the opposition, which by this time had been weakened but not destroyed. Time and again this opposition had revealed how cleverly it could, by insidious and indirect means, subvert the revolution and turn it to its own conservative advantage. This situation, in fact, served as a springboard for a new offensive against the rebels, which brings us to the second phase of the February countercurrent.

The Attack Against the Mass "Rebel" Organizations

What threatened to deprive the avant-garde groups of a portion of their support from the Party militants was their own mistakes.

The opposition was quick to move in and take advantage of the situation wherever it could: it exploited the discontent created by the spontaneous excesses; it posed as the defenders of ousted cadres; it castigated the prevailing disorder; it tried to rally the hesitant, the malcontents, and various moderates; and, finally, it attempted to discredit the whole notion of the transfer of power.

In so doing the opposition was once again employing the tactic which consisted of "waving the red flag while combating the red flag." It was also not above spreading false and insidious rumors claiming that the "rebel" leaders were thoroughly corrupt and ambitious. It was at this time that the "theory of lineage," which had already been raised by dissident Red Guards back in November 1966, recurred. To discredit certain revolutionary organizations, some people spread the rumor that they were made up of reactionaries and the sons of the bourgeoisie. In the factories sons of peasants were tagged as sons of landlords, and once again the slogan "From a reactionary father, a vile son!" reappeared.

What the opposition was trying to do, of course, was to confuse the situation so that the people could no longer act with confidence. Key to this was convincing them that the "rebels" were really anti-Party. It was difficult to pretend that the transfer of power was anti-Party, since the official press and radio were constantly singing its praises, but even here the opposition managed to turn the situation to its advantage. In the Ministry of Agriculture there had been certain transfers of power which were really false transfers; similar deceitful transfers occurred in Canton. Using these, the opposition reported: "In some places the *tso tze-pai* have feigned transfers of power in order to fool the masses. They have pretended to give up their power," it claimed, "but in fact they have simply handed it over to reactionary organizations which they still control and direct." The result was a veritable plethora of false transfers.

In various schools and factories disputes over the transfer of power became frequent. When the members of the new revolutionary committees called general meetings the opposing groups would try to shout them down and turn the meeting into a shambles. But that was the least of it. In some places a more disturbing pattern emerged: taking advantage of this confusion and division, the opposition managed to set up new conservative organizations, or to further strengthen already existing ones, and through them physically attack the revolutionaries.

Thus it was that in a group of factories and in some cultural and administrative services in Peking there ensued what came to be known as the "quarrel of the seals."[5] This consisted of an attempt by the opposition to prevent the revolutionary committees from taking over the various seals of the local Party committee which were needed to validate their documents, and resulted in a whole series of fights. When one group had got control of them, that did not put an end to the tension, for in many cases their opponents attacked the premises where the seals were held and physically tried to regain possession of them. In many places work was disrupted because of the rising tension, as anti-Maoists kidnaped "rebel" leaders and then themselves were the victims of "rebel" reprisals. It was not long before the kidnaping campaign spread to the Party cadres, who were seized in turn by "rebels" or conservatives, depending on where they stood politically. They were released after a few days' detention; the experience supposedly meant only to serve as a warning to those involved, but one can imagine the state of confusion that typified this period.

Nonetheless, although the atmosphere was tense to say the least, it rarely if ever exceeded the level of scraps and group clashes. To speak of deep troubles, or even as some did of civil war, was a gross exaggeration. With rare exceptions, the balance sheet of clashes was still light, but during the coming months, as the antagonisms worsened, it would be another story.

3.   The Failure of the Countercurrent

A Point of Clarification

It would be wrong to think that the difficulties the Cultural Revolution encountered, which I have just described, were general. They were not. The extent of the disorders and obstacles in the way of the revolutionary movement varied from place to place. The three provinces and two municipalities where the power transfers had originally taken place constituted a solid bastion for the "rebels." What is more, it did not mean that the opposition was in charge everywhere else. Actually, revolutionary committees had been formed in a great many places by this time, but the authorities did

[5] Similar struggles occurred in the provinces.

not always rush to endorse them, preferring to allow them to broaden their popular bases and consolidate their positions. In addition, the divisions and disorganization of the Party committees caused by excessive haste in ousting cadres were not as widespread as has been sometimes made out. The February countercurrent, too, was not a generalized phenomenon; the rehabilitation of revisionist cadres involved only two ministries, and the counterattacks against the "rebels" was limited to a few areas. In short, while there did exist a negative countercurrent of fair proportions, the Maoists were very much in control, and their basic concern was to make certain it did not spread. As the events of March 1967 will show, they overcame these obstacles in a reasonably short period of time.

The Countercurrent Smashed

The prime task of Mao and his followers at this point was to turn back the countercurrent, and to do so they launched a multipronged attack. The press denounced the attempt to whitewash the revisionist cadres. The rebels were praised and defended: they may have made errors in judgment, but never errors of line, it was stated. A series of directives based on these considerations were sent to the representatives of mass organizations. In both ministries where the February countercurrent had begun, the GCCR moved in to set the revolutionary movement back on the right track. Without giving any precise details or naming any names, the official press also went out of its way to denounce the rightist countercurrent.

Using the veiled terms that typify that paper's style, *Red Flag* warned against the attempt to reintroduce the *tso tze-pai* into the revolutionary ranks: "Those who persist in their mistakes, and who do not draw a clear-cut demarcation line between themselves and the people in authority taking the capitalist road, between themselves and the bourgeois reactionary line, must not be imposed on the masses, and arbitrarily pushed into the three-in-one provisional organs of power," it declared in a March editorial.[6]

Any number of similar articles were published in *People's Daily* and broadcast over the radio. Members of the GCCR began traveling into the provinces, multiplying their contacts with the local mass organizations to encourage and stimulate their efforts in the same direction.

---

[6] See *Peking Review*, No. 12, March 17, 1967.

A Delicate Problem

I have explained the reasons why Mao Tse-tung chose to utilize a major mass movement to overcome his opposition. As long as his victory was not completely assured, he would continue to use that weapon to the fullest. In February 1967 that opposition had still not been defeated: therefore, mass mobilization remained very much the order of the day, and the "rebel" groups Chairman Mao had chosen as his spearhead still played as large a role as possible.

What Mao had to do was try to steer a careful course between centralism on the one hand, and mass involvement on the other. The latter, by its leftist excesses, could engender rightist reactions.

The key to the situation was the problem of the cadres. In those schools and factories beset by divisiveness, the differences usually evolved around the question of the cadres. Structually there usually were two major factions opposing each other, with a myriad of satellite organizations revolving around each one. If one of the two defended the Party cadres, claiming either that they were revolutionaries or in any case reeducable, the other accused them of being revisionist, and vice-versa. As a result, where such a divisive situation obtained, few were the cadres who had the unanimous backing of all and could exercise real authority; most cadres were the object of criticism by one faction or another. This situation of overlapping conflict must be borne in mind to understand what followed.

The Party Center could not intervene directly to straighten out these problems without, by the same token, making the mass participation they so stoutly desired completely superfluous; to do so would also quash the movement's dynamic qualities and repudiate the principles followed up to now. It was the students and workers who still had to judge the value of the cadres. But, to be serious, these evaluations had to break with the abuses of the past and instead adopt the method of searching inquiries and extended discussions. Not only the cadres' activities of the preceding few months had to be examined; what was needed was a long-range assessment of their activities throughout their militant life. This would not only tend to discourage hasty dismissal of essentially good cadres, but would also prevent the reinstatement of dissidents.

The Party press, therefore, called upon the various mass organizations to unite. Efforts had to be made to eliminate any spirit of cliquishness, do away with dissensions of a secondary nature, and strengthen the Great Alliance. Here too there was a major difficulty.

In a certain number of places conservative mass organizations had been secretly influenced by the opposition and were in fact defending the revisionist cadres. There could be no question of joining forces with these groups on any hit-or-miss basis entailing risky compromises that could only result in the rehabilitation of dissidents. One had to join forces and unite, true, but not eclectically. What the Party press recommended, therefore, was a patient effort to explain, to persuade the partisans of these groups that they had been misled by Mao's opponents, and to bring them back to a revolutionary position.

A policy so subtle reminds one of those delicate works of embroidery of which only the Chinese have the secret. The artisan of that policy, the man chosen to implement it, was the master diplomat Chou En-lai. Indefatigable despite his then sixty-eight years,[7] Chou was everywhere: in the ministries, in the factories, in the schools; at Peking and in the provinces; talking to the workers and Red Guards, tirelessly explaining the sense and substance of Mao's directives and how to apply them. His powerful personality had a deep effect on the closing weeks of that first trimester of 1967; by what he did and said, by his physical presence in the factories and offices, by his cleverness and power of persuasion, he contributed enormously to sorting out complex and conflicting situations and creating order out of chaos.

A task as complex as this could obviously not be accomplished by the magic of words, by any simple directives no matter how adroit, or by the talent of any one man, no matter how exceptional. Only an organization, a solid structural complex, with experienced men as the backbone, could really bring it off. And where, under the prevailing circumstances, was one to find them? In spite of all the problems about the cadres, in many places they still had the people's confidence and had not strayed from the revolutionary path: where that situation existed, they could be used. But in other places, where it did not, a vacuum existed. The immediate necessities of carrying on the administrative functions in any given area, and reimposing political and organic centralism to a proper degree, called for other solutions.

It was the Chinese Army—the People's Liberation Army (*Renmin Jiefangjun*)—which under these circumstances was to become the valuable back-up for the cadres that the Cultural Revolution needed.

[7] Chou En-lai was born in 1898.

The PLA Steps In

The purely military responsibilities of the People's Liberation Army during the Cultural Revolution were extremely limited. During this period the army had a dual role. First it was given the job of making sure the sensitive areas of the country's basic functioning —both passenger and freight aviation, certain factories, printers, and the like—continued to operate normally. This aspect of its work was called "military control." It could also happen, as it did in Kwangtung, that the administrative responsibilities of an entire province were placed under military control. "Control" consisted of a relatively small number of soldiers, without weapons, who saw to it that offices and businesses operated normally in spite of the raging debates and discussions which were an essential part of the Cultural Revolution. The fact that these soldiers intervened in no way put a stop to the Cultural Revolution.

There was another aspect of the February countercurrent: a wave of economism in the countryside. It appears clearly established that T'an Chen-lin, the Minister of Agriculture, was largely responsible for it. In some communes, a number of people, following subversive directives, began to distribute their stocks (deposits of money in Chinese communes are extremely limited, for wages in cash are practically nonexistent), and work points were faked in order to reevaluate them and modify the tallies. In Fukien, Kiangsi, and Yunnan there were serious disturbances, and the agricultural output suffered both from absenteeism and from the disorganization of the Party committees which resulted in confusion.

The PLA, therefore, tried to counter the effects of this economist wave. Military cadres arrived to reorganize the production teams, and many soldiers went to work in the fields in areas where production was lagging and where the sowing season was just getting under way. Guarding goods and granaries was also part of their duties.

The other aspect of the army's duties was the support of the left, which was announced in an editorial of January 25, 1967; this involvement was stepped up during the February countercurrent. The army's job was to defend the "rebel" organizations against the counterattacks to which they were being subjected, and to prevent them from being isolated by their mistakes and then crushed. The support given these organizations also consisted of helping them undertake rectification campaigns and join with other revolutionary organizations, and urging them to treat the cadres better. The soldiers were asked especially to try and sort out the validity of the various contradictory and overlapping evaluations of the cadres from opposing groups. Obviously, the army did not get involved everywhere, but it did in the relatively few areas where there were acute problems.

It operated essentially with a light hand, through its well-known propaganda teams. These teams were made up of about ten soldiers, unarmed, who went to the schools, offices, and factories and took part in the discussions, in an effort to prevent them from degenerating into chaos. Bear in mind that they did not, wherever they went, replace the faltering Party committees: these teams had no power of decision. Their job was to see that a sufficient number of cadres were functioning in their posts to make sure the daily administrative work was carried out. Military control and the support of the left, therefore, were their twin roles in such cases.

The military propaganda teams could not give orders to the mass organizations. What they tried to do was sort out the differences that separated the students and workers, delicately trying to distinguish the revolutionary from the conservative trends, and then persuade both students and workers to apply what conformed to the Maoist line. They had both to convince the conservatively oriented organizations of the errors of their ways and to persuade the revolutionary organizations to desist from certain of their malpractices. They constantly had to remind both groups that the real target of the Cultural Revolution was the "handful," the 5 percent of the cadres who might qualify as *tso tze-pai*. Since the propaganda teams were under strict orders not to use force, and since they were not in any real position of authority, their work, which was basically political and ideological, was a marvelous display of diplomacy and patience, two virtues in generous supply in the Chinese character.

I had the opportunity of talking with several soldiers doing this kind of work in a Peking factory, and they explained to me how they went about their job. First, it was a hard-and-fast rule that the members of the propaganda teams participate in the work processes of the factory or office under exactly the same conditions as the workers and employees. They lived with them and ate at their canteens with them; thus they had close relationships at the grass roots. On all problems that created differing opinions, they not only consulted the heads of the mass organizations but solicited the opinions of as many workers as possible. They did their best not to support any one faction or organization, but to support proper initiatives wherever they came from. They made a special effort to distinguish the really antagonistic from what was not; to point out differences of opinion within the ranks of the people from differences with the enemy. And yet they had to make sure that, on the matter of basic principles, there was no compromise. Thus they often organized study sessions in which the works of Mao were chosen for discussion as they applied especially to the problems this or that group was facing; in so doing the teams led the workers and students to think in Marxist-Leninist terms. Finally, the soldiers did their best to see that full freedom of expression was maintained, and that no organization tried to stifle another's freedom to speak or put up posters.

Three Special Traits of the PLA

To understand the role of the PLA in the Cultural Revolution, it is imperative to understand clearly certain of its characteristics. Here again a number of Western newspapers, by their exaggerated and fantastical accounts, portrayed China at this time as being in a state of total chaos, a semiapocalyptic situation in which factories were shut down and the workers were either quarreling and fighting or gallivanting around the country. The army, went the Western reports, was sent in to put an end to the strikes and make the workers go back to their jobs.

The Chinese Army is the only army in the world which clearly predicates the primacy of the political over the military. The primacy of man over material, and that of ideology over technique, are the principles that govern its actions. I cannot elaborate here on the significance of these principles, nor on their scope or application: suffice it to say that the soldiers of the PLA are political militants as much as they are armed men entrusted with the defense of their country. The soldiers of the PLA are educated to play a political role in society, and this role is not subsidiary to their military task but considered fully as important. The involvement of the military in the Cultural Revolution basically corresponded to the exercise of its political role. How can one understand this fact if it is portrayed as soldiery indulging in repression?

On the contrary, for the Chinese Communist regime it is a tremendous asset to have been able to build an army that not only enjoys the people's confidence but has immense prestige among them, especially considering the fact that in pre-1949 China the soldier was a hated symbol of the many militarists who ravaged the country and exacted exorbitant payments and taxes from the people. The only way the Chinese Communists managed this about-face was to keep their life style very simple and selfless, and by having their soldiers play an important social role in the life of the country; too, they established relationships of criticism and self-criticism both between the army cadres and the ordinary soldiers and between the army and the population at large.

It is difficult for Westerners to envisage clearly such an army, whose members are as much political participants as fighters—and I say this without trying to paint an idyllic picture of the Chinese military. But I can say from personal experience that the involvement of the Chinese Army in the Cultural Revolution in February 1967 consisted mainly of a vast exercise in the art of gentle persuasion, and was typified by patience and careful attention to detail. The army, then, was the trump card by which the Party Center could inject into a complex social and political situation an element which would help strengthen the movement without compromising a mass mobilization whose purpose was nothing less than revivifying the Party and the Communist regime.

The State Reasserts Its Authority

The renewal of centralism was accompanied by a growth of governmental activity directly affecting the evolution of the Cultural Revolution. A number of public utterances made it eminently clear that in the ministries and their administrative dependencies transfers of power were forbidden—a step which in no way affected the right to criticize one's superiors. In fact, at one time or another *every Chinese minister* was publicly criticized in posters. And yet a minister could be dismissed only by the Politburo itself. What was more, no revolutionary committee could be substituted for a Party committee in any ministry. The Politburo reserved to itself the right to name new persons to high-ranking posts upon the recommendation of revolutionary organizations.

Other posters, sporting government recommendations, urged the people to work their full eight hours a day. They also preached against absenteeism, asked the workers to use their tools and machines carefully and not to waste material. And an appeal was launched asking the peasants, as winter drew to a close, to make sure the spring farm work was done. This same message also reminded the peasants that the vast majority of the cadres in the countryside were good or relatively good, and added that those who had made errors should be given a chance to redeem themselves. A few weeks later a similar appeal was launched, aimed at the workers and cadres in industry and commerce.

Finally abandoning their aloof attitude of the preceding period, the Party and government organs decided to take police action against the organizations which were hostile to Maoism. The Ministry of Public Security announced that two such organizations were outlawed and at the same time announced the arrest of some of their leaders who had broken the law: the United Action Committee (*Lien Tung*) and the Red Workers' Army, some of whose activities we described earlier. This resulted in the occupation of the ministry by members of both organizations as a protest against the measures taken against them.

The Three-in-One Combination

Centralism had to be reestablished, but with velvet gloves. It was therefore out of the question to try to reinstate the former organizational structures. For the moment, the presence of the army propaganda teams provided a basis for strengthening centralism, but that was not enough.

What was needed was a new formula which allowed for as rapid a movement as possible between the center and the periphery, between the leaders and the people. What was needed was a structure that would not hinder the mobility of the masses but at the same time would brake the spontaneism and disorder. What was needed was the abolition of a rigid hierarchy and the installation of organs in which the lines of communication between the leaders and the led were close. And to make these organs viable, a sufficient number of experienced cadres had to be integrated into them. The three-in-one revolutionary committees were intended to fill these needs. They were to be made up of equal numbers of the following three categories: representatives of the people, designated by them; Party cadres faithful to the Maoist line, who would also be named by the masses; and representatives of the army. Members of the military sat on these committees only at the municipal and provincial level. In the factories, offices, and schools they were replaced by members of the militia, who were also named by the students and workers.

In this way the revolutionary committees brought together an elite of militants and gave impetus to the trend toward centralized leadership of the Cultural Revolution through a method that was democratic. It is undeniable that the formula for the revolutionary committees, which I saw operating in living fashion, gave the Chinese population greater control over their future leaders. The three-in-one combination was different from the Paris Commune, however, in that the Commune provided for election by the people of committees at every level, and committee members were subject to dismissal by the electors at any time.[8]

The army representatives, who constituted one-third of the revolutionary committees at the municipal and provincial levels, were not named by the masses but by the Military Commission of the Central Committee. The difficulties of the preceding period obviously explain this break—which today seems definitive—with the model of the Paris Commune.

Strict measures were taken to make sure that the revolutionary committees did not in turn move away from the masses and become bureaucratic groups. These committees were structured into three group divisions: one was in charge of administration; another was a permanent group whose function was to investigate the complaints of the administered and listen to their suggestions and demands; and the third functioned as regular workers in various establishments. These three teams switched periodically, each assuming the other's functions. If, as seems likely, these committees continue to function in this manner, they could well prevent any resurgence of bureaucratism.

New Progress in the Cultural Revolution

If the revolutionary committees were to grow and prosper, the Great Alliance had to develop. There had, in fact, to be a large degree of unity among the masses in order for them to name their

---

[8] The members of the revolutionary committees are also elected and subject to dismissal. The difference from the Paris Commune is that in the Chinese setup those elected must belong to one of the three categories, and only a third of the members can come from any one category. See, Jean Daubier, "*La célébration de la Commune de Paris*," in *La Nouvelle Chine*, No. 3, July, 1971.

representatives and the revolutionary cadres. The strengthening of organic centralization was part of this effort. Therefore the central leadership, with Chou En-lai in the vanguard, made a point of stressing unity.

On February 22, with Chou En-lai present, the Congress (one could also say Association or Meeting) of Red Guards from the Peking upper schools was created: the *Hong Dai Hui*. At this time the three Red Guard headquarters of the capital, whose differences during the months of November and December we have already detailed, came together. This meeting had resulted from a number of factors: the outlawing of the *Lien Tung* and the arrest of some of its leaders, and a number of conversations between the representatives of the three headquarters on the one hand and the members of the GCCR on the other. Since December, and the elimination of T'ao Chu, the conservative and divisive influences among the Red Guards had tended to diminish. A manifesto was published, as well as an appeal to the Red Guards, calling on them to follow the Peking example. As time went on similar meetings were organized in many large and middle-sized cities of China, all of which contributed to the desired unity at the grass roots.

In the ringing, lyrical style that typifies so much Red Guard literature, the manifesto paid homage to Mao Tse-tung and his doctrine. It was interesting to see that it also contained an endorsement of the principles of organization based on democratic centralism. It also emphasized the necessity for the left, in light of the circumstances and possibilities of the moment, to join forces with the masses in order to isolate as much as possible the rightists—the key principle of the Cultural Revolution.

The manifesto further insisted on the need to take power away from those who had strayed from the revolutionary road, from the proletariat and socialism. It further noted that in those areas where the demands made themselves felt the Marxist principle which stated that the old machine of state should be broken ought to be applied. It also reminded the people that the dictatorship of the proletariat had to be strengthened, and a new revolutionary order installed and consolidated—all of which meshed with the concerns of the moment.

This same text also stressed the essential roles of the Great Alliance and the three-in-one combinations, and the leadership role that the working class had to assume. Finally, it recalled the importance of going back to the works of Mao Tse-tung and thereby transforming one's concept of the world, of constantly recalling his devotion to the collectivity and to the people in the struggle ahead.

On March 19 a conference of peasants of the Peking region was held, with Chou En-lai present. He stressed the importance of making sure the spring sowing went on as usual, and therefore asked that there be no power transfers within the brigades. Ch'en Po-ta was also present, and emphasized the same thoughts.

On March 22 the most important of the conferences held during this period took place, that of the workers and employees of the capital. The speeches given reflected most of the major concerns we have already heard: the reestablishment of revolutionary discipline; care to make certain production was not interrupted; revolutionary unity; destruction of revisionist structures; and the continuing struggle against the countercurrent. Chou En-lai noted that an appeal on March 18 to the industrial concerns had not fallen on deaf ears, emphasized the leadership role of the working class, and alluded to the countercurrent in these words: "The class struggle is being waged under very acute and complicated circumstances. We hope, dear workers and staff member comrades, that you will heighten your revolutionary vigilance, form a great revolutionary alliance, uphold the policy of the revolutionary 'three-in-one' combination and resolutely beat back the adverse current aiming at a counterrevolutionary restoration of capitalism."[9]

These points were summarized in a resolution which also contained a new and very important measure: a radical transformation in the management of business enterprises, aimed at both reducing the number of nonproductive employees and considerably speeding up the wheels of administration. The Resolution of March 22 called for the basic transformation of the "revisionist system of management and of the plethora of bureaucratic organs installed in many offices and factories by the counterrevolutionary clique of the former Party Committee for the Municipality of Peking." Out of this conference was created the temporary organ, the Workers Congress (*Hong Dai Hui*).

About this time a "Congress of Peking Higher Education Red Guards" was formed which extended and completed the movement of the Great Alliance. Some time before, the Central Committee had asked that courses in these schools be resumed at the same

[9] See *Peking Review* No. 14, March 31, 1967.

time the Cultural Revolution and the critical examination of the school curriculum and teaching methods were being carried out, with a view toward revolutionizing the latter.

By the end of March, then, the chaos which the opposition had tried to exploit was well under control, and the Maoists had largely stabilized the situation. Nonetheless, the problems were not basically resolved, and there were still many difficulties ahead.

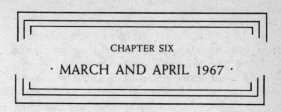

CHAPTER SIX

· MARCH AND APRIL 1967 ·

The Aftereffects of the Countercurrent

Chou En-lai's Delicate Position

"In the leadership organ you have set up, there is no cadre from the political department.[1] Could you tell me why?"

"Because they are all conservatives."[2]

The man to whom that answer is given is Chou En-lai. For a moment he surveys his guests, young workers from one of the propaganda departments whom he has received along with representatives of various mass organizations in the capital, to sound out the situation of their respective enterprises. His finely chiseled features are still surprisingly youthful, and the intensity of his expression is often tempered by cordiality. The special quality that seems to emanate from him as he converses is his extraordinary intelligence.

From the start of the interview, the youthful delegates have obviously been impressed by both the clarity and the quantity of questions Chou has asked them, by his astonishing memory, by his capacity to go immediately to the heart of any matter and to extricate the main threads from any problem, however confused it may seem.

"You must learn to distinguish," he says, "between the organized

---

[1] At the factory or office level the "political department" is a collective of Party cadres in charge of political and administrative work.

[2] The conversation from which I have quoted was recorded by a revolutionary group and broadcast to the personnel of the office where I was working.

conservatives and those who simply happen to express conservative ideas. As for the cadres of the political department, you must proceed from a class analysis."

Periodically top Party leaders or important members of the GCCR received in like manner the representatives of various city or provincial mass organizations which had been formed during the Cultural Revolution to lead the ideological battle. The leaders both talked and listened, learning what was going on in this or that section of the country and in turn informing their visitors of the overall situation in the rest of China. They would give advice and make practical suggestions—which were unofficial but were recorded and widely disseminated through posters or tape recordings.

The February countercurrent forced the Premier to utilize all his considerable ability. He did his best to persuade the revolutionary mass organizations to revert to a fairer policy with respect to the cadres and to be less harsh with them: it was a delicate operation which had to be carried out in such a way that the rightists would not be able to use it to exploit the errors of the left. Nor should it stymie the pugnacity or stem the impetus of the rebel forces. To preserve the Party spirit in this tumultuous revolution, full of conflicting tendencies and ideological currents, was difficult but vital. Balance and flexibility were required, for the rule that the masses must "educate and free themselves" could not be infringed. Some groups were very touchy about this principle, and the Premier was well aware that voices were rising to criticize him.

At T'ien-an-Men posters had appeared calling for the criticism of Chou En-lai. As he addressed the young revolutionaries who filled the auditorium in the center of Peking called the Reception Center of the State Council, Chou must have felt the full weight of the responsibilities that were his.

Yes, you have to fight, with your eyes always turned toward the future! And for that you have to call upon all that is best within you, to spur on again and again that hope symbolized by the red flag in China for the past fifty years; you must extol the pure, stir up enthusiasm and courage, provoke joy and anger, call for combat, for destruction and rebuilding, for loving and hating, for, as Mao Tse-tung has so aptly put it, the revolution is a drama of passion.

At T'ien-an-Men workers and students had also put up posters countering the attacks on Chou En-lai: "Chou En-lai is Chairman

Mao's close comrade-in-arms," they proclaimed, while others declared in big characters: "Those who oppose Chou En-lai are counterrevolutionaries."

How One Conflict Gives Rise to Another

The struggle against the February countercurrent could be effective only if it corrected the excesses which had made it possible. Chou En-lai was instrumental during this period in helping to check the abuses and disorders that had surfaced in some ministries during the criticism movement: he spoke often and eloquently, stressing the need for discipline in one's work, a more tempered approach to evaluating the cadres, and urging more rapid progress toward the Great Alliance.

If some leaders had been upset by the rightist trend condemning the "rebels," now others were concerned by the measures taken to turn back the February countercurrent.

If some leaders had thought that the "rebels" of the mass organizations had gone too far, now others found that the movement was going too far in the opposite direction. Wasn't the concern to foster the Great Alliance going to entail the risk of making hasty, eclectic compromises between revolutionary and conservative organizations? By insisting that the cadres be treated more solicitously, hadn't they engendered an opposite trend in some ministries to whitewash them, a trend that ought to be quashed immediately? In the eyes of those who expressed such reservations, it was a mistake to emphasize the problem of the cadres. The battle was first and foremost one of politics and ideology, and since it was far from over, to make sudden, empirical decisions might well compromise the movement. Any concession would be interpreted by the opposition as a tendency toward conciliation and exploited as such by it, for its own ends. The rehabilitation of rightist elements by T'an Chen-lin was ample evidence that this was true.

Nor should intervention by the army be indiscriminate. It would be wrong for the army to move in at the first sign of any disturbance. Disturbances were normal, since the Cultural Revolution thrived on mass mobilization. How could the masses fight and eliminate the *Zu Zi Pai* if there was too much centralism and the masses' freedom to speak and act was curbed?

Those within the GCCR who expressed these views could,

given the circumstances of the time, be thought of as representing the ultraleftists. They showed themselves more concerned about the roles of the masses and the "rebel" organizations than about the cadres and the army. As time went on, those who held to this view revealed themselves to be increasingly inclined toward those spontaneous excesses which had marked the end of January and the first weeks of February: this gave rise to a new conflict between trends, which characterized the second half of 1967.

Chou En-lai's position seemed to straddle the two extremes, which doubtless explains the reputation he has among some foreign observers as a moderate. But such terms as "moderate" can be misleading, for in the context of a situation as confused and turbulent as the one we are describing, Chou En-lai's "moderation" derived from a very acute political sense, and was thus quite relative. For him, the reinforcement of centralism was a necessary correlative to the mobilization of the masses, and one could not emphasize one to the detriment of the other without deviating from Marxism. Both cadres and army alike played an indispensable role, and neither should be interfered with. The army especially, under Lin Piao, was a bastion of the revolutionary forces, and had to be given a full vote of confidence. Moreover, if one wanted to count on the masses' support, there was no reason to be afraid the Great Alliance might favor compromises with the conservatives. Such fears were based on an exaggerated opinion of the influence and number of these people.

Chou's thinking must have been influenced by another consideration. Among the members of the Central Committee who did not agree with all of Mao's views, not all were firmly opposed to his policy. It was therefore worth-while winning them over, if necessary by careful doses of tactical concessions. The support of these more or less centrist elements, who were not systematically dissident, could be key for certain meetings and votes, as in the course of an eventual Party Congress. Thus they should be reassured rather than frightened by an extremist stance. It was doubtless in this spirit of reconciliation that someone like T'an Chen-lin, whose position was severely compromised as a result of the February countercurrent, was allowed to remain at his post and carry on his work with the help of the "rebels" in his ministry—an intermediate step between dismissal and out-and-out support. This tendency toward clemency aroused the indignation of the Young Turks of the GCCR, who looked on it as an intolerable concession.

Toward the middle of March a meeting of the leadership of the Cultural Revolution was held, with little attendant publicity. A *ta-tzu-pao* in the streets of Peking laconically announced it. The same poster indicated that the meeting would be marked by a struggle between two lines. Somewhat later another poster appeared announcing that the meeting had been held and had produced "satisfactory results." There is reason to believe that the struggle against the February countercurrent was the main item on the agenda, and that Chou En-lai succeeded in imposing his viewpoint. It is also probable, as we shall see later, that more radical elements on the left managed in turn to wrest some concessions from the meeting.

But in any revolution, problems follow hard on the heels of one another without respite. The future course of events would, in quick succession, reignite the flames of conflicts that had been only lightly covered by the ashes of compromise.

Postscript 1973

I think I rightly described the problems analyzed in Chapter 2, "The February Countercurrent," as "enduring problems." Certainly the question of the cadres remained unresolved, and we know that a factional struggle over the matter went on until very recently, involving an antileftist campaign that resulted in the elimination of Ch'en Po-ta and the attack against the late Lin Piao, both of whom would have tended, had they had their way, to eliminate too many cadres.

The arrest of some leaders of the *Lien Tung* to which I alluded in Chapter 3 was also a source of discord among the Chinese leaders. Hard information on this score is hard to come by. In September 1972 a number of articles in the Chinese press encouraged the cadres to send their children into the countryside to share the peasants' way of life, a move doubtless inspired by the Party's fear of seeing a revival of the spoiled-youth syndrome such as that of the *Lien Tung*.

In Chapter 2 I may have gone overboard—again in an effort to counterbalance the stereotyped views promulgated by the Western and Soviet press—in stressing the democratic and nonviolent nature of the military teams. In all fairness, I know now that these teams also made errors. In the beginning some of them tended to exert pressure on groups which had somewhat hastily been tagged as conservative because they had not approved the transfers of power. In fact, things were more complex, and according to the Sixteen Points, the minority should not be restricted or prevented from voicing its opinion. Later on the soldiers acted with greater prudence.

It can still be said, in all objectivity, that the Chinese soldiers went about their task with a rare measure of patience and diplomacy, which is to their great credit and the credit of the Communist Party that educated them. Nonetheless, I am not so naïve as to believe that the Chinese Army consists of saints. The section called "The Army Steps In" describes a general orientation on a nationwide basis. Locally there were some abuses of authority, with especially serious problems at Canton and Wuhan.

It is worth noting here that if the military participated in the revolutionary committees only on the municipal and provincial levels, things changed after April 1969, when the number of military personnel increased at all levels of administration. This accentuated the problem of the precise relationship between civilian and military authority and prompted a press campaign during 1971 and on through the summer of 1972, whose essence was: The army must obey the Party. Clearly, Lin Piao's opposition to that dictum, and his subsequent disappearance, are closely linked to this struggle.

The student at Tsinghua University, Kuai Ta-fu, whom I mention in the section of Chapter 1 called "The Situation Changes," is now under considerable fire in China. No one disputes the credit due him in the early phases of the Cultural Revolution, but later he slipped into a spirit of cliquishness. Like ultraleftists the world over, he was convinced that anyone who did not espouse his views had to be a counterrevolutionary, and in 1968 he launched several attacks against a rival student group that resulted in a number of deaths. In July of the same year Kuai went so far as to arm his commandos with grenades and pikes against a team of workers sent to the university. The toll this time was five workers killed, and hundreds of wounded on both sides. Kuai recognizes his responsibility for those incidents, although he steadfastly denies ever having belonged to Wang Li's May Sixteenth Detachment.[3]

---

[3] For a complete description of Kuai's activities and the events at Tsinghua University, see William Hinton's *The Hundred Day War: The Cultural Revolution at Tsinghua University*, Monthly Review Press, New York, 1972.

As for the revolutionary committees' abandonment of the Paris Commune principle, which I discussed in Chapter 2, it was Mao himself at the time who advised setting up the Three-in-One Alliances. The Commune, Mao told Chang Ch'un-ch'iao, should not become a stereotyped model, for that would act as a brake on the mass movement.

III

APRIL TO SEPTEMBER
1967

THE GREAT TUMULT

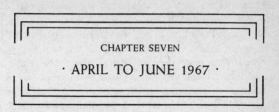

CHAPTER SEVEN

· APRIL TO JUNE 1967 ·

1. The Great Mass Revolutionary Criticism

"China's Khrushchev"

In April 1967 the Maoist line was to resume the offensive and score a number of points. It seems to be part of Mao's character that even in the face of the gravest difficulties he remains unalarmed and continues to exude confidence and optimism. The events of the preceding period had been tumultuous and fraught with peril. Even among the Maoists themselves there was division, with some emphasizing the role of the masses and others stressing that of the cadres, all of which created a second conflict superimposed on the struggle against the Liu Shao-ch'i faction. The organisms of leadership of the Cultural Revolution, especially the GCCR, which the Chairman had been careful to staff with his followers ever since the elimination of T'ao Chu, were threatened with schisms. Such a situation would tend to strip the movement of its direction and, in the agitation of the time, to foster anarchy. Thus it was that in July 1967 posters appeared in the capital quoting Mao as having declared that this phase of the Cultural Revolution had been especially critical. Any other leader would doubtless, in a similar situation, have deemed it wise to hold aloof, and might perhaps have abandoned an undertaking which seemed so dangerous. Mao, on the contrary, judged the time ripe for again moving to the attack.

It was on his orders that the struggle against Liu and his followers was intensified through a movement of criticism which was mainly ideological. It was to touch upon all areas of political, military, and economic life where the head of the Republic, Liu Shao-ch'i, had been influential. It was to be carried on throughout the country, at all levels of society, with the population participating actively in countless meetings and study sessions.

Liu Shao-ch'i was by now out of power and incapable of any direct political activity, but his influence was far from ended, since its roots went deep into everything conservative and traditional in Chinese society. By entering a new phase of more profound criticism, Mao was hoping that the masses would be better able to make out the common goals of the struggle, and thus solidify the unification effort. In the Party Center, where the struggle between two lines was also evident, this heightened movement would serve to accomplish the same ends.

Since the left wing of the GCCR was afraid that the struggle would be called off while only halfway to what it considered the objective, this new offensive was to its liking. It was at this juncture that a new phase in the anti-Liu struggle began: the Party press, which till now had refrained from naming him, would begin a campaign against him. And yet even that condemnation could only be termed semiofficial until such time as the attacks against Liu by name would appear in the *People's Daily* and *Red Flag*. Even when he was mentioned he would be referred to in ambiguous terms, a subtlety at which the Chinese are past masters: "The highest-ranking official who has taken the capitalist road," he would be called; or again, "China's Khrushchev."[1]

This new phase of the attack against Liu was to become known in China as "the great mass revolutionary criticism." Indeed, the entire Chinese population was to take part in it: in all the schools and universities, the factories and service branches, the mass organizations, groups or ordinary individuals began to write and post *ta-tzu-pao* in which they explained what forms revisionist tendencies had taken in their school or place of work. The goal of the Maoists was a further effort in raising the political consciousness of the people, and through this vast exchange of ideas they were learning not only

[1] In Chinese political life a high-ranking member of the opposition is officially named only after his case has been decided and political sanctions—usually expulsion—have been made. In the case of Liu Shao-ch'i the official press referred to him by name only in the fall of 1968, after the Twelfth Plenum of the Central Committee, once his expulsion had been voted. The same had been true for Kao Kang, the main target of a Party purge in 1954, who was not officially named until 1955. It is ironic that the chief accuser of Kao Kang was Liu Shao-ch'i.

to educate themselves but also seeing specifically the many facets
that revisionism could take.

The number of posters put up was unprecedented. There were
no longer enough walls to go around, so new places had to be
found: poster panels were built in factories of wood sidings covered
with straw matting. Canteens were also a favorite spot: steel wires
were stretched overhead from one side to the other, and the posters
were clipped to them, thus transforming the canteens into one vast
labyrinth of rustling *ta-tzu-pao*. Every time I stepped into one of
them I was struck by the lingering odor of ink.

"Patriotism or National Betrayal?"

This time all the propaganda forces at the command of the Party
Center were brought into action. On March 31 the national radio
and official press began to denounce Liu Shao-ch'i's political orientation—still referring to him by euphemisims.

Ch'i Pen-yu opened fire in the Party's *Red Flag*, of which he was
now one of the editors, in a long article entitled "Patriotism or
National Betrayal?," which was to have wide repercussions.[2] Ch'i
Pen-yu appeared on the political scene at the time of the Cultural
Revolution; before that little was known about him, since his earlier
duties had been relatively unimportant.[3] He belonged to that group
of young ideologists who emerged after May 1966 and assumed
more prominent positions. He was a member of the GCCR, and
although a poor speaker, wrote well and incisively. He appeared to
be about forty and had the look of an intellectual: his thick-rimmed
glasses gave him a rather forbidding air. His consistent stands as an
ultraleftist resulted in his eclipse in 1968.

In his article Ch'i made a rather detailed indictment against Liu
Shao-ch'i,[4] whom he accused of having used his influence as far
back as 1950 to help disseminate in China a film conceived and
written, some time before 1949, by a film maker who later became
a refugee in Hong Kong. The film, *Inside Story of the Ch'ing Court*,
exalts the role played by the Emperor Kuang Hsu at the time of the

[2] See *Peking Review*, No. 15, April 7, 1967.

[3] I did hear while I was in China that he had been a philosophy professor at
Peking University.

[4] In the article Liu is referred to as "the top Party person in authority taking
the capitalist road." Teng Hsiao-p'ing is "another high-ranking leader who is following the capitalist road."

Boxer Rebellion. Kuang Hsu represented the reformist tendency within the aristocracy which was opposed to Dowager Empress Tz'u Hsi. According to Ch'i Pen-yu, this film presents Kuang Hsu and his followers as patriots desirous of regenerating China without properly emphasizing the role of the foreigners who were the real exploiters of the country. He also claims that the film portrays the "Boxers,"[5] whom the Chinese call the *Yi Ho Tuan*, in an unfavorable light, whereas in reality they represented at the time the real movement of popular resistance against imperialism.

Ch'i Pen-yu then attempts to demonstrate that Liu's efforts to distribute this film clearly show that his basic orientation in ideological matters is bourgeois. As further proof of this allegation he reminds his readers that it was Liu who in times past favored maintaining a private sector in both agriculture and industry. He blames him for having tended toward compromise during the war against Japan, and later in the war against the Kuomintang. He also accuses Liu of having been opposed to the Great Leap Forward and to the Socialist Education Movement. And the article especially stresses the role he played at the time of the work teams during the Cultural Revolution.

None of this came as any surprise, for similar attacks and accusations had been made against Liu by the Red Guards and the proletarian revolutionaries in their poster campaigns, but this was the first time an official Party organ had opened its guns against the still legally elected head of state.

In this same issue of *Red Flag*—among a number of articles on the subject of Liu's revisionism—was a report of an inquiry into the role of the work teams at Tsinghua University during the months of June and July 1966. The connection was obvious: Liu's wife, Wang Kuang-mei, was in charge of these teams. In all these articles the nefarious role Liu and his followers had played in trying to set up the cadres in opposition to the masses was emphasized, the point being that in so doing he was trying to prevent unity of action in the revolutionary struggle.

At about this time a great number of articles on the same theme began to appear in the Party press: again and again it ham-

---

[5] The term "Boxer Rebellion" derived from an English mistranslation of the Chinese term for the secret society that led the uprising. The society's real name was "Righteous Harmony Band," which was erroneously, and by confusion with the name of another society, translated into English as "righteous harmonious fists"—and from the "fists" came the notion of "boxer."

mered away at the fact that the mass revolutionary movement of criticism then getting under way had to foster the Great Alliance, help bring about three-in-one combinations, contribute to the struggle of the proletarian revolutionaries, and turn back the countercurrent once and for all.

During this period the streets of Peking were filled every day with tens of thousands of people, as every mass organization under the sun paraded in turn, shouting as they went: "*Da dao Liu Teng T'ao!*"—"Down with Liu, Teng, T'ao!" There was also a resurgence of caricatures and posters. One especially appeared throughout the city in thousands of copies: it pictured Wang Kuang-mei during an official visit she and her husband had made to Indonesia two years before. Numerous photographs, crossed over with X's[6] showed Wang Kuang-mei dressed in a close-fitting traditional Chinese dress slit up one leg. She was all smiles as she sipped champagne and danced with former President Sukarno. Films taken during the Indonesia trip were screened, showing Liu and his wife participating in a great many worldly functions scarcely in keeping with proletarian practices.

Inside Story of the Ch'ing Court was also widely shown throughout the country at the time so that the people could see it and judge for themselves. In China it is common practice to circulate quickly and on a national scale any document of general interest. In the case of films many copies are printed and sent to the four corners of the country, where they are shown free in schools, universities, offices, and factories.

Similar manifestations took place in Shanghai and Nanking, in Shanshi, Shantung, and many other provinces. Meetings were also widely held in the army. In all, this criticism movement lasted for several months.

April 10, 1967, marks an important date: it was on this day that a huge mass meeting was held, with over 200,000 people present, at Tsinghua University, at the very place where, some ten months before, bitter clashes had taken place between revolutionary students and the work teams. On this occasion a series of accusations were made against Wang Kuang-mei and her assistants. Detailed reports about what had gone on were presented to the public, and several people who had suffered at the hands of the work teams offered their accounts as evidence. The defendants were there too:

---

[6] As a sign of hostility and contempt.

Wang Kuang-mei herself, together with ex-minister Po I-po. A documentary of this meeting was filmed and many photographs were taken; both film and photos were distributed throughout China. The texts of the speeches made at the meeting appeared both in the parallel press of the various mass organizations and in countless mimeographed handbills given out in the streets.

The Hsiu-yang

One major element of the movement of mass revolutionary criticism was the meticulous study of the book by Liu Shao-ch'i entitled *Lun Kung-ch'an-tang Yuan ti Hsiu-yang*, which literally means "On Self-Cultivation of Communists" and is generally known in English as *How to Be a Good Communist*. At the time Mao Tsetung himself directed that the book be read and evaluated by everybody. He further stated that it should be discussed and criticized in a lively manner, relating its contents to the particular problems that existed in each work unit. In those days the book was sold in the streets, so that any revolutionary who wanted it could easily find it.

The evaluation of this book was important, for it constituted a prime factor in the political education of the masses which the Party Chairman so desired as an integral part of the Cultural Revolution. Outside China people have sometimes been amazed that the Chinese criticized *How to Be a Good Communist*. Many observers thought of it as completely Marxist, and throughout the world pro-Chinese groups had it on their recommended reading lists. And then the Chinese attacked it as revisionist and anti-Maoist! Yet a careful reading offers a number of interesting revelations, though perhaps not with the explicitness to which Westerners are accustomed.

The chapter entitled "Attitude Concerning Erroneous Ideas and the Struggle Within the Party" is characteristic. In the very beginning Liu's ideas on the subject are classically Marxist: "Reject all trace of liberalism," he says. "Don't be afraid of necessary struggles within the Party." "The Party must be pitiless in weeding out errors of principle," he notes at another point. But what Liu does is comment on and modify these assertions to death, until finally you find him far removed from the original subject. In so doing Liu is trying to show that a tendency exists, which he calls "leftist" and "dogmatic," to start arguments and polemical discussions within the Party. The essence of what he is saying in this chapter is that those who, according to him, have an "extremist" attitude, who have a "mania about fighting" and "reject out of hand any compromise and are forever creating tempests in teapots," should be castigated. "According to these people, who must be of unsound mind," says Liu, "any kind of peace in the Party midst is blameworthy." The text goes along in this vein for page after page. All this may seem to have no special significance, but the informed reader cannot help but detect a veiled allusion to Mao Tse-tung and the P'eng Teh-huai affair. The person of "unsound mind" who has a "mania about fighting" is clearly Mao himself, and the former Defense Minister he dismissed is a victim of his "extremist" attitude.

Here a further point of clarification is in order: Liu Shao-ch'i's book, written in 1939, was republished in 1962. The passages cited date from the 1962 edition, which the author revised at the time P'eng Teh-huai was asking to be rehabilitated. It is also characteristic that these attacks against "leftists" and "dogmatic elements" date from 1962. In the history of the Communist movement 1962 is a crucial year: it was the year when the differences between the Chinese Communist Party and that of the Soviet Union became public. It was the year when the Soviet leaders, under the direction of Nikita Khrushchev, emerged from the Twenty-second Party Congress having adopted a political line that the Chinese termed revisionist and energetically opposed. The position of the Chinese Communist Party at this time was that the principal danger to the Communist movement was a revisionist danger from the right. The position of Khrushchev and his followers was that the danger was coming from what the Soviet press termed the "leftist" and "dogmatic" clique led by Mao Tse-tung. That Liu launched an attack in his book against "leftists" and "dogmatic elements" without even mentioning revisionism and the opportunism of the right can only be interpreted, given the circumstances of the time and the political mores of the Communist movement, as an expression of views closer to those of the Soviets than to those of Mao.

Other passages in the book were also denounced as attacks against Mao. Liu suggests that the Party should not have any "heroes" or "great men." At another point he alludes to people "who always try to enhance their own merit." These people, he notes, "try to play on any differences in the Party, to speak ill of some people then of others behind their backs, to get involved in intrigues and sow discord." This kind of attack also goes on for several pages, and provided the Maoists with ample ammunition to claim that *How to Be a Good Communist* was a work intended to prepare public opinion and the Party cadres for a kind of "de-Maoization" similar to the "de-Stalinization" campaign that had taken place in the Soviet Union. It heralded and laid the groundwork for a document comparable to Khrushchev's famous secret report to the Twentieth Party Congress.

Liu's work was also criticized for being, in essence, an outline of Confucian reminiscences filled with idealistic, feudal influences. This may be a facet of the book difficult for Westerners who have only a nodding acquaintance with Confucian thought to detect. But the Chinese public is naturally more familiar with this aspect of the attack on the book. Confucianism has left a deep imprint on the habits and customs of China, and there is a whole heritage of formalism and moralism that still weighs heavily on many Chinese. One of the targets of the Cultural Revolution, in fact, was Confucianism, or rather the ritual and customs which have become so deeply ingrained in China as to help mold the national character. As we have seen, revisionism is a corruption of the revolution through a reversion to, or because of the influence of, tradition.

According to the attacks that we have just described, the personality of Liu Shao-ch'i, his thought and his work, therefore had to be situated precisely at the intersection between tradition and revolution. His theory about the individual perfection of the Communist which is at the very core of his book betrays the Confucian influence. The complete list of recommendations he makes, intended for the militant Communist, is based on a cult of individual moral values, egotism, and self-education, and is reminiscent of the Confucian atmosphere. This individual self-education is called *Hsiu-yang* in Chinese, a term which appears in the title of Liu's book and also means "nobility," "good manners," or "breeding." If that seems obscure to most Westerners, it is crystal clear to anyone familiar with ancient Asian philosophies. In fact some Western sinologists have drawn the logical conclusion. Etiemble,[7] for one, in his book on Confucius, wrote that Liu Shao-ch'i, in contrast to Mao Tsetung, was not desirous of stamping out the influence of the master philosopher of old China, and called *How to Be a Good Communist* a synthesis of Marxism and Confucianism.

There was nothing academic about the criticism of Liu's book; on the contrary, it was lively, profound, and free of formalism. It was based on the assessments of young students and workers whose

[7] French philosopher and sinologist.

millions of posters were very often penetrating and lucid. Here again we can only regret that one of the most interesting aspects of the Cultural Revolution was virtually passed over in silence abroad, and that the foreign-language Chinese papers chose to publish only greatly oversimplified material about Liu Shao-ch'i, except for two long pieces from *Red Flag* and the *People's Daily*.[8]

2. The Contradictions Persist

May 1, 1967

This new offensive against Liu Shao-ch'i was meant to satisfy two contradictory currents. On the one hand it stressed the break with the former number-two man in the Party, thus giving new impetus to the revolutionary movement that some had feared would go down in a morass of compromise and inefficiency; on the other, it pointed up the necessity of dealing rationally with the problems of the cadres and of maintaining a proper degree of centralism, thus allaying Chou En-lai's main anxieties. A good part of the anti-Liu campaign of April 1967, in fact, consisted of condemning the extremist attitude of the work teams he had directed in June 1966, which in some universities had been responsible for the massive dismissal of Party cadres.[9] The reminder of these already ancient events served as an indirect warning against the "spontaneist" tendencies that had surfaced in recent weeks. These ideological combinations, whose entanglements are reminiscent of a polypary, are typically Chinese. They obviously do not make it any easier to explain the Cultural Revolution. Let us say, therefore, in an effort to simplify and explain, that the April 1967 campaign against Liu Shao-ch'i clearly stressed the fact that the abusive attacks against a great many Party cadres, like the effort to discredit or repress the avant-garde revolutionary elements, were wrong. Mao's revolutionary line, then, appeared as a middle road between these two tendencies. It could not on the one hand stand idly by and see the revolutionaries and the masses persecuted to the point where they turned passive; but on the other hand, it could not allow their mobilization to obviate

---

[8] "Patriotism or National Betrayal?" and "Betrayal of Proletarian Dictatorship Is Essential Element in the Book *On Self-Cultivation*," in *Peking Review*, Nos. 15 and 20, April 10, May 12, 1967.

[9] " 'Hit Hard at Many in Order to Protect a Handful' Is a Component Part of the Bourgeois Reactionary Line," in *Peking Review*, No. 15, April 10, 1967.

the role of the cadres. The intermediate road had to be followed,
which consisted of mobilizing the masses while at the same time
allowing most of the cadres to join them to guide and organize their
struggle. The Three-in-One Alliances, as we have seen, were an
effort to solve these concurrent demands.

Considerable success in this direction was achieved, the most
spectacular example of which was the creation, on April 20, of the
Revolutionary Committee of Peking. It resulted in a mass meeting
held at the Workers and Peasants Stadium with most of the Party
luminaries in attendance. Chou En-lai, Chiang Ch'ing, and Minister
of Security Hsieh Fu-chih gave speeches that day, extolling the
victory of the revolutionary line. They also took the opportunity to
remind the audience what the guidelines of the Cultural Revolution
were, and to launch several appeals for unity throughout the
country.

Still, overall progress toward unifying these two trends remained
slow. In the course of the following months very few revolutionary
committees were set up on the municipal and provincial levels, while
a considerable number of committees hastily created in the schools
and factories continued to be a source not of unity but of discord
and dispute, and could not be really considered representative of
the masses.

At the beginning of the summer the press announced the creation
of a revolutionary committee in the province of Tsinghai and, a
short while later, the inauguration of the Three-in-One Alliance at
the Academy of Sciences. Earlier, we had read official reports about
a revolutionary committee set up at the Aeronautical Institute. But
all in all the balance sheet was unimpressive. It was becoming
increasingly clear that the contradiction which had appeared within
the Maoist leadership between Chou En-lai and his leftist detractors
was not going to resolve itself but would crystallize into an ever
more bitter struggle which would spill over into the mass organizations and block, for some time to come, both the possibilities of the
Great Alliance and the measures of consolidation taken in March
and April, with their incipient steps toward unity.

According to the wall posters which appeared in June 1967, this
division was again apparent as early as the beginning of May. There
re a number of reasons to date the renewal of this conflict, which
had been temporarily quelled during the months of March and
April, as May 1. On May Day that year, to the surprise of foreign
observers, a number of personages who had been severely criticized

earlier appeared on the official viewing stand, including old Marshal Chu Teh and the economist Ch'en Yun. On that day it was also noted that, despite the concerted poster campaigns against them during the preceding two months, Ch'en Yi, Minister of Foreign Affairs, and T'an Chen-lin, Minister of Agriculture, who had been implicated in the February countercurrent, were both present and in their usual order of rank in the hierarchy. It seemed obvious that this was the fruit of Chou En-lai's pacification efforts to erase the resentment and concern felt by many Party cadres who had been roughly treated by some mass organizations during January and February.

This was noted in China and abroad, and was seen by certain GCCR members as a dangerous sign of conciliation. They therefore decided to fight the trend.

The "Extremists" of the Cultural Revolution

Four leaders of the GCCR can be considered proponents of this current.

The first is Wang Li, a young cadre of the former Municipal Committee of Peking, where he was one of the first to come out against the influence of P'eng Chen and his "Black Gang." Like his three colleagues, he was little known, and it is virtually impossible even to sketch in his background. It is uncertain whether he belongs to the military, for even the civilian members of the GCCR generally wear uniforms at important gatherings (as do all members of government). But the fact that he always wears the olive-green tunic tends to make us think he does. He looks to be young, between thirty-five and forty, is tall, rather portly, and full-faced, almost cherubic. At this time he was in charge of the propaganda machine, a post which, indeed, has seen its share of controversial title holders.

The second member, Kuan Feng, is physically the opposite of Wang Li. He is small, thin, and wears thick glasses. He is extremely nervous, unable to sit still for more than a few seconds, and chain smokes during meetings. At the time of the battle against the *Lien Tung* he became very popular because of his support of the Third Headquarters. I have always seen him wearing the uniform of the PLA, and therefore assume he is a member of the military.

Even more popular was Ch'i Pen-yu, to whom we have earlier alluded. His popularity stemmed from the fact that he too had been a supporter of the Third Red Guard Headquarters, and what was more, had since early 1966 been in the forefront of the anti-P'eng Chen forces. He was, finally, the author of several famous ideological articles, including the recent "Patriotism or National Betrayal?."

These three men were also the three chief editors of *Red Flag*. In the course of the coming months all three would be the staunch advocates of a "tough" line within the GCCR. By September the first two would suffer defeats and eclipse. Ch'i Pen-yu, doubtless by disaffiliating himself from their uncompromising stance, remained in power somewhat longer, but he too would be ousted some eight months later.

The fourth member who advocated the "tough" line within the GCCR, whose role was doubtless as important as those of the other three but who remained more in the background, was Lin Chieh, about whom I unhappily know very little, though I often saw him in public meetings.

In the spring of 1967 all four of these men—and especially the first three—were at the height of their power and influence. They traveled around the country a good deal, and their influence transcended the student milieus and spread generally not only throughout the capital but also into the provinces. During the coming weeks their policy was to fall on receptive ears among many of the revolutionary groups. Among all the Party leaders at this juncture they were the youngest, with the exception of Yao Wen-yuan, whose orientation was different. There were many who thought of them as men of great future, and even as the leading candidates to replace the venerable leaders of China still in charge, after the latter had disappeared. It is quite possible that the interested parties were aware of all this speculation, and the later confrontation between them seemed to many like a conflict between generations.

The Question of T'an Chen-lin and Ch'en Yi

For these men, who represented the left wing of the GCCR, neither Ch'en Yi, Minister of Foreign Affairs, nor T'an Chen-lin, Minister of Agriculture, had played the role in the Cultural Revolution that should be expected of revolutionary leaders, and both ought to be ousted. Hadn't they committed serious errors of policy at the time of the work teams? Hadn't one of Ch'en Yi's sons been a member of the *Lien Tung*? As for T'an Chen-lin, had he not been responsible for the February countercurrent? The position of both men was very weak. They had been severely criticized, and many posters had gone so far as to call them counterrevolutionaries. But they had one very solid force behind them: Chou En-lai. The Premier had not shared in any of Liu Shao-ch'i's errors at any time. His past was well-nigh unassailable and his prestige enormous, both at home and abroad. Chou's position about the two was that, despite the serious errors they, especially T'an Chen-lin, had committed, it was too early to make a final decision about them. It was his opinion that they should stay on in their posts, make their self-evaluations, and be given a chance to redeem themselves. Conservatives? Perhaps. Revisionists? Far from certain. Therefore, to dismiss them would be premature to say the least.

Chou's thinking at the time probably went something like this: Ch'en Yi and T'an Chen-lin are both skillful ministers, and not easy to replace. What is needed at present above all is to reassure the cadres all up and down the line. Now, to eliminate leaders of high rank at this point would be to imply that Liu's faction is still strong and broad-based. Anything that happens at the highest levels of government has repercussions, direct or indirect, at the lower levels, on the battles going on. A new purge of top Party leaders could be interpreted as a signal for a new assault on the Party cadres —which we do not want. Chou En-lai, therefore, chose to discreetly protect not only these two ministers but also a number of others, and he made a point of being present at all meetings where they were the target of attacks or accusations.

It took a lot of courage on the part of even as powerful a personage as Chou to defend these unpopular ministers against young men who seemed to be sailing before the wind. As time went on, we shall see, the differences between them would grow to such proportions as to be transformed into antagonisms.

The divisions that beset the organs of leadership also affected the "rebel" groups. The left wing of the GCCR grew more and more irritated by the effort to spare the cadres. It viewed that effort as an obstacle in the way of the revolution, and undertook to denounce it. Various mass organizations influenced by the GCCR took the same position, and in some factories and universities there were renewed attacks against the cadres. The "spontaneist" current, which had been slowed in March, reappeared. Conflicts and divisions resurfaced in many other organizations, and the various alliances that had been painfully sought and in some cases won began seriously to be eroded, or even broken.

New Violence

In various sectors of the country the division into two major factions, which during March and April had seemed if not to disappear at least to have been attenuated, reappeared. The question of power transfers still remained a special source of discord. In spite of some progress during the preceding period, and despite not only the efforts of the propaganda machine but also the intervention of PLA teams, many were the places where transfer of power had not occurred and been followed up by the Three-in-One Alliance and the Great Alliance. Some revolutionary committees formed in February had not yet been officially endorsed and therefore remained a subject of dispute between some workers and students. In March and April some progress had been made toward reconciling cadres and revolutionary groups, but not enough to erase the differences. Now, in May, the left wing of the GCCR, by rejecting the policy of moderation and flexibility toward the cadres, could only deepen the disputes, intensify the discord, and overturn the still fragile results obtained over the preceding two months.

The two tendencies, which had confronted each other earlier without any clear-cut decision, were to meet head-on once more. The organizations which had transferred power to their benefit were often made up of dynamic elements of whom some came out of the Communist Party and some did not, people who had given impetus to the movement by their enthusiasm and passion. Other organizations contested the justice of what these groups had done, pointing out that they had failed to ally themselves with the cadres, and among the latter members of the Party and the Young Communist League tended to be in the majority. A fraction of these organizations were conservative and used this same argument to defend revisionist cadres, who themselves took advantage of the confusion of the time to attack rebel organizations, as had happened the year before in Shanghai and during the February countercurrent. Many organizations who contested the power transfers, though, did so in good faith, on the basis that they had been too precipitous and had led to the dismissal of good cadres, thus opening the floodgates to spontaneism and anarchy. In most cases the task was to reconcile these two trends without favoring the conservatives, who were waiting in the wings to turn the discord to their own advantage and return to power in the wake of compromise.

There was the rub, and one can understand the enormous difficulties facing Chou En-lai, whose task it was to sort out the situation through a subtle application of diplomacy and tact. In the provinces, conservatives were especially active, and in some places still clung to power, thus giving them a solid base from which to use the mass organizations for their own ends, by urging them to physical violence against the real revolutionaries. Sometimes blood did flow, in Szechuan for example, and in some other places conservative cadres manipulated the conservative tendencies among both their fellow cadres and the masses in an attempt to preserve their positions. The opposition was weakened and ousted from power in many places, but on the local levels at least, this kind of maneuvering still went on.

The four members of the GCCR whom we have just described were of the opinion that since the conservatives were still alive and struggling, there should be no compromise. On the contrary, an attack should be launched against them, using the only force that had proved effective up to now: the mass revolutionary organizations, whose dynamism and spontaneity had to be preserved and encouraged, and whose ardor should not be dampened by warnings and rectification campaigns which could only tend to discredit them.

Chou En-lai's tendency was to stress the role of the cadres: they had to be detached from any conservative influence. In his opinion, to prolong the errors committed in February with respect to the cadres, to launch once again an all-out assault against them, would simply have the effect of making them withdraw into their shells or, what would be worse, would force them over into the conservative camp and tend to make them support the line of Liu Shao-ch'i. No, what was needed was a real coalition of the left organizations and the revolutionary cadres who, by uniting, would isolate the Liuist forces and, by depriving them of any mass support, disperse their ranks.

During the month of May, Wang Li, Kuan Feng, Ch'i Pen-yu, and Lin Chieh crossed the Rubicon and unleashed a new offensive against what they termed the "bourgeois reactionary line," which in reality constituted an attack against Chou En-lai, whom they viewed as the proponent of that policy. It began with an unprecedented campaign against Ch'en Yi and T'an Chen-lin, with a number of mass organizations of Peking leading the way. The real target was not the two ministers, but Chou himself. Posters appeared in dozens of Peking streets detailing the errors of the two ministers and portraying them as revisionists. Slogans called for Ch'en Yi to be "bombarded,"[10] then "overthrown." One day we saw a big balloon floating over the center of Peking bearing a banner which read, in big characters: "Down with T'an Chen-lin!" At times—at first timidly but then more and more boldly—the diatribes against Ch'en and T'an would end with attacks against Chou himself. Accusations and counteraccusations flew thick and fast, involving power transfers, the role of the cadres, "spontaneist" trends—and at times name calling and invective developed into actual physical battles.

In Peking there were more and more posters with photographs of wounded people, while various groups accused one another of failing to respect the Sixteen-Point Party Decision which asked that reason, not force, be used to make revolution.

This led to the appearance in the *People's Daily* on May 21 of an editorial entitled "Stop the *Wudon.*"[11] *Wudon* is violent physical struggle, as opposed to *Wendon*, which is struggle through reasoning and persuasion. In Peking, groups armed with billy clubs and iron bars and wearing helmets fought one another at their places of work, and sometimes in the streets. I won't go so far as to say that these battles took place every day and were as widespread as has been reported, but there is no doubt that the atmosphere then was indeed very tense.

The month of June 1967 marked the tenth anniversary of the appearance of Mao's article entitled "On the Correct Handling of Contradictions Among the People." This date served as a propitious occasion to start a new propaganda campaign against violence and encourage peaceful discussion among contending groups.

In his 1957 article Mao had in fact explained that one should use force only against one's enemies. Contradictions existing within the population itself are in general of a different kind and ought to be resolved through discussion and persuasion. During the Cultural Revolution, the Chinese press went on to explain, antagonistic contradictions existed only between the Chinese people on the one hand and a handful of revisionists on the other. Therefore there was no point in one segment of the masses using force against another; differences among the people should be resolved by democratic means. When one segment of the masses is misled and joins a con-

[10] That is, "criticized."
[11] On May 14 the Revolutionary Committee of Peking had issued an Urgent Appeal on the same subject.

servative organization, one should not resort to violence just because one disagrees; on the contrary, explanation and persuasion are the means to bring these people back to the revolutionary path, all the more so since it makes no sense for revolutionary organizations to fight among themselves.

This campaign did tend to calm the waves of violence, but only temporarily, and by mid-June the disorders flared up once again.

3.   The Problem of the Army

Party, Army, and Masses

The conflict between Chou En-lai and the left wing of the GCCR, which was the basis for these confrontations, may seem difficult to understand for someone with only a nodding acquaintance with Marxism. But for the Chinese these problems are an intimate and passionate part of their lives, which they discuss and debate. Superficially complex, they all lead back, really, to the basic question which is as old as the Communist movement itself: What is the special role that the Communist Party ought to play in a revolution? Is a revolution the handiwork of the masses or of a Communist Party? The theoretical reply is that it is a mass movement directed by a nucleus of militants who all belong to a centralized Party. But one has every right to wonder which of the two—Party or people— predominates. There is no easy answer, and the truth of the matter is that it varies from situation to situation. Any Marxist will tell you that both people and Party are necessary ingredients for any successful revolutionary endeavor, and will refuse to say that one has priority over the other. Still, the fact remains that there are circumstances in which the Party leads the way for the masses, and others in which the reverse is true. In historical or social situations where the latter obtains, some militants tend to put their trust blindly in the masses. But if the situation changes and the Party catches up with the masses, then a blind faith in the masses can cause problems for the Party leadership. It was just such excessive reverence for the masses that Lenin criticized in *"Left-Wing" Communism: An Infantile Disorder.*

Any revolution is a process whereby the movement of history is speeded up, and it passes through many different phases. Those who are in the forefront at any given moment can very well, by failing to understand the later phases of the movement, take off on a wrong tangent and find themselves left behind. The French Revolution, the October Revolution, as well as the Chinese Revolution, each furnish examples too numerous to mention.

Among those who may be said to have fallen prey to this tendency during the Cultural Revolution are Wang Li, Lin Chieh, Kuan Feng, and Ch'i Pen-yu. In the vanguard of the movement in its early phases, they later found themselves in conflict with the new situation. Indeed, it was tempting for the young militants who came to maturity in the tempests of the Cultural Revolution to view the Chinese masses as a decisive factor in revolutionary progress. The Party, on the other hand, risked looking like some sclerotic organism whose ranks had been disturbingly infiltrated by revisionists bent on manipulating the masses for their own selfish ends. To view the Party thus was, to say the least, unfair, for all in all it had hewed to the Maoist line very faithfully. The relatively important number of anti-Maoists within the Central Committee was not a fair indication of the situation among the middle and lower echelons of the Party hierarchy, where Mao's policy and personal prestige were very high among most militants. Moreover, to try to dismantle the Party organization was to risk turning the administration of the country into chaos, not to mention the problems posed for the economy and national security. The fact that a fairly high proportion of local Party committees had ceased to operate from 1967 on was a situation that could not endure forever. Besides, it would have been very poor strategy indeed for the Maoists to neglect the cadres or strike out against them en masse, for this would simply have had the effect of forcing them all into the arms of the opposition, thus swelling its ranks.

What was needed was a careful and equitable evaluation of the cadres, not only examining their present attitudes and activities but also taking their past into account, ousting only those who were too clearly compromised with the Liu Shao-ch'i faction and retaining those who, though they might have committed errors, had essentially remained faithful to the revolutionary line. But to effect such analyses took time, and meanwhile there was a vacuum at the local committee level. As we have seen, it was the army that stepped in and filled this vacuum.

The "leftists" of the GCCR—Wang Li, Lin Chieh, Kuan Feng, and Ch'i Pen-yu—more sensitive to the efficacy of mass mobilization and mass democracy than to the needs of centralism, were going to be forced by the very dynamics of their position to question the role of the army. Here they assumed a responsibility that was to prove fatal to their respective political careers.

Political Problems in the Army

Since Mao Tse-tung (on January 21) had ordered the army to intervene in the Cultural Revolution on the side of the left, the PLA had found itself saddled with a heavy task. With all organizations claiming to be revolutionary, leftist, and followers of Mao and his policies, the army had the devil's own time trying to figure out which were truly revolutionary and which conservative.

At this stage, what was the situation of the opposition? On the highest Party levels, it was practically neutralized since the ousting of T'ao Chu. In the provinces, in some places it had been weakened, in others eliminated, but wherever the "rebel" forces had not been strong enough to ferret it out or overturn it, its tactic was to keep quiet, hang in there, and pretend to belong to the faithful but really work from within to corrupt or coopt the movement to its own ends.

One can see, therefore, the problems confronting the army, and although in general it operated with commendable prudence and discretion, the heated and troubled times made it impossible for it not to be criticized by some adverse groups.

Directives of the Military Commission, the result of an eight-point ordinance of February 1967,[12] were intended to protect the army against dissident attacks. It was strictly forbidden to trespass on military installations or attack military personnel with dangerous weapons. *The military, on the other hand, were forbidden to use their weapons.*

The left wing of the GCCR had expressed reservations about the army's intervention, doubtless fearing that such a step might act as a brake on the political activities of the masses. To allay these fears, on April 6, 1967, a new six-point ordinance was promulgated by the Military Commission presided over, we recall, by Lin Piao. To make sure the army's activities in no way hindered or burdened the masses, it was once again made clear that it was not to use constraint but persuasion in effecting its work.

The same ordinance forbade the army to dissolve any mass orga-

---

[12] The directives were publicized by posters put up in the streets of Peking.

nizations whatsoever, even if it appeared to be reactionary,[13] and to make any arrest except when there was glaring evidence that the people concerned were unquestionably guilty. Finally, it urged the army to make sure that rightist elements did not infiltrate to influence its political efforts and make it throw its support to bad organizations.

In spite of these moderating restraints—which alone explain the relative chaos that existed at the time in China—the "leftists" of the GCCR little by little came to question the PLA's activities. Convinced that the Cultural Revolution was marking time, and that revisionist leaders were still in power in high places, they saw in Chou En-lai—and in certain army chiefs they thought were following in his path—obstacles standing in the way of the evolution of the movement, people incapable of understanding the new phase of the Cultural Revolution and at best lukewarm toward seeing it carried forward to its ultimate goal.

Yet it was far from easy to attack the army and its leaders. Directed by Lin Piao, it was a bastion of Mao Tse-tung's political thought. What was more, the army was the key element of the power of the state, and for the moment the only organized force that, in those unstable times, remained stable. Its prestige and solidity were such that it was the only force capable of dealing effectively with the warring factions. The only concern was to make sure the army itself did not degenerate into factions. If it had divided into two strains, like some of the workers and students, nothing could have withstood the turmoil. It was for this reason that special directives were issued forbidding soldiers to form mass organizations and that, contrary to what was happening everywhere else, the ousting of Liuist followers among the military was not granted to the ordinary soldiers but handled by the Military Commission.

The fact was, with the exception of Lo Jui-ch'ing, the ex-chief of the security forces who had been compromised with P'eng Chen, no important military leader had been ousted, for the army was solidly behind Mao and Lin. One army leader had come under fire during the February countercurrent, but although he had been attacked he had retained his post and made an appearance at T'ien-an-Men

---

[13] As a result of this ordinance, members of the *Lien Tung* and the Red Workers' Army who had been arrested at the beginning of March were set free, except for a handful accused of murder. This ordinance was also publicized via the street route, that is, through posters put up in the streets of Peking.

Square on May 1, as had Ch'en Yi and T'an Chen-lin. As far as one could tell, the army was managed with great care, and its unity had to remain untouched.

In July, however, a serious incident occurred at Wuhan, wherein the army was led to support some conservative organizations. This was the occasion the "hard-liners" of the GCCR had been waiting for, and they used it to launch their attack.

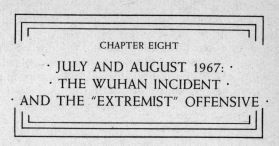

CHAPTER EIGHT

· JULY AND AUGUST 1967: ·
· THE WUHAN INCIDENT ·
· AND THE "EXTREMIST" OFFENSIVE ·

1. The Events at Wuhan

The Tribulations of Wang Li and Hsieh Fu-chih

Wuhan is really a triple city consisting of the three mid-Yangtze cities of Hankow, Hanyang, and Wuchang. The Han and Yangtze rivers have their confluence at the largest of the three cities, Hankow, and Wuhan is important not only because of its strategic situation as a port at the beginning of the most navigable portion of the Yangtze but also as a major iron and steel center, the home of the mammoth Wuhan Iron and Steel Works.

It was at Wuhan that Mao Tse-tung began his now famous swim in the Yangtze on July 16, 1966. It was here, too, that a man we have already spoken of, Wang Jen-chung, long operated. Mayor of the city, a member of the Central Committee, first secretary of the Party for the surrounding province of Hupeh, Wang had been a close collaborator of T'ao Chu, whom he had backed with his liaison agents in Peking in August and September 1966. In June 1967 Wang had been ousted and placed under house arrest. But nonetheless this was his bailiwick, and Wuhan remained a center where the opposition was strong and where friends of T'ao Chu retained important posts which they hoped to use to launch a counterattack. In contrast to certain Communist parties in the West, who are careful to rotate their Party cadres so that none is tempted to carve out a personal political fief for himself, the Chinese Communist Party has apparently not been afraid to leave the same civilian and military leaders in the same posts for many years. As a result, in some provinces bureaucratic feudalities grew up with great influence locally; during the Cultural Revolution they were revealed to be hotbeds of opposition.

In Wuhan, truly huge mass organizations had been formed. One of them indicates by its very name the scope and size of these groups: it was called "The Million Heroes." Of conservative bent, it was surreptitiously supported by and defended the local followers of T'ao Chu and Wang Jen-chung. It stood in opposition to other, equally powerful organizations: the Wuhan Workers General Headquarters, with strong alliances to other groups, especially university and middle-school students.

On June 19 these groups clashed, and violence flared on a bridge over the Yangtze, leaving several dead. The military commander of the region, Ch'en Tsai-tao, supported the Million Heroes, who he claimed represented the left.

This situation degenerated over the next few weeks, and Peking's concern became so great that it dispatched three high-ranking officials to Wuhan: Chou En-lai; Wang Li, member of the GCCR and propaganda chief; and Hsieh Fu-chih, Minister of Security and Chairman of the Peking Revolutionary Committee.

After a number of discussions during which he tried to get a clear picture of the facts, the press of other matters forced Chou to leave Wuhan. He flew back to Peking but left his two comrades behind to complete the mission.

The following account is based on the report of a messenger of the Central Committee who visited the Peking office where I was working to tell the staff about what had happened.

On July 18 a meeting was held in the office of the military commander of Wuhan between Wang Li and Hsieh Fu-chih on the one hand and the military leaders of the city on the other. The two emissaries from Peking told the others that the GCCR considered the support given by the military commander to the Million Heroes an error, since it judged that organization to be conservative.

Much to the surprise of Wang and Hsieh, the others refused to follow their advice. Further discussions ensued, with each side sticking to its guns. Ch'en Tsai-tao expressed his dissatisfaction, and the political commissar of Unit 8201 of the security forces stormed out of the room, slamming the door behind him.

The next day, July 19, turned to tragedy.

Learning what had happened the day before, the heads of the Million Heroes mobilized their followers. Donning helmets, and armed with clubs, knives, and spears, these men left their places of work and, transported in trucks furnished by the army, took up positions at strategic points around the city: highway intersections, the port, the railway station, and the airport. They were backed up by Unit 8201, which joined them in armored cars.

As dawn broke, the simmering city—the day was sweltering— awoke to find big-character signs and posters being plastered everywhere by excited gangs. They all said the same thing: "Down with Wang and Hsieh Fu-chih!" "Wang and Hsieh out of Wuhan!" From one end of the city to the other loudspeakers manned by personnel from the Million Heroes blared threats and abusive tirades against the two emissaries from the capital.

At 7:00 A.M. the house where Wang and Hsieh were staying was surrounded by members of the Million Heroes who prevented anyone from going in or coming out. An hour later a group of helmeted civilians armed with clubs entered the building to seize the envoys.

Hsieh and Wang faced them. Hsieh stepped forward and reminded them that he was not only Minister of Public Security but Vice-Premier. "Would you dare kidnap me, or kill me?" he demanded. Somewhat taken aback, the intruders hesitated. Maybe they had been unaware of the high rank of the man they had planned to kidnap. Wang Li, however, was less imposing. He was younger, and of lesser rank in the hierarchy. Who did this greenhorn think he was representing anyway? The attackers moved forward, but since Wang Li's bodyguards drew their guns, they again hesitated.

Both sides stood facing each other, their faces tense. Suddenly there was a noise in the house and an officer burst into the room, his jacket open. It was Ch'en Tsai-tao. The men moved aside to let him through. Had he come to protect the two men? No, he had come to make them retract their condemnation of the Million Heroes and hold him blameless of any accusation. "You can see what your intrigues are leading to," he is reported to have said. "The people are furious because of your attitude."

Wang and Hsieh remained unshakable. Ch'en withdrew,[1] at

---

[1] Various books on the Cultural Revolution have different descriptions of many incidents (for example, Jean Esmein's excellent book, *La Révolution Culturelle*). Some do not mention Ch'en's intervention; others say that at one point the situation got so out of control that Ch'en, summoned to Wang and Hsieh's room, was himself beaten by agitators who burst in and mistook him for one of the Peking emissaries. The problem is that, especially for the period we are describing, there was no official reporting of these incidents. We had to depend on unofficial accounts, wall posters, and what we heard.

which point uniformed men arrived, pushed the civilians aside, and leveled their machine guns at the bodyguards. Hsieh and Wang then asked their bodyguards to lower their guns. Wang was immediately taken away, while Hsieh remained a prisoner in the house.

Wang Li was dragged to a military vehicle and badly beaten along the way. He is reported to have had his arm broken and some accounts say that he almost lost the sight of an eye from the beating. Men from Unit 8201 bundled him off to the headquarters of the military commander, where a pushing, shoving throng made up of members of the Million Heroes was massed. Wang Li was pushed out onto the balcony of the building; his clothes were torn, his face bloody, as down below the crowd waved copies of the *Little Red Book* and chanted: "Down with Wang Li! Kick Wang out of the directorate of the Cultural Revolution! Wang Li does not represent Chairman Mao's Proletarian Headquarters!"

Someone grabbed Wang Li by the hair to make him bow his head. He resisted, and stumbled. Someone else suggested he be allowed to rest till the following day, so that he could be fresh for questioning. Furious, the crowd screamed: "No, question him here, right now!" Finally, his clothes in tatters, Wang is said to have been marched through the streets of the city, his face and body streaked with sweat and blood, with a sign hanging around his neck: "Wang Li, Revisionist." Crowds massed along his route to boo and hoot at him.

While these painful events were going on, other groups from the Million Heroes decided to launch an attack on the organizations hostile to them and finish them off. While their loudspeakers, scattered more or less throughout the entire city, blared in a frightful cacophony that the Million Heroes were the true followers of Mao and their opponents were reactionaries, the commandos, armed to the teeth, surrounded the university section of the city and part of the iron and steel works, the two focal points of student and worker resistance to the "Heroes." While armored cars covered their assault, the commandos pressed forward in a hail of fire from automatic weapons toward barricades that had been erected against them. They were met with a rain of Molotov cocktails. Soon this section of the city was a veritable center of civil war; the acrid smell of gunpowder and blood filled the air. After violent fighting, the university and industrial sections were taken by assault.

As soon as Peking learned of these events, prompt measures were taken. Chou En-lai immediately flew back to Wuhan, but just as he was about to land some officers in the control tower warned him he was falling into a trap. Ch'en Tsai-tao had taken part of his garrison and stationed them at the airport, together with some armored cars, as though he were receiving the Premier with all due honor. But in fact he had planned to place him under arrest. Chou's pilot beat a hasty retreat and, according to some accounts, set down at an alternate airfield.

Meanwhile, loyal troops, both infantry and airborne, arrived in the city and occupied strategic points. They also began negotiations with the Million Heroes and Unit 8201 to release their two prisoners and yield any remaining areas they were occupying.

According to one story related at Peking, soldiers of Unit 8195, who had remained loyal throughout all the turmoil, managed to wangle the task of guarding Wang Li, under the pretense that they were going to take him off to make his self-evaluation. They tried to sneak him away in a helicopter, but that effort failed. Finally, Wang managed to escape, thanks to the help of the political commissar of Unit 8195, and took refuge in the countryside outside of Wuhan, after a forced march of some twelve miles.[2] He was taken to a loyal military barracks and thence driven by military car to a nearby airport. To get there he had to pass through a number of roadblocks set up by the Million Heroes, who failed to recognize him.

The Reaction in Peking

How had things reached such a pass? Ch'en Tsai-tao and the leaders of the Million Heroes had managed to convince their followers and a portion of the military that it was they who were truly loyal to Mao's revolutionary line, and that Wang and Hsieh were reactionaries. As had been the case in Shanghai in November and December of 1966, these confusions were made possible to the extent that, as several factions each claimed to be true Maoists, the Party Center kept aloof and refrained from interfering. Whenever the neutrality of the central government ceased, and it disowned this or that group, the organization thus repudiated soon suffered a rapid eclipse, for the necessary ideological support was gone. This is what happened in Shanghai, we may recall, once the Detachment of the Red Defense had been disavowed by Peking. In Wuhan,

[2] In Esmein's account, Wang and the political commissar escaped just as the "Heroes" were about to assault the camp where they were being kept prisoner.

however, there had been a new development without precedent: a
faction criticized and disowned by the GCCR, in the person of two
high-ranking officials of that directorate, had refused to capitulate.
The fact that Mao had to intervene personally to restore order and
end the turbulence shows both the extreme urgency of the situation
and the enormous prestige Mao enjoys.

Mao sent messages not only disowning the Million Heroes but
explicitly supporting and encouraging the Wuhan Workers General
Headquarters and their Red Guard allies. The message of Mao's
support was broadcast over loudspeakers at every intersection of
the city, and navy personnel who had been sent to Wuhan handed
out leaflets by the thousands. It was not long before, thanks to the
extraordinary efficiency of the Chinese propaganda machine, virtually the entire population knew of the Chairman's stand.

Not only is Mao immensely popular, but his prestige is such that
when he takes a position the vast majority of the population listens,
and responds quickly to his directives. During the Cultural Revolution, whenever Mao made his wishes or position known the repercussions were considerable. In many cases they helped pacify warring factions and restore unity. The Wuhan incident offers a typical
example.

Shortly after the violence in Wuhan, another message was broadcast. As had been the case in Shanghai in January, it was signed by
the government, the Central Committee, the Military Commission,
and the directorate of the Cultural Revolution. Here are extracts
from that document, which clearly indicated Mao's support for the
students and workers and condemned the Million Heroes:[3]

> . . . Certain leaders of the Military Region of Wuhan have
> committed serious errors of orientation and policy. They have
> dissolved the Workers General Headquarters,[4] a revolu-
> tionary organization they have tagged as counterrevolu-
> tionary. They have arrested persons belonging to many other
> revolutionary organizations. This is inadmissible! Those per-
> sons must be liberated without exception and rehabilitated.
>   Some military leaders in Wuhan have utilized a portion

[3] To my knowledge no official publication of this document was ever made in
any foreign language.
[4] This dissolution took place in February 1967. Subsequently, in accordance
with instructions issued by the Military Commission on April 6, the Wuhan military leaders reluctantly authorized the Workers General Headquarters to function
again. Some handbills and pamphlets distributed at the time make no mention of
the facts; others give different dates.

of the masses misled by The Million Heroes. Resorting to slander and subterfuge, they have distorted the facts and tried to lead them in the wrong direction.

These leaders have shamelessly subverted the proletarian revolutionary line of Chairman Mao and the judicious directives of the Military Commission. They have incited people who are misinformed to combat the central Party organs and the Cultural Revolution Directorate. In so doing they resorted to barbaric, fascistic methods, assaulting and kidnaping people, even going so far as to physically attack emissaries of the Party leadership.

This grave political incident has aroused the wrath and indignation of the masses, the soldiers, and the revolutionary military cadres. The entire population decries and condemns them. The infantry, the air force, and the navy all condemn them throughout the country. They are overwhelmed by a tidal wave of reproach emanating a millionfold from every sector, military and civilian, of the country.

As for the handful of evil men and their followers who fomented and carried out this incident, they will be sought out and punished in accordance with the law.

In the city of Wuhan, the Workers General Headquarters, the *Kang 913*, the *Hsinhua Gong*, the Second Headquarters, the *Hsin Hu Da*, the *Hsin Hu Nong*, and the *San lian* have all stoutly defended Maoist thought and policy. You have followed the right road and acted properly. The proletarian revolutionary battle is in no way restricted to Wuhan. The victory is yours—workers, peasants, soldiers, revolutionary intellectuals—as it is the victory of our great Party and of Chairman Mao our great guide, and of his revolutionary line.

The Party Center calls upon the masses who have been misled to become aware of their mistakes and return to the Maoist line, to join the revolutionaries in their struggle against the common enemy, and to denounce the insidious intrigues of the military leaders of Wuhan and the handful of evil leaders of the Million Heroes.

The Party Center calls on all those who have erred to mend their ways, reminding them that if they do so sincerely and honestly they will not be held accountable for their acts. . . .

Measures to restore order were taken immediately. The Million Heroes were disarmed and its members turned in their arms to the military authorities; the occupation of strategic points was abandoned; work, which in many places had slowed or stopped, resumed.

Ch'en Tsai-tao was arrested and taken to Peking. New military leaders were named, under the leadership of Tseng Sze-yu, former deputy army chief of Manchuria. Calm was restored relatively quickly. A scant week after the incident a friend of mine—a non-Chinese—went through Wuhan; it is hard to believe that if the city were still in turmoil he would have been authorized to visit it. According to what he told me, he had seen signs of the fighting—scarred buildings, the remains of barricades, tanks stationed at intersections—but apparently the fever had completely subsided.[5]

There can be no doubt that the incident was serious—the most serious of the Cultural Revolution. Western papers whose headlines screamed "Civil War in China" exaggerated grossly; but so did those who passed it off as just another news item emanating from the Cultural Revolution, as did Paris' *Le Monde*.

As soon as news of the "rebellion" became known throughout China, huge demonstrations were organized from one end of the country to the other denouncing the "Wuhan reactionaries." In the capital, mammoth parades occurred, with the marchers rhythmically shouting their support of the Cultural Revolution's Directorate, acclaiming Wang and Hsieh, and booing Ch'en Tsai-tao. Hundreds of caricatures and thousands of big-character slogans stigmatizing Ch'en appeared overnight on the walls of Peking.

The pro-Wang and Hsieh demonstrations culminated on the afternoon of July 25 in a huge meeting. On the scale of mass meetings in China, the summit is those held on T'ien-an-Men Square, where a million strong can gather. This was such a meeting. Every school, university, office, and factory send part of their personnel, who march in shifts to the square, on a staggered schedule so that everyone does not arrive at the same time. The army also sends contingents of unarmed soldiers. Within the space of three or four hours it is possible to assemble a million people.

At 5:00 P.M. on July 25, the highest-ranking Party leaders ascended the rostrum at T'ien-an-Men to address the crowd. Mao was not there, but his then second in command Lin Piao was, next to Wang and Hsieh. His presence served to demonstrate forcibly that while the army commander of Wuhan might have committed errors of line, they did not involve the loyalty of the army itself.

---

[5] Some authorities note that at least pockets of resistance continued until the beginning of August. In any case New China News Agency reported on July 29 that the struggle for the city had moved into a new phase, with opposing factions lined up "on battlefields along both sides of the Yangtze."

2.   The "Extremist" Offensive

The PLA under Fire—the Canton Incidents

However serious they may have been in themselves, the Wuhan incidents were quickly brought under control. But the events there had one very important consequence. The militant extremists among the leaders of the Cultural Revolution used them as a pretense for launching an attack against the People's Liberation Army. Since a segment of the army had revealed itself to be less than wholly pure politically, the slogan began to circulate in China: "Strike down the handful of army leaders who have taken the capitalist road!" At first this slogan was disseminated unofficially, but it was soon picked up by the official Party organs, especially in various editorials that appeared on August 1, the anniversary of the founding of the PLA. An editorial in *Red Flag* No. 12, "The Proletariat Ought to Have a Rifle in Hand," stated: "At the present time there is a country-wide campaign aimed at that handful of high-ranking leaders in the Party and in the *army* who have taken the capitalist road. That is the general focus of the struggle." Similar admonitions appeared in other journals of the Party Center, among them the *Liberation Army Daily*, whose head, Cha Yi-cha, was subsequently dismissed.

In an interview with Edgar Snow in 1965[6] Mao Tse-tung indicated that the precise wording of slogans and watchwords in China was a very delicate matter, for they could at times have unforeseen effects on the vast majority of the population. Actually, the call for a campaign against the "handful of revisionists" in the army almost led the whole country into a state of disorder. If the army were purged, using the same methods that had been used to purge the civil machinery, it might splinter into factions. Besides, to suggest that there were revisionists in the army could undermine the army's prestige and badly hurt morale, thus severely impeding its efforts to support the left. The army's role as arbiter was in effect based on the tacit acceptance by the workers and students of its Maoist loyalty. Now dissident factions disowned by the army could counter by branding it as Wuhan-revisionist and refusing to follow its orders. The PLA propaganda teams' delicate task of fostering alliances and resolving the problem of the cadres was suddenly going to run into

[6] See *The Long Revolution*, Random House, New York, 1972, pp. 191–223, for complete text.

a serious roadblock, making it difficult if not impossible to play the role of centralist mediator. Having earlier played the masses against the cadres and the Party machinery, the leftists were this time going to set the masses against the army. It was at Canton that this conflict crystallized during the month of August 1967.

Canton is the capital of the province of Kwangtung, in southeastern China. Since it lies opposite Taiwan and Hongkong, its strategic and political importance is obviously great.

Kwangtung was one of those provinces where the opposition remained strong and deeply rooted. T'ao Chu had long been the top-ranking leader in this area, and he had many friends there. The opposition's method of operation was the classic one of coopting the Cultural Revolution or subverting it clandestinely from within. Claiming to follow Mao and his revolutionary line, it had managed to fool part of the population and keep it splintered into various factions, thus keeping the Cultural Revolution from developing effectively. The workers were divided into warring factions, as were the students. The origin of this division dates back to early 1967. An attempt to transfer power had taken place at that time, but only a portion of the mass organizations had been involved, without any real backing by the people. The Peking authorities had not given their endorsement on January 22; later on the city was split in half, one group favoring the Revolutionary Alliance Committee, the other opposing it.

The details of the various conflicts that ensued were extremely complex and confusing—the battles in Canton went on until September. The revolutionary committee installed in January was somehow taken over or maneuvered by the followers of T'ao Chu. Whether they had infiltrated it from the start or only later remains unclear, but in any case it was used against the revolutionaries.

As was often the case in China when transfers of power created lasting problems, the PLA was called upon and the province was placed under the control of a military commander. In Canton, the PLA refused to support the committee, denounced it, and threw its support to the committee's opponents.

On April 17, Chou En-lai paid a visit to Canton and apparently approved of the measures that had been taken. The partisans of the former committee, however, were reluctant to accept the Premier's advice, as they had resisted that of the army.

During the summer the Wuhan explosion gave them an initial opportunity to take issue with that advice: they claimed that the dissolution of the committee was analogous to that of the Wuhan Workers General Headquarters. Thus the watchword from the extremists among the GCCR to fight the revisionists in the army came as a godsend for them. They used it for their own ends and accused the military commander of the city, General Huang Yungsheng, of being the "T'an Chen-lin of Canton," claiming that the dissolution of the committee was a result of the February countercurrent and an attack against true rebels.

During the summer of 1967 the city was covered with wall posters calling for the ouster of Huang Yung-sheng. Since he had the support of Chou En-lai, the Premier too was taken to task in the poster campaign. The upshot was that the role of mediator that was supposed to befall the PLA became virtually impossible, leading to increasing violence which, during the month of August, reached the stage of armed struggle.

Almost every day there were fights in the city. Truckloads of armed men rumbled constantly through the streets, and bloody battles were fought as opposing groups with submachine guns attacked and counterattacked. On August 20, several people were killed. By 5:00 P.M., the streets of this city, which in normal times are the gayest and liveliest in China, had emptied out, and street fights between the opposing commandos had begun. The military patrols sent out to restore order were virtually helpless, for the organizations which favored the ex-committee did not hesitate to open fire on them. Fuel was added to the fire when a number of prisoners escaped from jail and proceeded to pillage a city already in a state of near-anarchy; vigilante groups were formed to pursue the criminals, and summary executions added to the climate of hate and turmoil.

The hasty watchword which the extremists of the Cultural Revolution popularized had set off an offensive against the PLA which, in the case of Canton, almost drowned the Cultural Revolution in a sea of chaos.

Chou En-lai, the Main Target of the Extremists

The attacks against the army were particularly notorious in Canton, but they also occurred in other areas. Groups that had been disowned by the army seized the opportunity and, applying the same logic—if the soldiers don't support us it is not because we are in error but because they are in the camp of the revisionists—counterattacked. In a number of sectors members of the PLA propaganda teams were accused of being under the thumb of Ch'en Tsai-tao and of emulating the "Wuhan revisionists."

The offensive against the army, however, was only one prong of the extremist attack, the other target being Chou En-lai. In China, any political campaign requires slogans or watchwords to try and persuade the masses. The slogan used in the effort to undermine Chou En-lai's position merits examination.

During May and June the Party press had discreetly put forward the notion that the Liu Shao-ch'i faction was well on its way to extinction. The ultraleftists disputed this allegation, saying that this was so only in the area of Party organization. True, they said, a number of ranking opposition leaders had been ousted, but the trend they represented remained strong politically and ideologically, and had to be fought. In other words, one could be guilty of revisionism without having been an out-and-out follower of Liu or his policies. The clear implication was that T'an Chen-lin and Foreign Minister Ch'en Yi in particular should not benefit from any extenuating circumstances but be classified in the same category with Liu and Teng Hsiao-p'ing. As a result there was a resurgence of big-character posters, with T'an and Ch'en as targets, which reached a peak in July and August. Frequently included in the caricatures that covered all the walls in the center of Peking at the time was the image of Ch'en Yi, who with his horn-rimmed glasses was easy to portray.

On the pretext that the Liu line was far from eradicated but threatened to recur and grow, the "ultra-Maoists" tried to get a certain number of Peking organizations to join forces in an offensive first against Ch'en Yi and T'an Chen-lin, then more and more clearly against Chou, who, they had decided, was protecting Ch'en and T'an and therefore, objectively, had to be in Liu's camp.

More and more frequently, as the people of Peking went to work in the morning, they discovered posters put up during the night which attacked the Premier. Even more serious was the effort made to discredit the government of which he was the operative head by trying to depict it as incapable of functioning because of the popular opposition to it.

This tends to explain a whole series of incidents which today seem anything but fortuitous, which occurred in Peking during the month of August, at the time the Foreign Ministry was occupied by members of its own staff and demonstrators from outside.

We should recall that during the Cultural Revolution employees could decide to fire a higher-up, but this practice did not extend to the ministerial level. Thus Ch'en Yi could not be ousted (except by the Politburo) and his functions taken over by a revolutionary committee. The occupation of the Foreign Ministry was an attempt to change that situation: the result was the proclamation of a power transfer not throughout the ministry but in the section of the Party that directed it. Later this power transfer was declared illegal.[7] Needless to say, all this tended to hinder the smooth operation of government.

What happened was a whole series of incidents aimed at harassing or embarrassing the diplomatic representatives of a number of countries with whom China's relations were strained. The incidents were also meant to embarrass the Chinese government: if it disowned them or apologized it ran the risk of being accused of compromise with the enemy; if it approved them, it became guilty of submitting to the dictatorship of the street.

On August 9 a Mongolian diplomat shopping in the capital was assaulted by groups of young Chinese. On August 17 the Soviet Consulate was attacked and ransacked and a diplomatic automobile burned. Even more serious, on August 22, following an anti-British demonstration involved with British policies in Hong-kong, the English Mission was attacked. The British Legation was set on fire and the chargé d'affaires, Donald Hopson, was seized and humiliated. Soldiers and police tried to fight off the attackers (an eye-witness reported that the resistance was more than token, with some defenders being injured) but were overwhelmed until reinforcements arrived, by which time the building was little more than a smoking ruin.

It is also likely that the same extremists who were exerting these pressures on the government, and were responsible for the resulting disorders, were also responsible for a number of diplomatic moves at the time. In one instance the Foreign Ministry cabled the Cambodia association for friendship with China virtually inciting it to revolution in the Khmer kingdom. Prince Norodom Sihanouk was understandably furious and reacted by threatening to cut off relations with China, a threat nipped in the bud by an apology by Chou En-lai. It is also likely that, in the conflict between Chinese Communists in Hongkong and the British government, the radical

---

[7] It was reported that Wang Li personally came to the ministry to encourage this power transfer.

elements in the Party organization in Peking gave encouragement to the former, whereas the official government position was much more subtle.

The burning of the British Legation in Peking was the straw that finally broke the camel's back. Chou En-lai, the extremists' ultimate target, was about to react energetically.

China in August 1967

The summer of 1967 was one of the hottest in the history of China, in more ways than one. It marked the culmination of tensions resulting from the Cultural Revolution, the most critical and acute moment of the struggle.

And yet, all in all the situation at this juncture was not all that unfavorable to Mao and his followers. In a certain number of cities and provinces power transfers had put true revolutionaries in positions of authority. In others, such as Inner Mongolia, Kiangsi, Honan, Hunan, Chekiang, and Kiangsu, committees established to pave the way for the Great Alliance were functioning. A number of anti-Maoists had been deposed, such as Li Ching-ch'uan in Szechuan and Liu Lan-tao in Shensi. Only in Kwangtung could it be said that the opposition was still solidly entrenched.

The increase in incidents during the summer of 1967, then, cannot be explained by the strength of the opposition, but by the movement started by Lin Chieh, Kuan Feng, Ch'i Pen-yu and their associates, one of whom was Wang Li. Since the events of Wuhan, in fact, Wang Li had become a hero and had come to think of himself as infallible.[8] This group introduced what amounted to a new contradiction into the political situation by enlarging the framework of attack to include Chou En-lai. They had a purpose in insisting that the struggle against Liu Shao-ch'i and his ideological influences was spreading: there was the clear implication that the Premier ought to be included among the future targets of the Cultural Revolution. The extremists had begun a vast campaign in Peking to familiarize the people with that idea. Every day Ch'en Yi, whom Chou had kept on in his post, was denounced, and to attack Ch'en

---

[8] Up to this point Wang Li had been thought of as a good militant and his disagreement with Chou En-lai had been taken to be nonantagonistic. There can be no question but that, after Wuhan, he acquired a swelled head and thought himself on an equal footing with the top leaders. But what China had condemned in July was aggression against the Party, of which he was the representative at Wuhan.

Yi and call him a counterrevolutionary was to embarrass the Premier who was defending him and make the notion credible that there were still revisionists clinging to power. During the summer, doubtless at the instigation of these extremists, various groups in the capital began loudly proclaiming that Liu Shao-ch'i should be "finished off" once and for all. What they were asking was that the Party Center officially announce his political condemnation and expulsion, and the usual campaign of posters and wall paintings was utilized. Here again this frenetic upsurge was meant to create the impression that the Cultural Revolution was being held in check. At the propitious moment, the masses would be informed that one person was responsible for this braking, and some even went so far as to utter his name: Chou En-lai. The demands of various groups to have done with Liu had led some of their members to proclaim a hunger strike in front of the former Imperial Palace, now the seat of the Central Committee.[9] They set up tents in front of the entrance and strung up posters calling for Liu to come out and make a self-criticism before July 31. To reply at least partly to these demands, a new meeting of the Party leadership had been called for August 5, during which, in fact, Liu did make a self-criticism. Loudspeakers set up outside enabled the crowds which had gathered to hear the exchanges that occurred during the session, after which the followers of the "extremists" gave up their hunger strike. But the hard-liners within the GCCR did not intend to leave things at this pass, and the following day, August 6, declared that Liu's self-criticism was unacceptable, that the activities of those who followed his line were greater than ever, and that far from being on the run they were moving over to the offensive. The upshot of this viewpoint was to sow further discord and create greater conflict. In many places work stoppages increased and teaching was interrupted. When the disputes were limited to the expression of varying viewpoints through posters it was bad enough, but too often the exchanges degenerated into violence and bloodshed in the provinces. More and more, groups of people fleeing from the violence in their own cities and towns came to Peking. There, profiting from the freedom allowed the masses, and the lack of repression on the part of the army and the police, there were outbreaks of delinquency, which up to then had been virtually nonexistent. Thefts were reported, and trafficking in a few commodi-

---

[9] Purportedly, Ch'i Pen-yu came to encourage them.

ties which the disruptions of the moment had caused to be in short supply, partly due to the split among the railway workers. Even Peking, generally the quietest of all Chinese cities, was that summer prey to an unprecedented violence. Armed groups roamed the streets, and there was an exchange of gunfire at the Hsitan Market followed by acts of random destruction.

The mass organizations tended more and more to split into two factions, and harsh quarrels ensued about the revolutionary committees formed in February, the arguments being based on whether the transfer of power was truly revolutionary or actually revisionist in revolutionary guise. Since June it had become increasingly common for workers to refuse to obey the committees' objectives. They did not go out on strike; they simply went about their work as they understood it, with all the troublesome consequences that entailed —in fighting, destruction of propaganda materials, and kidnaping of key personnel by the developing shock troops.

Never had the walls of the capital been more covered with posters and photos depicting wounded people and ruined buildings. Some of the photographic blow-ups were framed in black, as one group or another paid homage to one of its members who had fallen victim to the violence. The captions of these posters consisted of accusations and diatribes against the guilty. Other blow-ups portrayed people alive and whole . . . but perhaps not for long: these were the persons accused of crimes against group A or B, and the blow-ups called on the masses to arrest them.

Such was the situation, which if not anarchy was at least the brink of anarchy. With the authority of the army put in doubt and its role as mediator undermined, the task of creating alliances and forming revolutionary committees was severely jeopardized. The stage was set for a vigorous response.

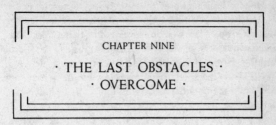

CHAPTER NINE

· THE LAST OBSTACLES ·
· OVERCOME ·

1. Mao Steps in Again

Mao's Second Absence

We recall that during the months of June and July 1966, Mao was away from Peking—and in my opinion away voluntarily. It was his intention to let the Cultural Revolution take hold as broadly and deeply as possible, and then, when the inevitable conflicts occurred, to step in and, with the help of his enormous political and moral prestige, resolve them.

In August 1967 we witnessed more or less a repeat performance of this tactic. During the time when the struggle between Chou En-lai and Wang Li reached its point of greatest intensity, Mao once again was conspicuous by his absence. Here again I am convinced he acted voluntarily, to allow the contradictions to develop fully, to the point where they would have to be resolved.

Mao Cuts the Controversy Short

In the beginning of September, Mao returned to Peking and settled the controversy by siding with Chou En-lai. *That was the major turning point of the Cultural Revolution.* Between the "spontaneist" current of the "ultraleft" on the one hand and the need for centralism on the other, Mao opted for the latter.

The criticism of Ch'en Yi that summer was an important element in the conflict. "During these past forty days," Mao said in more or less these words, "Wang Li committed more errors than Ch'en Yi committed over the past forty years." Mao's biting wit, which is well known in China, was in this instance once again widely disseminated. He also let it be known that the list of accusations drawn up against the Foreign Minister was grossly exaggerated and basically worthless. Ch'en, Mao went on, was going to stay on in his post, where he would try to redeem his past mistakes by taking into account the criticisms that had been leveled against him. As for the extremists, Mao accused them of being in the wrong and condemned both them and the groups under their influence in the Foreign Ministry.

Once Mao had thrown his support to Chou, the leaders of the GCCR, especially Ch'en Po-ta and Chiang Ch'ing, tried to explain and justify the Premier's positions to a number of hothead groups in the capital. Almost immediately the campaign against Chou ceased, as did that against Ch'en Yi and T'an Chen-lin.

Mao also went out of his way to state that he had full confidence in the army. Emphasizing that the errors of the PLA during the Cultural Revolution were so minor as to be virtually nonexistent, and that whatever they might have been they had been corrected, Mao demanded that all attacks against the army cease forthwith. He therefore called for a nation-wide campaign in support of the army. He issued special directives for Canton, and threw his support to Huang Yung-sheng. Chou received emissaries of rival Canton factions and again stressed that the Central Committee was backing Huang; he forbade them to compare Huang with T'an Chen-lin, and made them sign a twelve-point agreement aimed at settling their differences and fostering unity. A pre-Great Alliance group was set up in the province, with Huang Yung-sheng as its head. Some time before, on September 5, the Military Commission had ordered the rebel groups in Kwangtung to turn in their arms.

2.   The Restoration of Order

The Purge of the Cultural Revolution Directorate

It was high time order was restored. To effect it, a two-pronged move was initiated: on the one hand, a mild repression was ordered, to put a stop to the frenzied freedom that had brought some sections of the country to the brink of chaos; on the other hand, a real effort was made to bring together the various revolutionary groups which had been jeopardized by the earlier excesses.

Lin Chieh, Wang Li, and Kuan Feng were ousted from the GCCR. Ch'i Pen-yu was kept on in his post, but his role was greatly diminished. It was rumored that he had given his self-criticism on the subject of the events of that summer.

Via the standard routes of big-character posters and the official press, a vast campaign was undertaken to denounce the misdeeds of the ultraleftists. What the posters said in essence was: Beware of those who proclaim themselves far-leftists; they may well be rightists in disguise, bent on dividing the Proletarian Headquarters (an allusion to the attempt to make people think Chou was at odds with Mao) and the PLA. The exhortation to root out and eliminate the handful of revisionists in the army which appeared after August 1 was an error.

The wall press was much more explicit. It stated that Wang Li and his followers had created a secret organization called the May Sixteenth Detachment,[1] about which an inquiry was already under way. Little by little one began to see photographs appearing in the streets of Peking identifying the people who belonged to this group and who were responsible for the attacks against Chou En-lai. They were accused of having been responsible for the turbulence of the preceding months and for having willfully chosen the way of Wudon, that is, violent confrontation. Some of the leaders responsible for the sacking of the British Legation on August 22 were arrested. The slogan "Cut Off the Black Hand" began to appear on the city walls. In Chinese political slang the "black hand" refers to any secret, ill-intentioned force. A number of accusations were made against the May Sixteenth Detachment, which all came down to the following idea: the bourgeois, reactionary line of Liu Shao-ch'i[2] had been forced to change its tactics as it was progressively defeated. What happened was that the rightist leopard pretended to change its spots, but in reality was only using leftism as a disguise to undermine the Cultural Revolution and splinter the Maoist proletarian unity.

As for Wang Li and Kuan Feng,[3] it would be too facile to accept unequivocally the *unofficial* accusations leveled against them of

---

[1] The name was taken from the Central Committee Circular of that date in 1966, which disowned P'eng Chen's Outline Report. See Appendix 2 for text of the Circular.

[2] Even though Liu had long since been rendered inoperative politically, his name was still cited, for in China ideas need human incarnation.

[3] I do not know what has become of Lin Chieh. As for Ch'i Pen-yu, at the time I am speaking of he had not been condemned politically.

having applied the Liuist trend in another form. During the early phases of the Cultural Revolution they had been cited as among the staunchest supporters of Mao. It is nonetheless undeniable that their tendency had made Chinese politics steer a most perilous course. The rashness of some of their slogans and directives and their lack of political sense were ultimately unacceptable to the Chinese leaders. It is certain that some conservatives who were opposed to Mao were able to and did utilize the current created by the extremists to launch new offensives of their own and try to drown the Cultural Revolution in chaos. This became especially apparent in Canton. That the errors of Wang Li and Kuan Feng helped the opposition is unquestionable. That foreign or Taiwanese agents seized the opportunity of turmoil and trouble for their own ends is not inconceivable. But that the two men were implicated with any such foreign agents, or that they were involved in counter-revolutionary plots,[4] seemed farfetched, at least on the basis of the specific information available at the time.[5]

Mao Tse-tung's Directives

During the second half of September it was common to see little knots of Chinese at every intersection reading long wall posters. After they were read, and often copied, the posters became the subject of heated discussions. Most of the mass organizations went on to reprint them in the form of brochures and handbills, or to record them on tape, after which they were disseminated throughout the length and breadth of China. Either the exact text or some fair

[4] Such accusations were made in China, but only in wall posters and Red Guard papers, not in the official press.

[5] After his return from Peking in 1971 Wilfred Burchett alluded to this affair and spoke of a plot. But his article (published in the United States in the *Guardian*, May 12, 1971) really does not throw any new light on the situation. It is true that the May Sixteenth Detachment voiced its hostility toward the "former government" (meaning the government prior to the Cultural Revolution, which had been headed by Chou En-lai). The former Chinese counselor to Peking's embassy in Indonesia, Yao Tung-shan, was purported to be in line to replace Ch'en Yi as Foreign Minister. What, precisely, was Yao's role in the May Sixteenth Detachment? And what was the involvement in that same organization of the American Sydney Rittenberg, once thought of as a "three-hundred-percenter" and later considered a "revisionist" and "counterrevolutionary"? Why at the height of the crisis were the files of the Foreign Ministry robbed? Why did the May Sixteenth Detachment replace the slogan "Down with Liu-Teng-T'ao [Chu]" with "Down with Liu-Teng-Ch'en [Yi]," an indirect way of rehabilitating T'ao Chu? These questions still remain unanswered.

paraphrase thereof was quoted for many months thereafter. Not long after this period I took a plane to the interior of China and was surprised to hear the hostess read the complete text of these directives from the Party Chairman. If nothing else, this incident reveals both the importance accorded this material and the degree of intensity with which Chinese propaganda operates. And yet it was a long time before this text appeared in the official Party press, for it was reprinted only in local papers such as the *Peking Daily* and Shanghai's *Wen Hui Pao*, and not in such nation-wide or official publications as *Red Flag* or the *People's Daily*. One sometimes wonders why such a text appears in one place and not another, and although the reasons may be many, publication in the "parallel press" lends only a semiofficial endorsement to the directive or text in question and makes it easier to change course if the political situation subsequently requires it.

I have never been able to find a complete translation of this important text, and was thus unable to include it in the appendixes of the present volume. But it is nonetheless worth noting the salient points.

The Party Chairman began by indicating that during the past few weeks he had been away from Peking, touring the northern, eastern, and south-central provinces. The situation was excellent, he said—a statement which may seem surprising in light of the turbulent events we have just described. But Mao wanted above all to give the lie to assertions by the "extremists" among the members of the GCCR that the Liuists were again on the offensive. The main benefit of the Cultural Revolution, according to Mao, was the fact that the masses had been fully mobilized in a vitally important political struggle, thanks to which their level of political awareness had been measurably raised. He noted with considerable satisfaction that the Cultural Revolution had become the most important subject of conversation not only in the factories and offices, but also in every section of every city and town, and even in virtually every household. I can personally attest to the validity of Mao's claim: there can be no question that the Chinese people are the most politically aware in the world.

Mao dwelled at great length on the problems of the alliance of mass organizations and offered advice on how to create revolutionary committees made up of the three-in-one combination at all levels of the administrative apparatus. The key to the triple combination, he said, was to "free" a great many Party cadres.[6] Mao's recommendation was one that had been reiterated many times since the August 1966 publication of the Sixteen-Point Party Decision, but because of the winding course of the Cultural Revolution and its spontaneist detours it had seldom been applied.

Mao had seen in his travels around the country that the cadres in many levels of the administration had been criticized. He had also been somewhat surprised, he went on, to note the degree of animosity toward certain cadres on the part of the masses in some places. Even taking into account the slogans used by the spontaneists and the ultraleftists, Mao concluded that what he had seen was not a superficial situation but one that was deeply rooted. He declared unequivocally that "these cadres had cut themselves off from the masses." Why had they been criticized and sometimes roughed up by the workers and students? Why had they been make to wear dunce caps and carry ignominious posters—practices which Mao not only deplored but had forbidden? Mao said that the reasons were simply that some cadres were better paid and lived in more comfortable homes than their colleagues, and some had cars at their disposal; all this explained both the divorce between them and the people and the latter's lukewarm feelings toward some of the cadres. In addition, the attitude of certain cadres was very authoritarian; they tended to make decisions without consulting their fellow cadres or the people. The clear implication, of course, was that Mao strongly felt all that had to change.

As for the alliance among mass organizations, it should come about only after mutual consultation. The pretension of some organizations, said Mao, to form an alliance only if they were the nucleus, should be eliminated without further ado. "No organization," Mao remarked wittily, "can declare itself the nucleus. And those that do are the most idiotic."

Alluding to mass organizations of conservative bent, Mao offered the opinion that they were very few. To make arrests, in his opinion, was a poor way of going about things. The government should arrest few people, and then only at the request and with the help of the masses.

Mao emphasized the importance of the alliance in the working

---

[6] Some foreign commentators were quick to note and interpret the meaning of the word "liberate" as proof that they had been imprisoned. In Chinese political language "freeing the cadres" means simply that those who have made their self-criticisms and mended their ways are allowed to resume their posts.

class and called for the cessation of in-fighting among the workers. His words on this subject were repeated endlessly; almost every day one could find them quoted in the Party press: "There is no fundamental conflict of interest within the working class," said Mao. "Under the dictatorship of the proletariat in particular there is no reason for the workers to split up into organizations belonging to two major antagonistic factions."

Mao's directives consisted of several pages of thoughts and evaluations. Their widespread dissemination led to new phases of the Cultural Revolution, which were to be marked by progress toward unity and the appearance of new revolutionary committees.

Calm Returns

The Party propaganda machine was to undertake a two-pronged attack aimed on the one hand at strengthening alliances and on the other at opposing the spontaneism of the extremists. To counter the latter's claims that the bourgeois reactionary line had taken over the offensive, the Party asserted that this line was to all intents and purposes defeated. For the first time the official press declared that a clear-cut victory over the reactionaries had been won and the headquarters of the bourgeoisie destroyed. What this clearly meant was that the principal leaders of the Liu Shao-ch'i faction had been ousted from positions of power and henceforth were incapable of mounting any significant offensive.

Calls to support the army were legion too. A whole host of laudatory articles about the army appeared in which it was called, among other things, the pillar of the dictatorship of the proletariat. It was thanks to the PLA that the Cultural Revolution could continue. Unity between the army and the people was essential to the movement's success: Do not attack the military!

As had happened in April, there was a resurgence of attacks against Liu Shao-ch'i. The purpose once again was to foster unity by pointing to a common enemy. There was a resumption of what was called mass revolutionary criticism: Liu's texts were examined line by line; so were his policies in every area—political, scientific, educational, military, industrial—and they were branded as infamous. Once again thousands upon thousands of posters were written and pasted up. In the city streets we saw wooden scaffolding being erected outside the buildings of virtually every enterprise, on which information and caricatures were posted at regular intervals and constantly renewed. The purpose was to let any passer-by know what was going on inside the factory or office without having to enter the building. These scaffoldings must have come as a welcome breather for the weary walls and windows of the city's stores, which had all but disappeared over the months with a multilayered, and not always very esthetic, blanket of posters.

Chou En-lai's position as solidly entrenched Premier was reestablished. One color poster, distributed at this period literally by the millions, portrayed Chou in a group of five with Mao: the other four were Lin Piao, Ch'en Po-ta, Chiang Ch'ing, and K'ang Sheng. Thus everyone in China was reminded that he belonged to the group of leaders made up of Mao's closest colleagues, which in China are often referred to as the Proletarian Headquarters.

On October 1, 1967, to considerable surprise, Ch'en Yi reappeared during the celebration of the eighteenth anniversary of the founding of the Republic. The campaign against him had been going on for several months, since February of that year. Endowed with a great sense of humor, for which he is famous, Ch'en had in the beginning responded to the attacks against him without ever losing his smile. Numerous anecdotes about him went around in China at the time, one of which reveals his mordant wit and sense of irony, at least insofar as the Red Guards are concerned. When other ministers were trembling in their boots before the Red Guards, Ch'en refused to be intimidated and seldom lost an opportunity to hold them up to ridicule.

Once when he was on his way to the Peking airport to greet some foreign delegation, he was challenged by a group of Red Guards. Ch'en got out of his car and seemed to listen with rapt attention as the young people lectured him, interspersing their sermon with liberal quotations from Mao's work. When the lecture was over, Ch'en Yi thanked his youthful critics and climbed back into his car. Before driving off, he leaned out of the car and opened his own copy of the *Quotations*.

"Now it's my turn," he said. "Allow me to quote for you from Chairman Mao, page 320.[7] Chairman Mao has said: 'Ch'en Yi is a good and faithful comrade. He belongs to the Red Gang!' "

Saying which, Ch'en drove away, leaving the furious Red Guards shouting imprecations after him.

---

[7] There are only 270 pages in the Chinese edition.

Another story about Ch'en told of a public self-evaluation session held in the presence of various mass organizations in Peking. At one point a group of Red Guards had come to the stage to heap abuse on Ch'en. One of them waxed particularly vehement. As he was ranting on and on Ch'en got up and walked over to him, bowed low, stood up again, and in a quiet voice said to the assembled throng: "Ch'en Yi won't ever do it again!" provoking long peals of laughter.

In the long run, though, Ch'en Yi's morale must have weakened, for he was reported to have sunk into a depression, and the rumors going around about his bad health were not the usual "diplomatic" kind. I saw him at the banquet held on the eve of the October 1 celebrations and he looked pale and thinner. Mao had defended him, though, and he retained his posts in both the ministry and the Politburo, but his prestige and popularity were never what they had been prior to the Cultural Revolution.

By autumn, order had been essentially restored throughout the country. From this point on Mao's efforts were directed toward consolidating the victory. It would be safe to say that the Cultural Revolution had weathered the storm and was entering calmer waters.

Postscript 1973

Today the origins and manifestations of ultraleftism are better known. The struggle against this trend continued from 1967 through 1972. In 1971 it resulted in a number of spectacular and dramatic events, the most notable of which were the fall of Ch'en Po-ta and the attack against Lin Piao, followed by the accusation after Lin's death that he had been plotting against Mao.

Nonetheless, even if we know more today about the nature and importance of the ultraleftist movement than we did when I was writing this work, there is still a sad lack of information on a subject so important and so full of international implications.

What we do know for sure is that the attacks against Wang Li, Kuan Feng, and Ch'i Pen-yu have all been made virtually official. They were accused of having formed the May Sixteenth Detachment, a secret counterrevolutionary group which at one point was very influential in the area of propaganda and tried to take effective control of the Ministry of Foreign Affairs. The charges against them ranged from the familiar "ultraleftist" accusation to allegations that the group was serving not only American imperialism but Soviet revisionism.

Yao Tung-shan, the former counselor to the embassy in Indonesia and also a member of the May Sixteenth Detachment, had at one point all but supplanted Ch'en Yi as Foreign Minister. The spirited attacks against Ch'en were really aimed at Chou En-lai and his foreign policies: Chou was accused of not furnishing sufficient support to various national liberation movements and of supporting nationalist regimes in Southeast Asia and Africa. As soon as he returned to Peking in May of 1967, Yao inspired an intense vilification campaign designed to discredit Ch'en Yi and Chou, implying that they were responsible for the failure of Chinese foreign policy in the area where he had been stationed. His campaign continued throughout the summer and early fall, until his arrest in October.

For Mao and the leaders of the Cultural Revolution the movement was intended to stress the following areas: education and teaching, literature, journalism, public health, and internal administration. In these areas revisionism was a threat in varying degrees. It was said that such was not the case in foreign affairs, even if in this sector errors had been committed that needed correcting.

There can be little doubt that the direction Chou En-lai has given and continues to give to foreign policy had, and continues to have, Mao's approval and support. Moreover, in his complex sector where strategy and tactics impose subtle and often difficult maneuvers, no important decision is made without Mao's approval. Naturally, Mao and Chou have met with some difficulties in foreign affairs. But in attacking Chou En-lai in the realm of diplomacy Yao Tung-shan would have been hard-pressed to really make anyone believe he was defending Maoist policy.

During the few months that he was a power in the Ministry of Foreign Affairs, Yao made a number of strange and dangerous moves. He got the Chinese government to break off relations with Burma and was on the verge of doing the same with Nepal. Both these countries, geographically close to India, were on good terms diplomatically with China, as was Pakistan. They were all headed by reactionary regimes, but, confronted with the threat of India, which had the support of the Soviet Union, it was strategically important for China to maintain good relations with them. It is known that Yao Teng-shan tried to use the Chinese minorities in both Burma and Nepal to stir up revolutionary trouble that could only have been superficial, and that he did the same thing in Cambodia, then headed by Prince Norodom Sihanouk. All this revealed not only a simplistic conception of foreign policy but an abysmal ignorance of the international situation.

At about the same time the incidents occurred between the Chinese and the British authorities. Yao's reaction was to serve the British with an ultimatum, then organize the burning and razing of the British Legation in Peking, an act all out of proportion with the nature of the dispute. At a time when Soviet-American collaboration made China's role in the world delicate if not dangerous, Yao offered China's enemies ample ammunition which could be, and was, used to discredit her.

Internally, the aim of the May Sixteenth Detachment was to make Chou En-lai the target of its attacks, much as Liu Shao-ch'i had been earlier. What it was looking for, in essence, was the disgrace of the "former government," that is, the government headed by Chou before the Cultural Revolution. The movement's logic went something like this: Implying that Chou was a revisionist, its attacks focused on the cadres, many of whom it claimed were corrupt. The Party needed a massive purge. In defending the cadres, the Premier, in its eyes, was hindering the revolution.

One of the slogans disseminated by the ultraleftists in the summer of 1966 was characteristic: "Fifty Days or Seventeen Years?" they asked. The implication was: Had the more or less serious errors committed by the cadres during the "fifty days," with the help and temporary influence of Liu Shao-ch'i, gone on for only "fifty days," or had a revisionist trend been going on for seventeen years? It was not enough to talk about the cadres' errors during the month of July; one had to delve deeper and reveal "all the crimes that have been committed since 1949." In fact the ultraleftists were implying that, contrary to the Sixteen Points' contention, the "black line" had been dominant ever since Liberation. It was a difficult thesis to defend, but its obvious corollary, for those who believed it, was that a great many cadres had to be purged.

As for the attacks of the May Sixteenth Detachment against the army, it appears that Wang Li and Kuan Feng were the principal instigators of those that occurred in the North, where they utilized Kuai Ta-fu's group at Tsinghua University.

Today we also know that three high-ranking army officers (referred to in Chapter 11), when they were purged in 1968, were accused of belonging to the May Sixteenth Detachment: Acting Chief of Staff Yang Ch'eng-wu; Fu Ch'ung-pi, commander of the

Peking garrison; and Yu Li-chin, political commissar of the Air Force.

After the incidents at Wuhan described earlier, there were further serious attacks against the army not only in Canton but also in Nanking, where the activists took as their chief target Hsu Shih-yu, military commander for eastern China. According to reliable reports, Kuai Ta-fu was involved here too, having sent some of his followers to Nanking.

It is also certain that the May Sixteenth Detachment was responsible for a fair share of the violence that occurred during the summer of 1967. According to its pronouncements, which were endlessly repeated, the revisionists were returning in force, recovering the positions from which they had been ousted in January 1967, and had to be stopped by armed might. On August 1, Army Day, a campaign was started on the theme of one of Mao's sayings: "Political power grows out of the barrel of a gun." Such a slogan, repeated twenty-four hours a day, week in and week out, was, in the context of the times, adding fuel to the fire. Fights between rival civilian factions reached an unprecedented intensity, and attacks against soldiers resulted in thousands of victims, as Chou En-lai was to tell Edgar Snow three years later, in the fall of 1970.[8] One should recall, too, that all the activities of the May Sixteenth Detachment were carried on under the guise of a campaign in defense of Mao and Maoist doctrine.[9] Thus Yang Ch'eng-wu wrote an article at the time entitled: "Let Us Implant Ever More Vigorously the Absolute Authority of the Thought of Our Great Commander-in-Chief Chairman Mao Tse-tung," in which he made an out-and-out apologia for the personality cult. Mao, as noted, was neither flattered nor taken in by this kind of tactic.

So much for what we know for sure about the May Sixteenth Detachment. That the errors committed by Yao Tung-shan, Wang Li, Kuan Feng, and Ch'i Pen-yu were serious is indisputable. The evidence may even seem overwhelming. And yet at this time, as well as in other periods, we have seen that other Chinese leaders had made mistakes which could be qualified as serious without being treated as counterrevolutionaries. They were roundly criti-

---

[8] See *The Long Revolution*, Random House, New York, 1972, Vintage Books, 1973, p. 103.

[9] The ultraleftists, we remember, had strongly infiltrated the propaganda bureaus of the Party.

cized, harshly reprimanded, but generally without being defamed or disgraced. They had not reached the point of being considered "antagonistic," and thus, having mended their ways, could be reintegrated into the revolutionary struggle. Such for instance was the case of Teng Hsiao-p'ing, the former general secretary of the Party, who in radical attacks had often been coupled with Liu Shao-ch'i. The military commander of Wuhan, Ch'en Tsai-tao, has also been rehabilitated, according to some sources. What is the difference, then, and what are the criteria for determining when a contradiction is or is not antagonistic? In China it would appear that to be considered counterrevolutionary there must be a combination of solid proof, serious errors, many accusations, and cross-substantiation.

Certainly the case against the ultraleftists is serious. However, at least abroad, it is only partly known. Some observers will wonder whether the May Sixteenth Detachment was not among those who wanted to go too far too fast, and for that reason fell into the trap of violence and bloodshed. How can any commentator answer this question, about which the Chinese leaders themselves have revealed but little? On the other hand, their opinion is clear-cut: the May Sixteenth Detachment was indeed counterrevolutionary. Does this mean that the Chinese leaders had more than the ordinary reasons to condemn its members? The implication—and it can be no more than that because we still do not have much hard information to go on, despite additional clarification since 1969—is that the May Sixteenth Detachment had been infiltrated by foreign agents, had been working hand-in-glove with some enemy power. There was also talk of secret documents that had disappeared from the archives of the Foreign Ministry. But all this still remains in the realm of speculation. Will it ever be completely clarified?

One of the most disturbing aspects of the revelations made about the May Sixteenth Detachment is that higher-ranking leaders than those already named were implicated in its activities. Some say that the group was merely a tool for Ch'en Po-ta's machinations. Many meetings over the past two years in China have denounced Ch'en's conspiratorial activities. Ch'en, one may recall, was head of the GCCR, and at the Ninth Party Congress which opened in April 1969 was a member of the Politburo Standing Committee, that small group which, in addition to Mao himself, at that time included only Lin, Chou, and K'ang Sheng. This fact in itself suffices to surprise the foreign observer, especially since nothing of what transpired in these meetings has leaked out to the West. In William Hinton's book on the problems of ultraleftism at Tsinghua University there is scarcely any mention of Ch'en Po-ta. All one can say is that in 1967, when Wang Li was at the height of his power and prestige, he was working under the authority of Ch'en, who was the director of *Red Flag*. Is it possible that the ultraleftists were able to use the propaganda machinery as they did without the knowledge and consent of Ch'en? It is a question still to be answered.

During my stay in China I occasionally heard allusions to a disagreement between Ch'en and Chou, but I never heard anything specific.

The case of Lin Piao is even more murky. It was in the latter half of 1971 that foreign observers began noting Lin's absence at public functions, but no one thought too much about it.[10] The mystery deepened, however, when it was announced that the traditional October 1 parade would not be held in 1971, nor would the ranking Chinese leaders appear at T'ien-an-Men. Rumors then began to circulate according to which Lin Piao had been accused of trying to assassinate Chairman Mao. Somewhat later we heard that Lin had tried to escape aboard a military aircraft headed toward the Soviet Union, which had crashed in Mongolia. Most of these reports emanated from American sources, and seemed so incredible that few people really believed them. Yet the Chinese press soon launched an attack against ultraleftism, referring to "phony Marxists," and "political swindlers of the Liu Shao-ch'i ilk." It was not long before it became apparent that this campaign was aimed at what came to be known as "apriorism"—a term which included stereotyped propaganda styles, excessive use of the cult of Mao, subjectivism, and doctrinal rigidity. A complicated article praising Mao's essay "A Single Spark Can Start a Prairie Fire" revealed that this press campaign was really aimed at Lin. In fact, it turned out that Mao's essay was actually a letter he had written Lin back in 1930 criticizing some of his military ideas. Other articles followed attacking the ex-Vice-Chairman's notions of both the role of the militia and the apportionment of the national output under a socialist regime. At the same time the press pounded away at the theme that the army must submit itself to civilian control, that is, to the

---

[10] Wounded several times during the Anti-Japanese War, Lin was often ill and out of public view.

Party. Other essays appeared, of considerable theoretical interest and representing a sharp break from the mediocre propaganda pieces which appeared during the Cultural Revolution. They tended to emphasize that Lin had strayed from the Marxist-Leninist path. But theoretical errors are not counterrevolutionary acts. And yet on various occasions it has been affirmed that Lin tried to assassinate Mao and seize control of the Party leadership. Mao himself spoke of it to the French Minister Maurice Schumann, and also to the Foreign Minister of Ceylon, Mrs. Bandanaraike. During a press conference in Latin America the Chinese Minister Pai Hsiang-kuo officially confirmed the accusations against Lin. But no details were mentioned in any of these instances.

Taipeih has published various documents claimed to have been stolen by its secret agents on the mainland and to be assassination plans against Mao drawn up by Lin. I have always tended to consider any documents emanating from Taiwan as worthless, and will continue to do so. The fact remains that the Lin Piao affair is still not clear.

For the moment it is difficult to understand why a man of such high station, only recently elevated even higher, to become Mao's close comrade-in-arms, and after the Eleventh Plenum named as his eventual successor, could suddenly have turned into a plotter and traitor. It is undeniable that Lin made mistakes. We know that he had too schematic an attitude toward Marxism and that he endowed some political events with the character of religious ritual, all of which tended to undermine the theoretical bases of the Chinese Communist Party and encourage spontaneism. We know, too, that in the struggle between the army and Party at the end of the 1960s and the early 1970s, Lin tried to resist efforts to place the army under the leadership of the Party. There were also basic differences concerning China's attitude toward the United States, with Chou advocating better relations and Lin apparently resisting. As the months passed it became increasingly clear that Chou's views were prevailing.

Some rumors have claimed that the real instigator of the May Sixteenth Detachment was none other than Lin. In *Le Monde* of April 26, 1972, the Dutch journalist Jaap Van Ginneken, who had just returned from China, asserted that Lin was behind a 1967 attempt to seize power, and that the May Sixteenth Detachment was supposed to be the instrument for the alleged takeover. But once again there was no hard proof. Van Ginneken cited some slogans alleged to be Lin's which could have been interpreted as being ultraleftist, but to utter slogans is one thing, to plot another.

The Lin Piao affair will continue to remain a mystery until such time as Peking decides to open its archives and reveal the proofs of treason. Until then, the observer can only ponder and speculate.

IV

OCTOBER 1, 1967,
TO APRIL 24, 1969:

FROM A DECISIVE VICTORY
TO TOTAL VICTORY

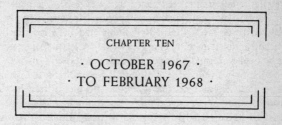

1. The Struggle Against Factionalism

Struggle, Criticism, Transformation

The thirteen months that followed October 1, 1967, were considerably different from those preceding that date. The struggle to eliminate a certain number of leaders opposed to Mao Tse-tung had for all intents and purposes been accomplished. From now on the vast welter of currents and countercurrents, accusations and counteraccusations, would largely be a matter of the past, except for a brief period in the spring of 1968. For Mao and his followers it was a time to methodically consolidate their gains, which would be consecrated in October 1968 at the Twelfth Plenum of the Central Committee.

Although the autumn did seem relatively calm compared to the fiery summer just past, and in spite of the official press's claims that "a decisive victory has been won," the fact is that the participatory method chosen to win the battle had shaken the Chinese society. Multiple schisms affecting mass organizations; internal quarrels; increased violence; the ousting of too high a percentage of Party cadres; the threat of splitting the army's unity—all these jeopardized the victory. For several months already, at least since February or March of 1967, there could be detected among the Party leaders a concern to reduce the scope of mass mobilization, with its inevitable disorder, and to extend the scope of centralism. Two obstacles had prevented them from acting more quickly or more effectively: the stubbornness of the opposition on the one hand, and the existence of the ultraleftist current on the other. In October both these obstacles were swept away, thus creating more favorable conditions for setting up revolutionary committees. Once that was done, one could think about rooting out any remaining opposition leaders, or those who in the course of the Cultural Revolution had been revealed to be either corrupt or tainted by bourgeois ideas. A Party Congress could then be held to formally sanction these changes.

Besides, it was time the Cultural Revolution moved from the phase of criticism and struggle—*Dou-pi*—to that of transformation —*Kai*. In Mao's mind, the Cultural Revolution had to include these three tasks: the masses had to overthrow certain leaders, to examine and evaluate all the negative aspects of their work, both political and ideological, and then to transform these aspects completely in a revolutionary sense. Art, teaching, and the state administrative machinery also had to be changed. This could be accomplished only by following an overall plan whose application called for a structural network of revolutionary committees in the factories, schools, and institutions of art and literature. The complex of these requirements dictated the direction the movement was to take over the coming months.

The Resurgence of Mass Revolutionary Criticism

The intensity of the factional struggles and divisions of the preceding period had tended to divert the combat from its main target and detour it into internecine quarrels. The attack against Liu Shaoch'i's policies in all their various manifestations which was begun in April had virtually ceased during the summer and given way to the conflicts we have described.

During the latter half of September, *Red Flag* No. 14 published an editorial entitled "Bring About the Revolutionary Great Alliance in the High Tide of Revolutionary Mass Criticism."[1] This was the first of a long series of articles that hammered away at the same themes. Mao's dictum, which was part of his directives, "There is no fundamental clash of interests within the working class," was especially emphasized. Red posters bearing the picture of Mao and this slogan in gold letters were put up by the thousands throughout China. The intent of the slogan itself and the attendant propaganda effort that went with it revealed the Party's deep-seated desire to

[1] *Peking Review*, No. 39, September 22, 1967.

bring about unity in the working class so that it could assume the role of avant-garde which, according to Marxist principles, it ought to.

Appeals for the Great Alliance and Denunciation of the May Sixteenth Detachment

At the same time that the press went about systematically attacking factionalism, reactionary trends, and narrow, petit-bourgeois attitudes of cliquishness and sectarianism. It also made the point that factionalism had been aided and abetted in some of its most extreme manifestations by people who feigned to be ultraleft while in reality harboring rightist views. This was the press's indirect way of attacking the May Sixteenth Detachment.

Once again the attack was carried out not by the official press but by the parallel news service, that is, through wall posters and workers' and Red Guard papers. Thus it was that in the streets of Peking we once again saw posters denouncing Wang Li, Lin Chieh, and Kuan Feng. From time to time we also saw another kind of poster, this kind bearing the picture of this or that member of the May Sixteenth Detachment. These posters carried various accusations that during the summer the people in question had fomented troubles and incited opposing groups to violence. Generally these posters were in color, with a streamer across them which said: "Cut Off the Black Hand!"

And yet the scope of this new poster-flowering was considerably less than that of its predecessors. Various newspapers were sold on Peking street corners which contained articles about the history and background of the May Sixteenth Detachment and named its leaders. But these papers were relatively few in number, and the information they gave was scant.

The reason for the scarcity of both posters and papers was that since the beginning of the month the struggle against factionalism and ultraleftism had been accompanied by appeals for revolutionary vigilance. The authorities had let it be known that the troubled atmosphere and near-anarchy that had developed here and there had been used by foreign agents for espionage purposes. This was also the time of the rumor that the occupation of the Foreign Affairs Ministry had resulted in a subsequent discovery that many high-level confidential documents had disappeared. At Peking University, Chiang Ch'ing had warned the students to be more careful and to make sure when they put up their posters that they did not contain any information that could be used by foreign agents or enemies of the regime. This is doubtless why the poster campaign against the May Sixteenth Detachment never had the scope of the earlier campaigns.

The Pursuit of Spies and Criminals

The unrest of the summer months had reached to the depths of Chinese society. All classes, all social levels, had been caught up in the ferment of the movement, including part of the criminal element.

Let me hasten to add that gangsterism in China today is no longer the organized, far-reaching world that it was before 1949. The strict control over daily life that the Communist Party exercises in normal times, as well as the fact that the Party has been able to endow manual labor with its proper value and dignity, have all contributed to reducing gangsterism and keeping it within controllable limits. But it would hardly be fair to claim that the Party had managed to eliminate it completely. In the big cities there are still various misfits, small-time criminals waiting for the opportunity to pull off something illicit. Obviously the Cultural Revolution, with its relaxed restraints intended to foster mass participation in the movement, and especially the nonintervention by the police and army during the summer of 1967, gave these people the occasion they were waiting for. During this time thefts, looting, and even murders were reported.

It would also appear, according to what some Chinese leaders have said—and I find it difficult to evaluate properly the accuracy of these allegations—that some of these antisocial types wormed their way into various political organizations, where they tended to give a style to their activities that seemed closer to that of the Mafia than to what one ought to expect from a revolutionary group. Part of this may have stemmed from the fact that in some factories—which are actually few in the overall picture—a portion of the personnel was made up of people who had committed "antisocial acts" of one kind or another and been sent there to be reeducated. It would have been normal for them to take part in the revolutionary debates and activities of their factories, but perhaps in the heat of the turmoil they could not help reverting to type and urging their colleagues to acts they otherwise would not have committed.

The authorities also seemed concerned at the time about the activities of various secret agents in China, as well as those of some hardened anti-Communists. Here again the nonintervention of the forces of order played right into their hands. Rumors at the time were rife that the factionalism, internal struggles, and violence that made the resolution of some problems virtually impossible, and that tended to impede the movement's momentum by destroying its upward impulse, were exploited or perhaps even fomented by them.

Every country, and every regime, tends to make too much of the subversive threats of foreign powers and to blame every problem and difficulty on these outside forces. China is no exception, but in all fairness it must be said that espionage and divisive maneuvers by foreign powers do exist in today's world, and China is doubtless a more obvious target than most countries.

In any case, these were the reasons cited by the Chinese leaders in their appeal to "cleanse the ranks" in an effort to rid them of the presence of any Formosan spies, *agents provocateurs*, or criminal elements. Inquiry committees were set up by the various mass organizations to see if any of their members had ideological files, that is, if they had a past history that made their loyalty questionable.

Two kinds of measures were taken. The first, a preventive measure, was to forbid anyone judged suspicious on such grounds from belonging to any mass organization. Among the categories were former members of the Koumingtang (with some exceptions), former capitalists and landowners, former gangsters, anyone who in times past had been branded a rightist, and anyone who had been closely associated with either the faction of P'eng Chen or that of Liu Shao-ch'i. As far as I was able to tell from personal experience, the number of people affected by this exclusion must have been somewhere between 5 and 10 percent of those who participated in one way or another in the Cultural Revolution. The people who fell into these categories, however, were not the subject of any punitive action, except that of being unable to take part in the Cultural Revolution.

There was a second category, though, made up of suspects from the first group whose files were more worrisome than most. They were given a more thorough check to see if they had committed any specific acts which might have harmed or impeded the Cultural Revolution. These files were gone through by civilian members of various mass organizations, then if necessary transmitted to the security forces, who would, if the facts warranted it, make arrests.

As had been the case in the attacks against the ultraleftists, the purge of troublemakers—in principal a drastic purge, but in my experience nonviolent—was obviously aimed at fostering unity in the factories, offices, and schools, thus facilitating the effort to set up revolutionary committees.

New Appeals in Favor of the Cadres

Since the establishment of revolutionary committees is based on three-in-one combinations, one-third of the posts were reserved for the cadres. What was needed was for the different groups which had previously attacked and in many cases ousted cadres who, while guilty of committing errors, could not be labeled revisionist to reconsider their stand and let the cadres resume their posts. What lay behind the reluctance to reinstate the cadres was the nagging fear of allowing revisionists to return to power.

A welter of articles was published at this point to try and dispel this fear. They stressed time and again that the cadres who could fairly be termed revisionist constituted but a tiny minority. Most of the cadres were recoverable, and the people should have the courage to reinstate them. One headline in the *People's Daily* in September read "Dare to Call on the Cadres." In a speech he gave in Wuhan on October 8, where he was welcoming an Albanian delegation whom he wanted to convince that the troubles of the past July were no more than a memory, Chou En-lai asserted that the Cultural Revolution was "an overall examination of and a rigorous test for cadres at all levels." We must now, he said, "intensify education of the cadres."[2] Chou's remarks, aside from showing his own concern for animosity toward the cadres being restrained, fit in with the Chinese adage: "Broaden the area of education and narrow that of attack." Also in keeping was the initiation throughout China of study sessions on the subject of Mao Tse-tung Thought which Lin Piao, in his October speech at T'ien-an-Men, announced would begin shortly.

The Study Sessions on Mao Tse-tung Thought

These courses were set up in the major cities. Various centers were outfitted and staffed with instructors from the PLA. A rotation

---

2 *Peking Review*, No. 43, October 20, 1967.

system was established so that all factories, offices, and schools could send in turn those of their cadres about whom there was some question. These cadres came to the courses accompanied by the heads of the mass organizations concerned. Thus discussions about them took place under the direction of military instructors who tried to come up with equitable solutions satisfactory to all parties.

These courses were aimed not only at settling the problem of the cadres but also at combating sectarianism and factionalism. With that extraordinary capacity for organization characteristic of the Maoist regime, other centers were organized to which not only the cadres and heads of organizations were sent, but also students and personnel of offices and factories. Thus the majority of the Chinese people attended these sessions, lasting for two or three days, in which Mao's articles on unity and on the correct handling of contradictions were read and discussed. All this fitted in perfectly with Mao's notion that an idea becomes an irresistible force once it has taken hold of the masses. Ultimately, then, the purpose of these minicourses was to create a powerful climate of unity in the country.

The study sessions were held under the slogan: "Fight Individualism and Attack Revisionism [*Dousze Pihsiu*]." The "fight individualism" part, in addition to its overall meaning of transforming people's ways of thinking and giving priority to the collective interest, had a more immediate purpose: numerous editorials at the time which heralded this slogan used it to stress the importance of everyone's thinking in a proletarian way, which meant ridding oneself of sectarian and cliquish habits, petit-bourgeois products that could exist only where one had an inadequate sense of what the collective interest was all about.

These study sessions went on for several months, while the articles calling for unity and the reinstatement of the cadres who "had understood their errors and changed their ways" kept appearing at regular intervals.

"Support the Army and Cherish the People"

To erase the aftereffects of the summer's troubles it was also necessary to counter the annoying tendency of some civilians to take the army to task. Thus a propaganda campaign in support of the PLA was undertaken at the same time as the others, stressing its contribution to the Cultural Revolution.

The Chinese press went into action and published a great many articles on this theme, together with specific accounts of sacrifice and heroism that had occurred over the preceding months. One soldier in particular was often cited—Li Wen-chung, who had drowned after diving in and saving several Red Guards who had fallen into a river. Li was given a high citation posthumously, along with his company, by Lin Piao himself. Such ceremonies were highly publicized throughout the country.

Meetings were held with both soldiers and civilians present in vast numbers, at which they were called upon to act together and work in concert: the people must support the army, and the army must "cherish the people." Thus was revived a slogan which would soon appear in profusion on the walls and in the papers.

At the same time the Party press announced that at regular intervals Mao was receiving army cadres in the Great Hall of the People. Although no details of exactly what went on in these meetings were ever published, it is likely that both Mao and Lin talked, to analyze past errors as well as to point out the direction to follow in the future. These meetings served to remind the people again of the confidence the highest-ranking leaders placed in the army, but they also served the purpose of trying to eliminate any vestiges of, or tendency toward, factionalism and divisiveness within the ranks of the PLA. For the events of the summer had not been without some harmful effects, and the possible dangers had been taken very seriously by China's leaders. Mao wanted to keep the soldiers from quarreling about events that were now past and about some of their leaders.[3] Using all his moral and political authority, Mao revealed unequivocally what his vision of the Cultural Revolution was and gave his personal opinions about some of the leading protagonists of the preceding summer's events. What this tended to do was to offer an official interpretation of these people and incidents, which would not have been the case had the interpretations been given by anyone less prestigious than Mao or Lin.

The Creation of New Revolutionary Committees

Little by little this many-sided effort began to produce results.

In a number of provinces where, as a result of factional struggles

---

[3] At the same time, military democracy was strengthened. Party committees in the army held their meetings with representatives elected by the ordinary soldiers in attendance.

and major disagreements, revolutionary committees had not been able to be formed, the hatchet was buried. As unity developed, it became increasingly apparent how important the reinstatement of the cadres was. And as support of the army grew, the possibility of three-in-one combinations became progressively easier, and in many cities and towns new leadership organs, represented by the masses, the cadres, and the army, began to function.

On November 1 it was announced with great fanfare that a revolutionary committee had been formed in Inner Mongolia. In December and January we learned of the formation of like committees in Kiangsi and Wuhan. Order was being restored at a quickening pace.

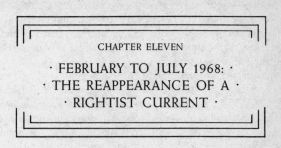

CHAPTER ELEVEN

· FEBRUARY TO JULY 1968: ·
· THE REAPPEARANCE OF A ·
· RIGHTIST CURRENT ·

1. The Revolution in Command

The Transformation of Teaching

The five months from September 1967 to February 1968 were a marked contrast to the turbulent times that had gone before. Compared to the epic style of the Red Guards, the revolutionary lyricism, the heated debates and general excitement of that early time, this period seemed almost monotonous.

The formation of revolutionary committees in various provinces was announced by the press at regular intervals: At the end of January, Kiangsu and Honan; in mid-February, Hopeh and Hupeh, the last-named, of course, being the province of which Wuhan, the site of the worst disturbances, is the capital. By February 14, revolutionary committees had been set up in every district of Peking.

University and upper-school students resumed their courses. Politics, of course, continued to absorb them. Under a new program they spent their mornings studying regular courses and devoted their afternoons to the Cultural Revolution. The subject of these afternoon sessions was how to move the Cultural Revolution past the stage of battles and polemics and create a truly proletarian educational system. This was perhaps the most positive and interesting aspect of the movement during these relatively staid months.

One of the first steps taken, in accordance with a directive issued by Mao, was to encourage physical culture courses and introduce military training. In November a great deal of publicity was given in the press to an experiment going on in Shanghai's Tungchi University, which specializes in training engineers and architects.

The university joined forces with construction units so that theory and practice would each contribute its fair share to the educational process. The former university administrative and teaching departments were done away with and replaced by committees consisting of teachers, students, workers, and technicians. Since politics remained very much to the fore, each committee had a political instructor and each class a political cadre.

Other important innovations were announced by the press: henceforth there would be no repeating a grade; age limits for students would be abolished; entrance examinations were also discarded, and hereafter political and social criteria would be used to determine scholastic eligibility. Stress was laid on the necessity for the schools and universities to give top priority to young workers, peasants, and soldiers.

What seemed to be happening was that the epic passions of the past were giving way to positive, constructive results.

The New Year's Day editorials at the start of 1968 made a special point of saying that the principal tasks for the coming year were to reinforce the Party organizations, some of which had been playing either a reduced role over the preceding months, or, at the grassroots level, in some cases playing no role at all. Having passed through the fire of the Cultural Revolution, the Chinese leaders were now setting out toward a new social order.

Supporting the Left but Not the Faction

Differences of opinion still existed, but now if they led to arguments or discussions they seemed to be less heated and rancorous, as many previously warring factions laid down their arms. Extra propaganda teams of the PLA were sent to new factories where they led the discussions and tried to turn them into something positive.

An editorial which appeared in the *Liberation Army Daily* on January 28, 1968, outlined the principles of what the Chinese leaders construed the present Party policies to be. The essential idea was bannered in the headline: "Support the Left but Not Any Particular Faction."[1]

"We must support all revolutionary mass organizations," the article said. "Favoring one while becoming estranged from another cannot be allowed. Nor is it permissible to support one at the

---

[1] *Peking Review*, No. 5, February 2, 1968.

expense of another, as you cannot support one faction against another." What the article was clearly implying was that among all the many mass organizations in China, few were truly conservative or manipulated by the opposition. It further implied that the debates and dissension dividing them were not, as had often been claimed, a struggle between two major tendencies, one revolutionary and the other conservative, but rather one huge and often sterile squabble among revolutionaries which tended to impede the progress of the Cultural Revolution. And, of course, it echoed Mao's oft-repeated assertion that the vast majority of the masses were good and only a handful were really bad.

Naturally, there had been conservative elements at work, and a good many people had been misled into opposing the revolutionary line; but all that should be forgiven and forgotten. "Even among those who were misled in the past," the article went on, "the majority have awakened and are standing on Chairman Mao's proletarian revolutionary line." It was, then, the time for reconciliation and forgiveness, for sacrificing pride and resentment on the altars of unity. "We must not negate and exclude from the revolutionary ranks," the editorial declared, "those people who have made mistakes at one time and those revolutionary organizations where some bad elements sneaked into the leadership."

Such emphasis on the need for unity brought with it, of course, the danger that hasty compromises would leave certain real political problems essentially unsolved, and that the hurried rehabilitation of the cadres would undoubtedly enable some members of the opposition to resume their posts. This had already happened during the countercurrent of February and March 1967, when the Party Center's appeal to deal properly with the cadres had been used by the revisionists to regain their berths. The Party leaders apparently judged the power of the opposition sufficiently defeated so that that risk could be taken. Nonetheless, a countercurrent did recur; it was, however, considerably less powerful than the one of the year before.

2.   The Second February Countercurrent

The Origin of the Second Countercurrent

For the Cultural Revolution, February seems to have been the cruelest month. It was in February 1966 that P'eng Chen had formulated a plan which was later denounced as counterrevolutionary.

Just a year later some leaders had taken advantage of the situation to start what came to be known as the "countercurrent." In February of 1968, a similar set of circumstances led the opposition to a similar kind of reaction.

The campaign against the ultraleftists led to a rightist countercurrent whose goal was to whitewash revisionist cadres. It was a phenomenon mostly confined to Peking, and existed primarily among the students. One notable characteristic of the forthcoming period was the rather remarkable unity and stability of the working class, in contrast to the upper-level students and young intellectuals, among whom strife and confusion often prevailed. This led to some important social shifts, among them a further reinforcement of the political role of the working class.

The origin of the second countercurrent is as nebulous as that of the first. Its first rumblings were heard in connection with an internal disagreement within the Peking Revolutionary Committee. In February 1968 some members of the committee questioned the loyalty of its Chairman, Hsieh Fu-chih, the Minister of Public Security whose role in the Wuhan uprising we have already described.[2]

One member of the Cultural Revolution Directorate who had had a hand in the ultraleftist current of the summer of 1967 was Ch'i Pen-yu. He had not suffered the same disgrace as had Wang Li and Lin Chieh, and had stayed on in his post. We can only speculate why, but it can be presumed that the top leadership was loath to oust someone whose prestige was great and who had been in the forefront of the struggle against P'eng Chen and Liu Shao-ch'i at decisive moments. It can also be presumed that Ch'i dissociated himself from his two colleagues and proceeded to make his self-criticism, after which he was authorized to retain his post.

In February 1968 Ch'i was removed from both the GCCR and the Peking Revolutionary Committee. Why? Again one can only speculate, but it can reasonably be assumed that he was a logical target in the continuing campaign against the ultraleftists. His ouster opened the way for some people to launch an attack against Hsieh Fu-chih, who had been considered a leftist and close to Ch'i. At the same time a campaign was begun questioning the exclusion of certain cadres both in administrative departments and in the

[2]Hsieh, the "hero of Wuhan," died of cancer in Peking, March 26, 1972.

universities which had come about at the instigation of or had been approved by Ch'i or Hsieh during the past few months.

Using the leftist excesses as their excuse, these groups sought to rehabilitate previously attacked or ousted leaders. It was a case of one excess leading to another, and the end result was too broad a reinstatement of cadres whose ranks included some revisionists. The struggle against the left was detouring to the right.

For and Against the Peking Revolutionary Committee

At the beginning of March the conflict within the Peking Revolutionary Committee spilled out into the streets of the city. Posters attacking Hsieh appeared, the work of students. Leading the attack was a militant member of the Peking Revolutionary Committee who had become famous overnight after she had, on May 28, 1966, put up the first big-character poster at the University of Peking, upon which Mao himself had commented: Nieh Yuan-tzu. This conflict between two persons whose reputations both as Maoists and as revolutionaries were virtually impeccable created considerable embarrassment for the top leaders of the Cultural Revolution, who tried to reconcile them. These efforts seem to have failed, and the polemics continued. One of the two leading student organizations at Peking University was called Chingkangshan, after Mao's famous mountain stronghold of the 1920s. With Nieh at its head, it stepped up the attack against Hsieh, who in turn found support among other student organizations, notably at the Normal School, the Institute of Geology, and at the People's University. Other groups came to Hsieh's defense, claiming that the rightists were out to sabotage the Peking Revolutionary Committee. Thus during the month of March, we got used to seeing endless parades, some pro-Hsieh, some anti-Hsieh, marching through the streets of Peking. Most of the commotion was limited to posters and parades, but there was violence on the campuses. In the course of one confrontation, Nieh Yuan-tzu was attacked by students with knives, and grievously wounded in the back of the head. Her assailants escaped and were apparently never captured. Nieh recovered.

On March 22 three senior army officers were dismissed for reasons that remained obscure: Yang Ch'eng-wu, Acting Chief of Staff, who had been named to that post after the dismissal of Lo Jui-ching; Yu Li-chin, political commissar of the Air Force; and

Fu Ch'ung-pi, head of the Peking garrison. The announcement of their dismissal was not made via the official press, of course, but through posters and wall paintings. Later we heard rumors that these three had wanted to arrest Hsieh Fu-chih, although they had not received any order from the Central Committee to do so. We also heard that they had been behind the attacks against Hsieh, and thus the expression of a rightist current. All of which, of course, was passed over in silence by official sources and therefore remained in the realm of speculation.[3] In any case, from then on none of their names appeared in any official press releases. Indications of the Party's confidence in Hsieh were reaffirmed in an article in the *People's Daily* of March 18, which made a point of stressing that it was Hsieh who had been chosen to accompany the New Zealand Communist leader V. G. Wilcox on his visit to a Peking factory. At about the same time Party leaders from Chekiang and Szechuan provinces who had come to Peking for consultations with the Party leaders were warned against the countercurrent which was moving too quickly to reinstate some cadres unworthy of rehabilitation. But few provinces were really affected by this movement, and over the weeks we learned that revolutionary committees had been formed in Kiangsu, Honan, Chekiang, and Canton.

Partial Renewal of the Conflicts

It is likely, however, that Mao may have judged the strength and scope of the rightist current greater than the optimistic assessments of the previous summer had made them out to be. Employing his favorite method, Mao apparently decided that the way to deal with the matter was to put it through the wringer of the masses.

What we witnessed, then, was a sudden shift in tactics, as the campaign against the "ultraleft" was succeeded by one against the right. Mao was running the risk, in making this shift, that the left extremists would regroup and factionalism would reappear, but it was apparently a risk he was willing to take. Perhaps he even speculated that a little dose of factionalism would not be all that bad at this stage of the revolution, when things had perhaps grown too calm. As we see, the guidance that Mao gave the Cultural Revolu-

---

[3] In Esmein's account Yang Ch'eng-wu is linked to the ultraleftists. The author reports, too, that during the summer of 1967 Yang was said to have backed a purge of the army.

tion was comparable to the constant tipping of a delicate scale to keep the movement in equilibrium between its extreme tendencies.

About this time Mao made a speech which was picked up and widely disseminated. In essence, he said that factionalism in itself might not necessarily be bad, since proletarian factions had to fight against bourgeois factions. When he called for unity, he stressed, he meant unity among proletarian factions, not among proletarian and bourgeois. Bourgeois factions, he concluded, had to be combated.

"Make a Class Analysis of Factionalism"

On April 27 the *People's Daily* published an article called "Make a Class Analysis of Factionalism,"[4] which elaborated on Mao's words in considerable detail. Once again new torches were being tossed to Chinese society to rekindle the flames which the leaders judged propitious to the moment. By inciting the left to the offensive, Mao and his cohorts were hoping for and expecting a reaction from the right, which again would help delineate its strength and scope, and reveal divisions.

These divisions proved to exist almost without exception among the students and among the employees of the administration, all of whom, in Chinese terminology, are called "intellectuals." It was these levels of the urban petit bourgeoisie that tended to harbor the last vestiges of rightist tendencies. The working class, on the contrary, remained stable and united, in sharp contrast to the scissions of the preceding summer. What this meant, in essence, was that the opposition was no longer in any position to influence the workers.

Another indication that the opposition was considerably weakened was the fact that the confrontations, when they did occur, were limited almost exclusively to Peking and to Kwangtung province, whereas in the earlier phases of the Cultural Revolution any major pronouncement or incident tended to have country-wide repercussions almost simultaneously.

During the months of May and June, factionalism in the various Peking universities and in the administrative services increased considerably. In the course of the Cultural Revolution various mass organizations had established contacts with other similar organizations. This horizontal network resulted in a kind of chain reaction:

---

[4] *Peking Review*, No. 19, May 10, 1968.

an event or incident in one university, for example, would often be followed by a similar event at a fellow institution. In the case of Hsieh Fu-chih, an attack against him by a Peking University organization set off further attacks by similar organizations in other teaching establishments, such as the Normal School, the People's University, and the Institute of Geology. But other groups opposed to these also maintained close connections, which meant that when they reacted they too operated in concert. Among the students the two major opposing groups were called "Terrestrial" and "Celestial." There had already been battles the previous summer between the rival coalitions, which some sources claim ended in several students being killed and several hundred wounded. In any case, the ease with which the split among students recurred a year later showed that the calls for unity had, at least in the realm of the university, fallen on deaf ears.

It was not long before the renascent quarrels had degenerated into physical violence. The western part of Peking, the university section, was transformed into a virtual battleground. Rival factions barricaded themselves in their buildings, or their portion of a building, and from that stronghold launched surprise attacks on their "enemies." Strategically placed lookouts kept close watch on their rivals' movements, and these surprise attacks could occur any time of day or night. Each faction had its share of loudspeakers, all of which blared imprecations and threats as loudly as they could.

Bricks were the most common projectile used, but later the roofs were literally stripped of their tiles for ammunition. At first they were thrown, but later catapults were made. In the early phases most of these "battles" were more picturesque than dangerous, but by June firearms had begun to be used and a number of students were killed. The authorities decided to step in and dispatched worker teams into the fray.

Meanwhile, throughout all these conflicts, there had been little progress in the realm of politics. True, certain conservative tendencies, more stubborn perhaps than had been thought, had been revealed among the students and the employees of administrative offices, and the conservatives were shown to be still capable of attack. Their attacks were aimed specifically against those militants who had played important roles in fighting the work teams and seizing power. But still, nothing had really been resolved, and after almost three months of struggle in the universities and the administrative services, chaos seemed to be the disorder of the day.

3. The Victory of the Left

The Facts Become Clear

The only other place besides Peking where turmoil recurred during this period—and never in the proportions of 1967—was the province of Kwangtung. In its capital city of Canton almost everyone—workers, students, officials—belonged to factions affiliated with one of two major groups, East Wind and Red Flag. For at least three months, from February through May, sporadic fighting among the rival groups continued, and on more than one occasion troops had to be called in. Even so, a number of deaths were reported. By mid-June, according to some sources, the army had imposed a dusk-to-dawn curfew.

In general, though, at this stage of the Cultural Revolution there were no more than three or four leaders in any given place over whom the people were still quarreling. These, however, were usually of high rank, which meant that a relative vacuum still existed. Without a three-in-one combination or a revolutionary committee it was out of the question for them to deal effectively with the problems of structural revisions, work methods, and teaching methods.

This delay was embarrassing, and it contrasted sharply with what was going on in the factories, where the workers had long since taken steps both to reform management methods and to lighten the administrative structures. The proportion of administrative workers as compared to workers actually engaged in production had been drastically reduced, as had the number of different categories of workers. To do away with bureaucratism before it started, rotation systems for the cadres had been instituted under which all employees, including supervisors and managers, spent one-third of their time on the machines as ordinary workers. They could either spend one-third of their work week, one-third of each quarterly period, or one-third of a year, as the case required.

In the universities, on the contrary, progress was almost at a standstill, and in the offices it looked as though it would be hard to institute any real revolutionary practices. Little or nothing had been done to modify either the existing structures or the work methods. Office employees had taken part in the debates and struggles on occasion during the Cultural Revolution, but the concrete results had been less than spectacular. The problem of the cadres had tended too often to revolve around the persons concerned, without touching basic political or ideological matters, and to get lost in a morass of petty quarrels. The problems of paper-pushing, of bureaucratic routines, were still present and unresolved. Unless these and other deeply ingrained habits were altered, little or nothing in these areas would have been accomplished, for the same causes would end up producing the same results.

The students had played an important, even a vital role in the early phases of the Cultural Revolution, but they seemed incapable of transcending that initial contribution and moving forward to consolidate their gains and create new methods and structures. In some universities a rather confusing theory was put forward: "polycentrism." Since the alliance among various organizations was not taking place as it should have, some voices arose saying the effort should be abandoned. To have two rival groups whose concept of the revolution differed might be a good thing, they argued. As two heads are better than one, so might be two revolutionary centers, which would stimulate and give impetus to the movement. What these suggestions would have accomplished if followed would have been simply to codify and institutionalize the factionalism and divisions that the central authorities were intent on stamping out. Editorials in *Red Flag* and the *People's Daily* during this period came out strongly against the notion of polycentrism.

"The Working Class Must Exercise Leadership in Everything"

In this situation, Mao and the Party leaders decided to call on the working class to get the movement going again wherever it had slowed or stopped. In July 1968 "worker control teams" were created, at the request of Mao himself, to be sent into the universities and offices. In an article that was as usual widely disseminated, Mao noted, "It is essential to bring into full play the leading role of the working class in the great cultural revolution and in all fields of work."

A few days later an article by Yao Wen-yuan was published under the title "The Working Class Must Exercise Leadership in Everything,"[5] in which he too noted that the "intellectuals"—that is, the students and office workers—were marking time at this point in the Cultural Revolution. "Certain people" in the schools, Yao's article accused, were "again active in secret. They incited the masses

---

[5] *Peking Review*, No. 35, August 30, 1968.

to struggle against each other, and set themselves to sabotage the great cultural revolution, disrupt struggle-criticism-transformation, undermine the great alliance and the revolutionary three-in-one combination." They were also trying to keep enemies of the people from being eliminated, and the Party organizations from consolidating. And he added, "Contradictions that the intellectuals have been quarreling over without end and unable to resolve are quickly settled when the workers arrive."[6]

The dispatch of the workers into the universities, then, was the curious reversal of the opening stages of the Cultural Revolution, which had begun with the students moving into the factories.

These teams of workers were selected on the basis of the militant role their members had played during the Cultural Revolution. Their first task in the schools was to disarm the factions, then to try and ferret out the leaders of conservative organizations. It was they, the workers, who were given the job not only of settling the question of the cadres but also of revising the curriculum. The results came quickly, but they did not always come without resistance.[7]

With the end of summer there was a flurry of new activity: There was to be a thorough transformation in the teaching establishment, which was to be much farther-reaching than anything previously announced. It was not merely, as Shanghai's Tungchi University had suggested, a matter of integrating the students more closely into the productive process. What was involved was nothing less than *doing away with students as a faction, a separate social entity*. In the future students were to be selected from among those workers and peasants who not only had a background of work experience but had also shown a high degree of political awareness.

This measure, which by now has been widely applied, was also aimed at further reducing the power and influence of the petty bourgeoisie by making sure that the student population would not, by its very living conditions, become or remain part of it. This same concern was behind the decision to drastically reduce the number of personnel in the administrative areas.[8] Here too worker control

[6] *Peking Review*, No. 35, August 30, 1968.

[7] In a conversation with a group of American members of the Committee of Concerned Asian Scholars, in July 1971, Chou En-lai disclosed that the worker team at Tsinghua University had been physically attacked, leaving five dead and 751 wounded. It was a long time before calm was restored.

[8] Reporting on his conversation with Chou En-lai early in 1971, Edgar Snow quoted the Premier as telling him that whereas there had been some 60,000 functionaries working for the central government, now there were only 10,000. See *The Long Revolution*, Random House, New York, 1972, p. 14.

teams acted both as mediators among warring factions and as investigators on the lookout for rightists. The structural changes they instituted consisted basically of whittling away at the top-heavy superstructures and cutting back on the number of administrative employees. This effort was completed by a country-wide movement which consisted of transferring these "excess" employees into the central regions of China where there was a real need for workers, whether industrial or agricultural. All this was part of a larger plan —which is not new in China—aimed at reversing the trend whereby the cities grew and developed at a faster pace than the countryside. By reducing the population of the big cities, the Cultural Revolution was both helping to implement this policy and satisfying other political exigencies. It was not only making the operation of the administrative offices more efficient—anyone who has ever spent any time in China can attest to the fact that there is an overabundance of office personnel, with two people doing the work of one— but also compensating for a lack of manpower in the agricultural area. That may seem surprising, given the size of the Chinese population, but when I have visited the communes I have often heard that they are shorthanded. This doubtless stems in large part from the fact that 65 percent of the Chinese population is concentrated on 30 percent of the territory, and from the fact that the mechanization of agriculture is still in its infancy.

This dispatch of worker teams to the administrative offices is something new in Communist countries.[9] Its purpose is to give real meaning to the notion of proletarian power. In principle the working class is the ruling class in socialist countries, but in practice it is often hard for it to retain control of either the Party or union organs. Leadership posts generally fall into the hands of intellectuals, either because of their training or their ambition, or both. It is even more difficult for the workers to keep control of their state, once capitalism has been overthrown. Here again responsibilities of government are rarely controlled by the workers themselves but pass to functionaries with little or no working experience, who tend to differentiate themselves from the workers by both their background and their functions. The presence of worker control teams in the admin-

---

[9] It should in all fairness be noted that the idea was Lenin's and that while he was alive an incipient effort was made to apply it. It was given up, however, after his death.

istrative offices, then, was aimed at resolving this problem, and was part of an overall plan whose goal was to bring leaders and people closer together.

The Victory Won—The Twelfth Plenum

During the summer we heard reports of further country-wide successes, as the Cultural Revolution continued to bear fruit: on August 18 the southern province of Yunnan, which borders on Vietnam, reported that its revolutionary committee had been established; on August 19 the province of Fukien did the same; on September 5 both Tibet and Sinkiang followed suit.

On September 7, 1968, both the *People's Daily* and the *Liberation Army Daily* were able to report in a joint editorial that the Cultural Revolution had been brought to a highly successful stage throughout China, and that the entire country was red.

What remained to be done was to draw up the balance sheet of the Cultural Revolution and to publicly sanction the defeat of the Liuist faction. Such was the purpose of the Twelfth Plenum of the Central Committee which began on October 13, 1968. This was an enlarged session, that is, not only members of the Central Committee participated, but others as well, basically the leading luminaries of the newly formed revolutionary committees. The communiqué published at the end of the session noted that both members of the Central Committee and alternates attended.[10]

This communiqué, dated October 31, 1968, is the only document we have to go on to learn what happened, and it is of scant help. As usual, the meetings were held behind closed doors. The communiqué tells us that Mao and Lin made important speeches. To date, these speeches have not been published, and it is likely they will not be for several years.

The communiqué also said that a report had been presented and approved by the Central Committee which confirmed, "with full supporting evidence," that Liu Shao-ch'i was a "renegade, traitor, and scab." In all likelihood this report detailed Liu's crimes over the years, doubtless going back decades, but precisely what these early

[10] The term "attended" can probably be taken to mean that the members of the revolutionary committees present had the right to vote. As for the term "members," it can be presumed that only those members loyal to Mao were present. See *Peking Review*, No. 44 (Supplement), November 1, 1968.

crimes were the report failed to say. Like the text of Mao's and Lin's speeches, the full report on Liu was not published.

Nonetheless, the Chinese people had a fairly good idea of the nature of the accusations against Liu, for all during the Cultural Revolution his crimes had been portrayed in newspapers and wall posters. The communiqué of October 31 is more interesting historically than factually: for the first time an official document publicly accused Liu Shao-ch'i of being a counterrevolutionary. His expulsion from the Party was announced and he was officially stripped of all his functions, as were his "accomplices."

Now that the Liuists were officially purged, the way was opened for the Party to be recast. It had long been planned that many of the militants who had come to the fore in the course of the Cultural Revolution were to be admitted into the Party: young Red Guards, young workers, heads of mass organizations, the leaders of the new revolutionary committees, were to become Communists.[11] These new elements were not only replacing the Liuists, but also those members who had been shown to be tainted by bureaucratism or who had lost their revolutionary zeal. It was, as *Red Flag* noted in its usual style, a sort of proletarian blood transfusion.[12]

The *Red Flag* article was important both for its rundown of the accomplishments of the Cultural Revolution to date, at a time when the movement was reaching its final phases, and for its projection of things to come. The Cultural Revolution had accomplished a number of vital things, the article said. For one thing, the Chinese people had acquired wide political experience. They had learned to detect revisionism even in its most veiled and labyrinthine forms, and to distinguish antagonistic from nonantagonistic contradictions. Out of the crucible of this experience had come a whole new wave of young, dynamic revolutionaries, both within the Party and without. The appearance of this valuable new wave of militants, who were going to help revivify the Party, could not have come about in any other way, *Red Flag* asserted. "Only by implementing this proletarian revolutionary line of Chairman Mao's and carrying out a Party consolidation movement of a mass character, not a movement behind closed doors, can we guarantee that the leadership of the

---

[11] The term "Communist" in China refers to Communist Party members. Out of a total population of some 800,000,000 there are a little less than 20,000,000 in the Party.

[12] "Absorb Fresh Blood from the Proletariat," *Peking Review*, No. 43, October 28, 1968.

Party organizations at all levels is truly in the hands of those Communist Party members who are loyal to Chairman Mao, to Mao Tse-tung's thought, and to Chairman Mao's proletarian revolutionary line."

How, precisely, was this "proletarian blood transfusion" to be accomplished? On the one hand, those persons who had distinguished themselves by their militancy during the Cultural Revolution and who were not Party members should be admitted to the Party; on the other, from among these old and new Party members, with first priority to the industrial workers, new leaders at all levels should be chosen. This included a proposed reshuffling of the Central Committee and the Politburo, which could only be done at a Party Congress. The period from October 1968 to April 1969 was preparing for the Congress.

Epilogue—The Ninth Party Congress

The Ninth Congress of the Chinese Communist Party opened in Peking on April 1, 1969. The preceding Party Congress had taken place in 1956. For thirteen years, therefore, the Chinese Communist Party had not held a general meeting. The reasons why it had not are today abundantly clear: the deep divisions that beset the Party would have made it impossible to adopt a revolutionary political line. If a congress had been held prior to 1969, it would probably have revealed serious disagreements.

Many China specialists tend to date the beginning of the conflict between Mao and Liu as 1958. I think 1956 is more exact, although in my Introduction I note the 1958 date as being key. In any case, some commentators—at least in France—have painted a picture of China's evolution during this roughly fifteen-year period which seems to me debatable.

This, in a nutshell, is how their version of the story goes: In 1958 Mao launched the Great Leap Forward in an effort to dissociate China from its Soviet socialist model. It was a complete failure, according to this script, and in 1959 a majority of the Central Committee refused to support continuation of the policy. At the head of the opposition at this juncture was Marshal P'eng Teh-huai. This was a major defeat for Mao, who was replaced as the titular head of government by Liu Shao-ch'i. Thus removed from power, Mao undertook, starting in 1962, to regain it, first through the Socialist Education Movement, later through the Cultural Revolution. In the course of the latter, by seeking support from groups outside the Party and making full use of the youth organized into paramilitary units (the Red Guards), Mao slowly succeeded in purging his enemies and stripping them from their posts (power transfers and the creation of revolutionary committees). He thus regained control and had his policies sanctioned and endorsed by a Party Congress and a Central Committee reshuffled to his liking. This, in essence, is the way many French "experts" summarize the situation. It is an assessment, though, which is full of flaws.

For one thing, the notion that the Great Leap Forward was a complete failure is a gross exaggeration. It is true that all its goals were not fulfilled; the gains were nonetheless often impressive. The people's communes date from this period, and they are unquestionably not only alive and well but flourishing. That Mao was outvoted in that 1959 Central Committee remains to be proved; in fact, if he was, how do we explain that he managed in the course of the meeting to push through the ouster of P'eng Teh-huai? That Liu was elected the titular head of government in itself proves little. Head of state in the Chinese People's Republic is not a key post; the same is true in most Communist countries, where the vital positions are head of the Central Committee, general secretary of the Party, and defense minister. Furthermore, if Mao had been outvoted at that meeting, he would not have been able to retain power. How then did he manage to impose his views concerning the class struggle under socialism during the January and August 1962 work sessions of the Central Committee? Even more important, how could a Mao who had been stripped of power have the views of Liu Shao-ch'i and his followers criticized as a right deviation during the Tenth Plenum of the Central Committee held in September 1962, as we later learned from various posters and handbills produced during the Cultural Revolution? One could go on: How could a powerless Mao have launched the Socialist Education Movement in 1963? The Socialist Education Movement was directed by Party organizations, and the intervention of outside forces did not materialize. How could he have had the line applied by Liu ni 1964, in Taoyuan, condemned, and how publish the Twenty-three Articles giving substance to that condemnation? How, ultimately, could a Mao who had been ousted from power have prevailed on the Chinese Communist Party to take its uncompromising stand with respect to the Soviet Union in 1962 and 1964? In 1964 the dispute with the Soviets took the form of a

"Twenty-five Point Letter"—called "A General Program for Communist and Workers Parties"—outlining the hard line for the Communist movement. Mao is known to have approved if not written that letter. And finally, how could a Mao who was powerless and without support on the Central Committee have unleashed anything so spectacular as the Cultural Revolution in 1965?

In my opinion it is unlikely that Mao was consistently in a minority position on the Central Committee, and even more unlikely that he ever lost the reins of power. On the other hand, there is no reason to dispute his word when he declares, as he did in July of 1967,[13] that he had only a slim majority on the Central Committee. That would in fact make plausible the evolution of Chinese politics from 1958 to 1969. With only a bare majority on the Central Committee, Mao could get his policies adopted but was in no position to demolish his opponents. Liu was condemned in 1962 and 1964 for deviationism but he was not ousted: such a step required a more solid majority and a major political campaign against the target. The Cultural Revolution enabled Mao to achieve these desired results.

It would be unfair to label the Ninth Party Congress uninteresting in itself. What made it significant, though, was simply that it could be held at all.

Some Salient Points from the Ninth Congress

Three documents published at the end of the Congress are worth noting. The first is the political report presented by Lin Piao.[14] It assesses the Cultural Revolution rather than outlining a plan for the future, and in this sense offers little new. It does depict the antecedents and history of the Cultural Revolution, but only in very summary fashion. The eight parts of the report echo the major themes of the Cultural Revolution: Support the Army and Cherish the People; Combat Individualism and Repudiate Revisionism; Attempt the Triple Task of Struggle-Criticism-Transformation; Grasp the Revolution and Promote Production; etc. It reaffirmed the parameters of the Communist Party, stressed the need to follow the mass line, and indicated the bases for Chinese foreign policy.

---

[13] See Appendix 4, "Mao Tse-tung Analyzes the Cultural Revolution."

[14] Subsequently published by the Foreign Languages Press in Peking as a separate brochure.

The new Party Constitution, however, contained a number of new elements. The emphasis seems to be on the desire to avoid excessive centralism and strengthen internal democracy. Also apparent is the fear that revisionist leaders may eventually utilize Party discipline and the rigidity of Party structures for their own selfish ends. It was as though the Party was leaving itself elbow room to deal with any new Liu Shao-ch'is who might try to take power. The wording of Article 5 relates to that concern and recognizes a certain "right to dissent":

> . . . Leading bodies of the Party at all levels shall regularly report on their work to congresses or general membership meetings, constantly listen to the opinions of the masses both inside and outside the Party and accept their supervision. *Party members have the right to criticize Party organizations and leading members at all levels and make proposals to them. If a Party member holds different views with regard to the decisions or directives of the Party organizations, he is allowed to reserve his views and has the right to by-pass the immediate leadership and report directly to higher levels, up to and including the Central Committee and the Chairman of the Central Committee.* . . . [Emphasis added.]

Not only is this totally new in China, it is new to the Communist movement throughout the world. For too many years the Communist leadership has tended to issue its directives as papal bulls to be followed blindly. This, then, is a remarkable political innovation on the part of the Chinese.

Article 12 is similarly revealing. The task of Communists is to "lead the Party members and the broad revolutionary masses in studying and applying Marxism-Leninism-Mao Tse-tung thought in a living way," and, in the spirit of the continuing revolution, "to give constant education to the Party members and the broad revolutionary masses concerning class struggle and the struggle between two lines and lead them in fighting resolutely against the class enemy."

The third document worthy of attention emanating from the Ninth Congress is the revised list of leaders, especially the members of the Politburo. Mao of course remained Chairman, with Lin Piao the only vice-chairman. Before the Cultural Revolution Chou En-lai and Liu Shao-ch'i had both been vice-chairmen of the Central Committee, but as of the 1969 Congress Lin was singled out as Mao's "close comrade-in-arms" and successor.

The all-powerful standing committee of the Politburo was reduced, with, in addition to Lin and Mao, the following members: Ch'en Po-ta, Chou En-lai, and K'ang Sheng.

More interesting perhaps is the list of those former members of the Politburo who had been dropped: Liu Shao-ch'i, Teng Hsiao-p'ing, T'ao Chu, T'an Chen-lin, P'eng Chen, and Lu Ting-yi. Replacing them was a massive infusion of loyal Maoists, including Mao's wife Chiang Ch'ing and Lin's wife Yeh Chun. Others were Yao Wen-yuan, Chang Ch'un-ch'iao, Hsieh Fu-chih, Wang Tung-hsing (an alternate member), and Huang Yung-sheng.

Two important personalities dropped from the Politburo although not from their posts were Ch'en Yi, who for the time being remained a member of the Central Committee and Minister of Foreign Affairs, and Li Fu-ch'un, who stayed on in charge of the State Planning Commission and as a member of the Central Committee. Despite pressures by the radicals for Chou to dismiss his two colleagues, Chou rejected their demands. For one thing, he needed the skills and support of both: Ch'en Yi, although it was difficult for Chou to defend him publicly because he was an outspoken critic of Red Guard excesses, was not only an able diplomat but a tough soldier and one of China's ten living marshals; Li Fu-ch'un, whose relationship with Chou went back decades to their Paris days together, was one of China's most skilled planners.

Ch'en Yi was a colorful figure, and stories about him abound. One of his best-known exchanges with the Red Guards who were trying to purge some of Ch'en's subordinates went something like this. "If you attack me for forty-eight days," the old soldier, who as head of the Third Field Army had captured Shanghai in 1949, said to his Red Guard assailants, "I'll attack you for forty-nine. If you use ten abusive words, I'll use eleven."

Another story that went around Peking told about a conversation he had with Mao just before the Ninth Party Congress. Ch'en informed Mao that he had decided not to participate in the Congress and, in fact, was going to retire from politics. Mao tried to persuade him to come to the meeting. Ch'en persisted, saying, "I'll cut a sorry figure. There were times during the Cultural Revolution when I took a rightist position. You hardly need my presence." To which Mao is reported to have replied with a smile, "Come anyway. You can be the representative of the right."

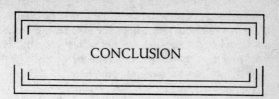

CONCLUSION

Did the Cultural Revolution achieve its goals? A number of foreign observers have expressed the view that the upheavals of the period brought with them such disruption in the social, political, and economic life of the country that China emerged from it considerably weakened. My conviction is that such a judgment is both hasty and erroneous.

Was the Cultural Revolution a complete success? To try and answer that question one must differentiate between different goals on various levels. As for the basic struggle between the Maoists and Liuists, there can be no question that the latter faction was completely eliminated. Many have raised the point that the price was very high: the "twists and reversals" as Lin Piao once described them, through which the Cultural Revolution went, the economic disruptions, and the resistance that the Maoists encountered are all cited. As for the turmoil, I think I have shown that far from being an accident that almost did in the enterprise, it was a planned, calculated risk from the start. Forty years before the Cultural Revolution, Mao had said: "A revolution is not a dinner party. . . . A revolution is an insurrection, an act of violence by which one class overthrows another."

What about the disruption of the economy? In general the economic life of the country was slowed and impeded, but that is a far cry from the exaggerated stories that often circulated abroad, which talked of economic crisis, stagnation, poverty, and famine. During the years of the Cultural Revolution I can honestly say that I never saw any real scarcity in the stores or markets. True, during the winter of 1968 we suffered from a lack of coal, but aside from that, foodstuffs and other goods were in sufficient supply, and were never rationed. Gas and electricity functioned normally, and transportation suffered only sporadic interruptions. If this represented my experience in Peking, I also talked to many people in a number of other cities, from Shanghai to Harbin, from Tientsin to Canton, and the story was much the same.

As for the oft-cited thesis that the length of the troubles indicated that there was indeed strong opposition to Mao, and that Liu enjoyed widespread popularity and support among the Chinese population, and that therefore Mao's victory was fragile indeed, I trust this book has shown that such is wishful thinking. At no moment in the complex and shifting situation of the Cultural Revolution was either the Maoist ideology or the Maoist regime in question. In the struggles between conservatives and revolutionaries no one claimed to be representing the views or opinions of Liu; all factions looked to Mao, thus enabling him to act as supreme arbiter. Moreover, the greatest disturbances did not stem from a conflict between Maoists and Liuists but from a division among the former. This split culminated in the summer of 1967 in the violence we have described; while often blown up out of all proportion, it was nonetheless very real. The risk that the army would divide and fight was also very real, but that too was an internecine fight among Maoists, and did not come about because part of the army was following Liu. If this violence existed, one should recall, it was also willed, though not always to the degree that it occurred. Mao was concerned to forge a new generation of young revolutionaries, and he was motivated by the knowledge that an entire generation of Chinese had never known the rigors of revolution. The Cultural Revolution initiated millions of young Chinese into the rough school of debate, dispute, and action, and made them aware of practical problems never before encountered.

What of this youth and its experience during the Cultural Revolution? This is perhaps the hardest aspect of the movement to analyze accurately. What we can say for a certainty is that the mass mobilization that Mao so ardently desired did take place, and that virtually the entire urban population of China was involved, with the youth unquestionably in the forefront. The youth revealed a certain propensity for battle, which must have pleased Mao, but it also revealed a tendency to be undisciplined and confused, with only a limited capacity to organize. To many young Chinese, the Cultural Revolution must leave a memory of a heady time of passionate debate, rebellion, and extraordinary freedom. The regime, which wants to reconcile freedom and discipline, centralism and democracy, still has, therefore, an educational task ahead of it.

Perhaps the most ambitious goal of the Cultural Revolution was the effort to extirpate revisionism and assure the supremacy of Maoist thought. This required a tremendous politicization of a country whose customs and habits go back for thousands of years. In my introduction I mentioned how, in Mao's view, socialism and individualism are ultimately incompatible; socialism is irreconcilable with individualism, the taste for personal pleasures, and the egocentric conception of the world. To recast men's mentality in order to create a totally collective man was Mao's ultimate objective. As we have seen, the task was difficult, for ancient habits and customs had often carried over and persisted under the new regime. The collision was essentially between Maoist collectivism and the Confucian ethic, and we have seen how Liuist views were affected by at least some aspects of the latter. Not only ingrained customs, but also superstitions, class feelings, mandarin tendencies and other carry-overs from the old regime also had to be constantly combated. What this requires is intense daily propaganda, to try to block off the various channels through which tradition filters, and in China today one can say that such a campaign is under way throughout the country. Revolutionary education is given everywhere, and everywhere small classes are held to study the texts of Mao Tse-tung. The Party propaganda machine talks constantly of revolution and class struggle. The radio constantly presents Maoist texts and does its best to maintain what we may call a "militant atmosphere." City walls, the façades of buildings, places of work, schools, restaurants, parks, all abound with revolutionary citations and appeals to activism.

Here again it is safe to say that important gains have been made. Political awareness is considerably heightened among the population, as witnessed by its reaction to references to the old regime, the Kuomintang, imperialism, or revisionism. Old-style clothes have virtually disappeared, as has old-style decoration of stores and homes. One feels, too, a new sense of pride among workers and children of workers, and a real, voluntary devotion to the collectivity. In this the Maoists have indeed succeeded in overturning values and accentuating altruism, the proletariat, and the revolutionary ideal. To say that the victory is won in this area, that proletarian ideology has triumphed once and for all over the bourgeois or feudal, would be an exaggeration. The gains are impressive, but tradition does tend to survive in new and often insidious forms, and has to be fought constantly.

One can see, for instance, a formalistic approach, borrowed from tradition to combat tradition, as it were. Quotations from Chairman Mao are read aloud in the morning before work; before any meeting wishes for long life and health are offered him. Scientific discoveries, medical advances, workers', soldiers', and peasants' exploits are said to be due to Mao's doctrine. Much of this, it must be added, is done in spite of Mao's desires, for he has expressly asked that any such "cultism" be avoided.[1]

Some commentators have said that Maoism is a new religion. Is that true? Hardly. What is true is that in China an effort is being made to replace the precepts and rites of Buddhism and Confucianism, which have impregnated Chinese thought for thousands of years, with revolutionary maxims and mores. In place of tradition, which weighs heavily on the conscience of the masses, conditions them, affects the conduct of their daily lives, an effort is being made to substitute a superior force: proletarian, revolutionary ideas. To combat tradition using methods taken over from tradition, however, runs the risk of helping tradition survive.

China is a country which by its very geography and historical heritage, as well as the political and military pressures exerted from without, is forced to live in relative isolation. Can such a country, with only limited exchanges with the outside world, find the energy and resources to not only break with the well-condi-

---

[1] In 1967 Mao personally disowned the description of him as "great teacher, great leader, great supreme commander, great helmsman," at the time of the H-bomb explosion. In 1968 he forbade anyone to refer to "inculcating the absolute authority" of his Thought. More recently he disapproved the mass production of metal likenesses of himself, saying it was a waste of metal for which better uses could be found.

In a conversation at a later date with Edgar Snow, Mao told his old friend and biographer that he deplored the excesses of the "personality cult." He also noted that it was hard to break the people's millennial habit of emperor worship, but said that "now things were different." Mao also said he found the four epithets applied to him a "nuisance." Sooner or later they would all be dispensed with, Mao said. The only one he cared for was "teacher"; he had been a schoolteacher and still was one. (See the following section, the "Afterword," for further developments in deemphasizing the "cult.")

tioned past but also create an entirely new social environment? To that momentous question the Great Proletarian Cultural Revolution provides the best, though still tentative answer, which has to be affirmative on the basis of the events and results of the four-year period 1965–69.

There is reason to believe that Mao Tse-tung's proletarian revolutionary ideal will manage to avoid being drowned in the sea of idealism and feudalism so deeply rooted among the Chinese. But for it to do so further tests and trials may be required. That may explain why, in 1967, Mao said: "The Great Proletarian Cultural Revolution presently going on is only the first of its kind. In the future other such revolutions will necessarily take place at several occasions. . . . All Party members, and the population at large, must refrain from thinking that all will be smooth after one, two, three, or four Cultural Revolutions. What we must watch for above all is never to relax our revolutionary vigilance."

Postscript 1973

New information now permits qualification and clarification of a number of important points in Part IV.

The article of January 28, 1968, "Support the Left but Not Any Particular Faction," and that of April 27, "Make a Class Analysis of Factionalism," were, purely and simply, contradictory. The second was an answer to the former. These conflicting viewpoints obviously reflected disagreements within the Party Directorate, with Ch'en Po-ta and perhaps Lin Piao in opposition to Chou En-lai.

We also know, thanks in part to Esmein and Hinton, that Yang Ch'eng-wu, the acting chief of staff dismissed in 1968, was in fact an ultraleftist and accused of belonging to the May Sixteenth Detachment. There can be no question that at the time of his disgrace the official propaganda organs were not stressing the fight against ultraleftism but against the right. At this time we who were in China thought that Yang's purge was part of this struggle against the right, and nothing in the official propaganda helped dissipate this misconception. I described him and his fellow officers in the subsection "For and Against the Peking Revolutionary Committee" as a rightist. The fact is that in those times of confusion it was not uncommon to find someone accused of being both "ultraleftist" and "rightist," depending in part on which extremism was then under attack. During the time I am referring to the emphasis was essentially leftist, which meant that most of those under attack were accused of being rightists. Even though today Yang is officially accused of being an ultraleftist, a close examination of the facts reveals that, if anything, my initial conclusions were closer to the mark, for he and his comrades had long been associated with both conservative causes and persons. Yang, as his actions and words show, was basically a law-and-order man. But whether he was tagged with a right or left epithet, the point is really not which extremism he espoused, but, for his opponents, that he was purged and stripped of his power.

The armed struggle at Tsinghua University was long and bloody —truly a "Hundred Day War"—and the victims many, both dead and wounded. The Chinese leaders were greatly upset by these incidents, and late in July of 1968 Mao is reported to have summoned five student leaders, representing the main Red Guard groups of the capital, including Nieh Yuan-tzu from Peking University and Tsinghua's Kuai Ta-fu. He is said to have bluntly reproached them for their improper attitude to ultraleftism, their sectarianism, and the mad, fratricidal combats in which they had indulged. Then, with tears in his eyes, he reportedly told them he felt that they had let him down. If the story is true, it would mean that Mao the educator had come to the sad conclusion that the student youth, the Red Guards on whom he had counted in great part to revive the regime, had failed their revolutionary exam. Had he already foreseen that the time had come to make concessions to more moderate tendencies?

Recent events have also shown that my evaluation of the unity of the Chinese leaders after the Ninth Party Congress was far too sanguine; the rupture between Chou on the one hand and Ch'en and Lin on the other is the most obvious example.

Other notes, comments, rectifications: Huang Yung-sheng, former chief of the general staff, is ousted. Ch'en Yi died in January 1972, and the honors accorded the Foreign Minister at the time of his funeral were tantamount to a complete rehabilitation. Finally, as of mid-1973 the National People's Congress was still not in session.

AFTERWORD
· FOR THE AMERICAN EDITION ·

Since this book was written many important political events have taken place in China. In addition to the Ping-Pong diplomacy, which led to the visit of President Nixon to China and the admission of China to the U.N., the most significant internal political events were the defection of Mao's previously designated heir apparent, Lin Piao, and the disgrace, after a long and spirited campaign against ultraleftism, of Ch'en Po-ta, who had been the head of the GCCR.

The basic purpose of my book was to relate the various ups and downs of the Cultural Revolution as I saw and lived them in Peking from 1966 to 1968. It did, I believe, help to shed light on a number of important facets of that second Chinese revolution, as well as correct a number of misconceptions and misrepresentations that, for whatever reasons, had been transmitted to the West and become common currency there. I think it also fairly emphasized the key role played by Chou En-lai in an effort to keep Maoist strategy and conflicts on an even keel in the midst of the mightiest storms. Indispensable to any understanding of the Cultural Revolution is the full knowledge of Chou's struggle against the "spontaneists" and the ultraleftist trends which surfaced during the movement. Those who were confused or baffled by these recent internal developments in China will, I trust, have a clearer picture of what really went on.

What has followed since 1968 has, it seems to me, not altered to any great degree this interpretation of the causes and objectives of the Cultural Revolution. Still, there were wrong emphases and conclusions here and there. I, no doubt like many Chinese, underestimated the seriousness of the problems that the manifestations of ultraleftism caused for the Party leaders. But Chinese politics is far less murky than it was formerly, and it is possible to isolate the origins, both internal and external, of the present problems of the Chinese Communist Party.

During the second half of November 1971 the Western press announced the disappearance of Lin Piao. In February 1972 a high Chinese functionary confirmed this fact to M. de Broglie, the head of a French parliamentary delegation visiting China. The news made a tremendous stir. There was other, surprising news: the intensification of the antileftist campaign in China; rumors of a plot, which were repeated in the Peking press; and the elimination of Ch'en Po-ta. Meanwhile Chinese policy at home and abroad continued to evolve: at home, more and more emphasis was placed on the leadership role of the Party; abroad, a renewed diplomatic offensive was launched, after the relative withdrawal during the years of the Cultural Revolution.

In my opinion, to explain the new developments in Chinese politics we must go back to the key events of the Cultural Revolution and to the recent shifts in the international situation. The following analysis does not pretend to be complete, and certain remarks may prove outdated by subsequent revelations. Nonetheless, I believe that by basing our conclusions on what is known about political life in China, and on the analysis of certain problems that surfaced during the Cultural Revolution—and by taking into careful account the risk of conflict between China and her neighbor to the north—we can at least fit some of the pieces of the puzzle together.

That Lin Piao was really ousted is today an incontrovertible fact. Before the Cultural Revolution the leading luminaries of China ranged from Mao Tse-tung to P'eng Chen, and included Liu Shao-ch'i and Teng Hsiao-p'ing. Six years later only Mao and his Premier, Chou En-lai, emerged unscathed from the cyclone. Those who closely followed the evolution of the Cultural Revolution were not surprised by the elimination of P'eng Chen's "Black Gang" and later that of Liu Shao-ch'i. But the five people who formed a directorate with Mao seemed united: Chou En-lai,

K'ang Sheng, Lin Piao, and Ch'en Po-ta. And it is harder to explain how it fell apart. Forgetting for the moment Chou En-lai and Chiang Ch'ing (who make discreet appearances), two of these leaders, Lin and K'ang,[1] have simply dropped from view, whereas Ch'en Po-ta is unofficially accused inside the country of divisive intrigues and even, it would appear, of plotting against the Party leaders.

To understand how things could have reached such a pass, we must go back to some aspects of the Cultural Revolution.

In some respects the Cultural Revolution was a dramatic event marked by constant crises within the leadership of the Chinese Communist Party. The elimination of P'eng Chen, Liu Shao-ch'i, and Teng Hsiao-p'ing preceded that of T'ao Chu, who, one may recall, vaulted to fourth in rank in the Politburo after the Eleventh Party Plenum. The struggle against the second wave of ultraleftists during the summer of 1967 led to the dismissal of Wang Li, Kuan Feng, and Ch'i Pen-yu. They were of lesser stature than those previously named, but their disgrace showed to what extent the Cultural Revolution had, at an ever increasing rate, taken its toll of the country's leadership.

Still, the remaining five members of the Politburo's Standing Committee seemed united, and were intact at the Ninth Party Congress. But there were flaws even in that unity. It was fairly common knowledge that Chou En-lai and Ch'en Po-ta did not see eye to eye, though why they did not remained a considerable mystery.

During the mass meetings of the Red Guards during the summer of 1966 two kinds of speeches were given, one by Chou and the other by either Lin Piao or Ch'en Po-ta. Mao remained silent. His silence was that of the arbiter allowing the representatives of both currents to express themselves. Of course the speeches given by all the men were very much alike, but a careful examination reveals differences of detail. Chou, unlike the others, made a discernible effort to exhort his listeners not to let the revolution harm production. At the height of the mass movements he sometimes stated that "proletarian discipline" should not be forgotten.

It was in 1967, during the mysterious episode of the Cultural Revolution known as the "February countercurrent," that the leadership team, which had already been purged of its Liuist opponents, underwent its most serious crisis. The wave of "power

---

[1] A New China News Agency dispatch dated January 10, 1972, listed K'ang Sheng in its account of those who attended Ch'en Yi's funeral.

transfers" which had begun with the January Revolution in Shanghai was accompanied by a great many disturbances. In various sectors the Party Committees crumbled after the massive dismissal of their cadres. In this situation some leaders, including Chou En-lai, fought for the rehabilitation of the middle and lower cadres, and of those who were not unduly compromised with the Liu Shao-ch'i faction. Others opposed this effort, on the theory that nothing should be done to impede the mass movement and that excesses were inevitable. Ch'en Po-ta was among this latter group.

At the time, Mao intervened and threw his weight to the cadres, that is, in support of his Premier. He made a special plea to refrain from violence toward leaders who came under attack—and as we have seen, self-restraint had not always been the governing principle. The official press also carried many editorials asking that the cadres be treated properly and decently, whereas the "rebels" were called upon to correct the error of their ways. Throughout this period Chou was omnipresent. He intervened personally in a number of ministries; he was forever receiving militants; he called for the "liberation" of the cadres; and he tirelessly visited factories and universities. It is interesting to note that during this same period Lin Piao was invisible.

This policy was exploited by the right to rehabilitate the followers of Liu Shao-ch'i and to counterattack the "rebel" organizations, all of which tended to embarrass the Premier and make him the target of criticism. Some of this feeling was translated onto the walls of Peking in the form of posters.

At this point the "leftists" clamored to smash the "rightist countercurrent."[2] The leadership team was on the brink of a split. During the middle of March a little-publicized meeting of the Central Committee brought about a partial reconciliation of opposing views. Still, a prolonged wave of ultraleftism continued to rise, with Chou as its target. It was not until September of 1967 that Chou, with the backing of Mao Tse-tung, managed to smash it. During the following period Chou En-lai was able to call for the rehabilitation of the cadres, with the exception of "a small handful of revisionists," and the unification of the mass organizations.

This trend seemed to be definitive. And yet in February 1968 the right still was capable of exploiting this situation to its own ends. A second "countercurrent" resulted in the rehabilitation of

---

[2] Minister of Agriculture T'an Chen-lin was behind the countercurrent.

some "revisionist cadres," which in turn led to a further leftist reaction, to which Mao gave some backing. The editorial of April 27, 1968, "Make a Class Analysis of Factionalism," probably written by Ch'en Po-ta, marked the return of the leftist current. The predominant role of Chou En-lai appeared to lessen. It was unofficially rumored in Peking at the time that Chou and Ch'en Po-ta were at serious odds.

Nonetheless the Ninth Party Congress seemed to consecrate the overall unity and provide it with a solid base, with texts and resolutions massively distributed throughout the country and abroad. How was it possible, then, that a scant two years later the dissensions were so acute that the leadership team was on the verge of rupture? It is a hard question to answer in any detail. One can surmise, though, that the struggle against an enemy personalized by Liu Shao-ch'i tended to bring the leaders together, but that after that enemy had been beaten any underlying divisions resurfaced, a phenomenon not all that uncommon in history.

Playing the arbiter's role, Mao helped preserve that unity and keep the disagreements in the realm of "nonantagonistic contradictions." He would encourage now one, now another, keeping them in balance and making them control each other; these divergent currents became the very motor of the development of the Cultural Revolution. The contradictions at the top, moreover, stemmed from the contradictions in the mass movement itself. In the final analysis, they were the expression of the class struggle taking place in Chinese society. On this point, Mao wrote that if there were no contradictions in the Party, and no ideological struggles to resolve them, the Party would wither and die.[3]

Mao also likes to quote these words of Lenin: "The unity of opposites is . . . relative. The struggle of mutually exclusive opposites is absolute." For a long time the contradictory tendencies within the leadership of the Chinese Communist Party have coexisted in unity and in struggle. Today this struggle has burst the framework they had managed to fit into. The elimination of Ch'en Po-ta and the current antileftist campaign mark that break as they do the success of the policies incarnated in Chou En-lai.

This analysis is purely theoretical. It is difficult to know the precise ups and downs of the Chinese Communist Party between 1969 and today. But we can venture an analysis of the various

[3] Mao Tse-tung, "On Contradiction," *Selected Works*, Vol. 1, Foreign Languages Press, Peking, 1965, pp. 311–47.

external factors, that is, the factors of international politics, that have possibly affected the already existing internal contradictions, and study the various problems emanating from the Cultural Revolution which have tended to impose new tensions on Chinese society. The new and spectacular turn of events in Chinese policy is, in fact, the culmination of a long process in which complex and contradictory forces—both internal and external—have met head-on.

By unleashing the Cultural Revolution China projected the image of a country concerned with preserving the revolutionary ideal and trying to give communism a shot in the arm, as it were. In essence it was a double challenge: first to the materialism of the West, the society of consumption; and second to the Soviet Union, which seemed intent on emulating that society.

Subsequently the problems the Americans encountered in Southeast Asia, the emergence of a Palestine resistance movement, the unrest in Eastern Europe, and the appearance of a New Left in the West, led some Chinese to think in terms of a vast complex of revolutionary attempts on an international scale.

There is no doubt that at least some Chinese leaders who were in favor of the Cultural Revolution thought of it in exactly these terms, and judged that Chinese policy should be based on the notion of world revolution. During the past few years the Peking press often used the theme "the Cultural Revolution is shaking the world." There is also no doubt that this style of thinking implies forgoing diplomacy for contacts with the world-wide revolutionary movement. The recall of most of the Chinese ambassadors in 1967 clearly attests to it.

Men involved in revolutions do not work under the ideal conditions that their minds may suggest to them but under conditions, both social and historical, which impose upon them choices that are often as unforeseen as they are painful. Mao Tse-tung has said the class struggle is independent of human will. What this means is that it is not within the power of capitalism to supress it; nor is it within the power of the revolutionaries to spur it on or direct it at will. Mao Tse-tung and Chou En-lai are too subtle and artful politicians not to be painfully aware of these truths. The whole art of politics, in fact, consists essentially of ridding oneself of illusions.

How closely, then, did the notion of a new, world-wide revolutionary movement correspond to reality? What we can say is that the appearance of China on the international scene, the stalemate or defeat—take your pick—of the United States in Vietnam, the crisis in Czechoslovakia, the unrest in Europe and America, have all put an end to the previously existing bipolar equilibrium. The period of growth that capitalism has known since the end of World War II seems to be ending, and monetary crises are becoming ever more serious. The Soviet Union has its own economic difficulties, and its positions of strength in Eastern Europe seem threatened; numerous forces of considerable strength are at play within its own sphere of influence. For both empires, which seemed determined to carve up the world between themselves, a period of crisis and instability has begun.

Nonetheless, it does not appear that the various revolutionary movements are in any position to take immediate advantage of the situation. This stems both from the varying levels of development of the areas involved and from their lack of unity and maturity. Outside Southeast Asia movements that look to Mao for their inspiration are notable for their inadequate grasp of Maoist strategy and tactics. In various places popular uprisings have in fact temporarily failed.

Moreover, if the Cultural Revolution helped to solve some of the problems of the international Communist movement, it was far from resolving completely the crisis that arose from the U.S.S.R.'s Twentieth Party Congress of 1956. This is due in part to the limitations of the Chinese propaganda machine, which failed to explain fully and effectively the complex events comprising the Cultural Revolution. This propaganda, such as it was, ran head-on into the immense counterpropaganda of both the Western and Soviet mass media, and when it was under the influence of ultra-leftist elements, and out-and-out dogmatists who cared nothing for public opinion abroad, it had a primitive air about it. Outside China the Cultural Revolution did not inspire a true renewal of the Communist movement.

From 1966 to 1969 China remained relatively isolated because of a number of factors: there was hostility not only from the West but from the Soviet Union; during those three years there was little or no diplomatic activity; there was no solid revolutionary alternative on a world-wide scale.

With the passage of time, this situation became serious, and all the more so as the threat of an open military conflict with the Soviet

Union became an increasing possibility. The reasons that could push Moscow toward a showdown with China are many. For one, the failure of the Kremlin's policy, based for the past decade or so on closer relations with the United States to maintain the world-wide status quo, is unquestionable, as is the lack of any alternate policy among the Russian leaders. This lack of perspective leads some Russians to think in terms of a military adventure against China. In this respect, the vast psychological campaign of anti-Maoism in Russia today is a disconcerting symptom.

Faced with threats from their northern neighbor, the Chinese leaders are obliged to emphasize internal unity and, on the inter-national front, to practice a politics of openness so as to emerge from their isolation. For China it is imperative to cultivate as many friends as possible in the Third World, to establish relations with countries having varied social systems, and to avoid having to con-front simultaneously both the Soviet Union and the United States by playing on the differences between them and on those which divide them from their allies. In this area—and taking into account the urgency of the situation—diplomacy is obviously the supreme weapon. A political viewpoint such as we have just described could only run counter to the ultraleftist tendencies which appeared dur-ing the Cultural Revolution.

Chinese policy today is based on an awareness of all these ele-ments. While fully cognizant of the crisis the two superpowers are facing, the Chinese leaders know that it will not lead to a general revolutionary offensive in the near future. Although they may keep that perspective in mind as a remote possibility, the Chinese leaders want above all to make sure that no "united front" is formed against them.

Such thinking could only act to the detriment of those in Peking who believed in a rapid development of world revolution. The ousting of Lin Piao could well have derived from a basic disagree-ment between him and Mao Tse-tung and Chou En-lai on the question of the international situation. But the success of Chou En-lai's trend derives from the ever increasing strength, over the past three years, of the Premier's position, and from the visible sup-port given him by Mao Tse-tung. The new direction of Chinese policy is the result of a new internal equilibrium. Foreign policy is an extension of domestic policy, and a particular conception of revolution prevailed in China.

Some will see in Chou En-lai the representative of a Party apparatus determined to reestablish its ascendancy over political life and, in order to do that, to suppress the spirit of the Cultural Revolution. Here, as always when dealing with realities in China, one must be careful of oversimplifying.

In the fall of 1970, Chou told Edgar Snow that it was not the army that exerted the power in China, and he said further that in the coming months this truth would become clear.[4] Chou's words went virtually unnoticed at the time, but today they become very meaningful. The problem of the political role of the army had already been posed in the top echelons of leadership, and perhaps even resolved. At present Chinese propaganda centers largely on one very precise theme: "Strengthen the leadership role of the Party."

Power, therefore, must be exercised through regular Party channels. The members of the military who came in to handle management and administrative tasks when the Party committees were not completely organized, and when the question of which cadres would be kept and which ousted was still not settled, are doubtless going to find themselves relieved of these responsibilities little by little. This trend is already evident.

The importance of the army in Chinese political life seems destined to continue to diminish. It is possible to speculate that such a change has not occurred without a certain amount of dispute and tension among the Chinese leaders. Some may have felt that the Army provided the best guarantee that the major accomplishments of the Cultural Revolution would continue to be applied. Wasn't the slogan "Learn from the PLA" one of the most often heard over the past few years? It is probable that the Lin Piao affair is linked, directly or indirectly, to this change.

How could Chou En-lai, no matter what his intelligence and prestige, impose his own policy and make it prevail over those of men as powerful as Lin Piao and Ch'en Po-ta? And why did the army fail to react? Chou En-lai could count on the support of the Party apparatus, but this machine was badly shaken by the Cultural Revolution and is still fragile today. Still, it did have one support which proved decisive: that of Mao Tse-tung.

By inviting President Nixon, and by personally receiving him while he was in China—as he had done earlier with Haile Selassie of Ethiopia and the Burmese chief of state, General Ne Win—Mao

---

[4] See *Le Nouvel Observateur*, April 5, 1971.

made a clear point that foreign policy was not the sole prerogative of the Premier and that he, Mao, supported him. There is every reason to believe that he did the same domestically, and threw his full weight, which is both political and moral, behind current internal policies.[5]

This explains the leading role the Premier has continued to play over the past few years. The notion held by some that it is Chou who is calling the shots is simply not plausible. Mao is a man who does not let anyone impose his will on him.

Mao's choice of options was followed by the break with Lin Piao, in spite of his having been named Mao's successor by the Ninth Party Congress. Such a decision must have been made under the most dramatic of circumstances, and only after a long, hard look at the exigencies of China's domestic and international situation.

We have seen what these exigencies were internationally. But what were they domestically? Here, where information is hard to come by, we can only offer educated guesses. First we must come back to the Cultural Revolution, which enabled Mao and his followers to eliminate powerful opponents from the Party Center. This was not its sole objective. This "elimination" was to come about as a result of a mass movement which would reveal clearly the web of contradictions existing within Chinese society. In this way the Chinese population would gain a greater awareness of the problems involved in building socialism, and thereby educate itself politically. This concept of revolution required a daring and broad-mindedness seldom if ever seen before. It resulted in the triumph of the "revolutionary line" and the disgrace of Liu Shao-ch'i. But the price was a great deal of disorder and confusion.

Today, the problem is to retain the benefits of the movement and at the same time reduce the tensions and distortions suffered by Chinese society. The part played by the military in the administration of the country is one such "distortion."

Some may evoke the special bonds between the Party and the army in China, the popular and egalitarian nature of that army, its participation in the process of production, and the principle of "politics in command" which it follows, to deny that there can be any opposition between the army and the civil authorities. But this

---

[5] During Mao's last conversation with Edgar Snow, as reported in *Life* on April 30, 1971 (and widely disseminated in China), the Chairman was at pains to criticize the activities of the ultraleftists who had made Chou the focal point of their attacks during the Cultural Revolution.

opposition does exist simply because there is a difference, and the oft-repeated slogan "The Party commands the gun, and the gun must never be allowed to command the Party" is in fact meant to resolve the matter.

In many sectors the Party organization had collapsed, thus creating a vacuum which the army filled. Such a situation can only be temporary, and demands the search for new balances. It would be naïve to believe that such an equilibrium can be achieved without stresses and strains. Though the relationship between the army and the civil authorities in China may not be what it is in various countries of the Third World, where a situation of constant conflict tends to exist, nonetheless there can be tensions.

What is more, the problems must be viewed from the perspective of thirty years hence. The future of the regime after the disappearance of its founders is one of the major concerns of current Chinese policy. The principles of Leninism to which they adhere, as well as their entire ideological background, will guide the Maoist leaders toward making the Party, and not the army, the heir and guarantor of the future. This serves to explain the current campaign exalting the role of the Party leadership.

These same considerations explain the measures taken to put an end to the cult of Mao. In November 1970, in his interview with Edgar Snow,[6] Mao admitted that the cult did exist, and he announced that it would be "cooled." Since then, portraits and statues of Mao have tended to disappear, and he is quoted much less often in the press. The Chinese have been taught to sing the "Internationale" without omitting, as had hitherto been done, the famous words: "There is no supreme savior. Not God, not Caesar, not democratic leader."

This cult is also one of the by-products of the Cultural Revolution. In the propaganda service people who thought they were very left felt compelled to exaggerate and praise Mao to the point of absurdity. Mao told Snow that these people were hypocrites pure and simple. He added that this "cult" had been necessary for a certain period. What did he mean? Here we have to be careful not to slip into the false notion, so widespread in the West, that such a cult was intended to buttress the power of a ruling bureaucratic class. Actually, the opposite was true: its goal was to fight against bureaucratism and transcend it. It allowed a strong leader to short-

---

[6] See *The Long Revolution*, Random House, New York, 1972, pp. 5, 19.

circuit the Party machinery and, by so doing, the opposition of certain hostile factions.

During the Cultural Revolution this "cult" allowed Mao to appeal directly to the masses and neutralize the Liu Shao-ch'i and P'eng Chen factions. Now that the Party has rediscovered its revolutionary dynamics, this method becomes useless and disappears. At the same time the leadership role of the Party is reaffirmed.

By maintaining the strategic orientation, by defending the Communist cadres who were unfairly ousted, by limiting the excesses committed by the "spontaneists" and "splinter groups," Chou En-lai emerged as the man who, with Mao's frequent backing, proved himself, more than any other leader, capable of maintaining the Party spirit during the Cultural Revolution.

All the changes in the leadership team can be explained in terms of the preeminent role of the Communist Party. In the final analysis, Mao's choices have always been based on that premise. The men whom the Cultural Revolution swept away, whether they were rightists or ultraleftists, are those who threatened the Party, because they represented interests or special groups which were either too independent or too powerful.

APPENDICES

1.

Teng T'o's *Evening Chats at Yenshan* Is Anti-Party and Anti-Socialist Double Talk

This document offers a fairly good idea of how the opposition operates within the Chinese Communist regime. Resorting to allusion and innuendo, to varied and often ingenious figures of speech to camouflage its real meaning, the opposition never appears openly or in its real guise.

COMMENT: In our opinion, Teng T'o's *Evening Chats at Yenshan* is a lot of double talk against the Party and socialism. Therefore, we have made our own compilation of passages from the *Evening Chats* and added a number of comments. It is our hope that the readers will make a comparative study of our extracts and those compiled by *Front Line*, the *Peking Daily*, and the *Peking Evening News.*

1. Venomous Attacks Against Our Great Party

Attacks Against the Scientific Thesis: "The East Wind Prevails Over the West Wind"—Treatise on "Great Empty Talk" and "Clichés"

Some people have the gift of gab. They can talk endlessly on any occasion, like water flowing from an undammed river. After listening to them, however, when you try to recall what they have said, you can remember nothing.

Making long speeches without really saying anything, making confusion worse confounded by explaining, or giving explanations which are not explanatory—these are the characteristics of great empty talk.

We cannot deny that in certain special situations such great empty talk is inevitable, and therefore in a certain sense is a necessity. Still, it would be deplorable if this practice should spread and be indulged in at every possible opportunity, or cultivated as a special skill. It would be even more disastrous if our children should be taught this skill and were turned into specialists of great empty talk.

As chance would have it, my neighbor's child has been in the habit of imitating the great poets and recently he has written a lot of great empty talk. . . . Not long ago he wrote a poem entitled "Ode to Wild Plants," which consists of only empty words. The poem goes as follows:

> The Venerable Heaven is our father,
> The Great Earth is our mother,
> And the Sun is our nurse;
> The East Wind is our benefactor,
> The West Wind is our enemy.

Although such words as heaven, earth, father, mother, sun, nurse, the East Wind, the West Wind, benefactor, and enemy catch our eye, they are used to no purpose here and have become mere clichés.

Recourse to even the most beautiful words and phrases is futile, and the more such clichés are used the worse the situation will become. Therefore I would like to advise my friends who are given to great empty talk to read more, think more, say less, and when it next befalls you to have the floor, beg off and go get forty winks. In that way, you will not only be saving your own time and energy, but also the time and energy of other people.

("Great Empty Talk," *Front Line* No. 21, 1961.)

COMMENT: "The East Wind prevails over the West Wind" is a scientific thesis advanced by Chairman Mao Tse-tung at the Meeting of Communist and Workers' Parties on November 18, 1957. It says by way of a vivid image that the international situation has reached a new turning point and that the forces of socialism are prevailing over the forces of imperialism. The East Wind symbolizes the anti-imperialist revolutionary forces of the proletariat and of the oppressed people of Asia, Africa, and Latin America. The West Wind symbolizes the decadent forces of imperialism and reaction in all countries. It is entirely correct to praise the East Wind and to detest the West Wind. Why then should Teng T'o pick up the statement, "The East Wind is our benefactor and the West Wind is our enemy," and malign it as great empty talk and a cliché? We know that the Khrushchev revisionists have incited people to "oppose the dogmatic theories concerning a mythical competition between 'the West and East Winds' more boldy and more resolutely." Thus Teng T'o is here singing the same tune as Khrushchev.

From this derives the insinuation that the leadership of our Party is "full of vanity" and has "nothing but disdain for the masses"

The wisdom of a man is never unlimited. Only an idiot fondly imagines that he knows everything and has an inexhaustible supply of wisdom, for that in fact is absolutely impossible. Some people appear clever, but strictly speaking they are only seemingly clever or only clever in a trifling way and cannot be considered really clever, let alone wise.

Lao Tze took an extreme position in this matter, and later the Kings of the Six Kingdoms went to the other extreme. The former wanted to obliterate all wisdom and good sense and negate everything, whereas the latter relied on their own wisdom and became blindly conceited. Naturally, neither attained good results. Their error derived from the fact that they failed to attach sufficient importance to the wisdom of the masses.

The best ideas can come only from the masses. During the reign of the Emperor Yuan of the Han Dynasty, Prime Minister Kuang Heng memorialized the Emperor: "I have heard it said that one should consult the multitude and follow their advice, and in so doing one is doing as Heaven wills." The famous scholar Cheng Hsing, who lived at the time of Emperor Kuang Wu of the same dynasty, also advised the emperor "to seek advice on all sides and accept suggestions from below." Fan Ya-fu, the son of Fan Chung-yen of the Sung Dynasty, gave the following advice to Szuma Kuang: "I hope you will be modest and take into consideration the opinions of the masses. One need not plan everything oneself. When a man plans everything himself, flatterers will seize the chance to say things that please him." The views of these ancients are all very sound. Fan Ya-fu's idea that "one need not plan everything one-self" is deserving of special attention. Some people, however, are always boastful and conceited; they look down on the people and make all decisions themselves in the hope of achieving success with original ideas and reject good advice from below. If such people are not aware of their shortcomings and do not try to overcome them, they will eventually suffer heavy losses.

> ("Is Wisdom Reliable?" from *Evening Chats at Yenshan*, Vol. LV, pp. 17–19, first appeared in *Peking Evening News*, February 22, 1962.)

COMMENT: Why should Teng T'o dwell today on such old stories as that of Kuang Heng advising Emperor Yuan to "consult and follow the multitude" and of Cheng Hsing advising Emperor Kuang Wu to "accept suggestions from below"? He is obliquely attacking our great Party as "being conceited and looking down on the people." This becomes clear when we compare what he says with the slanders about us spread abroad by the Khrushchev revisionists. Are not Teng T'o's words identical with the modern revisionists' vilifications of our Party?

In which our Party is spoken of disparagingly and accused of "going back on its word" and of being "untrustworthy"

Many are they who suffer from afflictions of one sort or another [. . .]; one of the afflictions is called "amnesia," and he who suffers from it cannot easily be cured.

The symptom of this affliction is that the person suffering from it often goes back on his word and fails to keep his promises; one is even inclined to suspect him of feigning stupidity, and he is therefore unworthy of one's confidence.

In *New Stories from Aitse*, Lu Ch'ou, who lived in the Ming Dynasty, relates a typical case of amnesia:

A man from the kingdom of Tsi was so absent-minded that once he had started walking he would forget to stop, and once he was lying down could never remember to get up. His wife was very worried, and gave him a piece of advice: "I've heard that Aitse is an ingenious man full of wisdom," she said, "and that he can cure all sorts of worrisome afflictions. Why don't you go and see him?" "All right, I will," her husband replied, and off he went on horseback, taking his bow and arrows with him. He had only gone a short distance when he was overtaken by a terrible urge. He dismounted, stuck his arrows in the ground, and tied his horse to a tree. When he had relieved himself, he turned his head to the left and saw the arrows. "Lord, that was a close shave! Where did those arrows come from?" he exclaimed. "They just missed me!" He turned his head to the right and, when he saw the horse, cried happily: "I had a terrible fright, but I've gained a horse!" He was about to remount the horse and set out again, with the reins in his hands, when he stepped in his own stool. He tapped his foot and whined, "Damn! I've stepped in dog shit and ruined my shoes!" He gave the horse a swat and set off on the way home. When he arrived he hesitated in front of his own door and asked himself aloud: "Where am I? Is this the Honorable Aitse's house?" When his wife saw him ruminating, she understood that he had once again lost his memory and began scolding him. The man, taken aback, replied: "Madam, we haven't had the pleasure. Why are you saying such unkind things about me?"

To all appearances, this man offers a case of serious amnesia. One cannot yet say precisely what form it will take when it reaches its peak, but in all probability madness or imbecility.

According to ancient books of Chinese medicine [. . .] one of the causes of amnesia is purported to be the abnormal functioning of what is called the "breath of life." This is why the patient not only suffers lapses of memory but little by little becomes *unpredictable*, has great difficulty speaking, becomes *irascible, nonsensical, and a raving lunatic*. Another cause: a brain tumor. The sick person grows numb from time to time, blood rushes to his head, which tends to provoke fainting spells. If he is not cared for in time he will become an idiot. Anyone who discovers that he is suffering from these symptoms must take steps to make sure he gets complete rest, and desists from speaking and from any activity, for if he persists in speaking he is courting disaster.

Aren't there any tried and true methods for treating this illness? There are, of course. For instance, [. . .] when the moment of crisis occurs, take a pail full of dog's blood and empty it on the sick person, then throw cold water on him to clarify his mind. According to Western medicine, one method consists of hitting the patient on the head with a blunt instrument specially made for that purpose, in order to put him into "deep shock," after which measures are taken to bring him around.

("Special Treatment for Amnesia,"
Front Line, No. 14, 1962.)

COMMENT: The attacks contained in this article clearly reveal a deep-rooted hate of our great Party. Nowhere in any medical books is there mention, as a symptom of amnesia, that the person afflicted "goes back on his word and does not keep his promises," is "unpredictable," "nonsensical," or "a raving lunatic." Nor is there any mention made therein of any treatment involving dog's blood or blunt instruments. Lu Ch'ou's *New Stories from Aitse* fall into the category of political satire, and have no relationship with anything medical. The fact is incontrovertible.

In which the leadership of our Party is vilified and called a "Weeping Choukeh Liang"

There is nothing more pitiful that a weeping Choukeh Liang. This nickname appears in an anecdote entitled "Kou Ni compares himself to Choukeh Liang," in volume 15 of the Pillowbook of Yue Ko, the grandson of Yue Fei. The story goes:

When he was head of a garrison to the east of the river Huai, Kuo Ti had walls constructed around two cities. With him was Kuo Ni [. . .] Kuo Ni was so overbearing that no one dared challenge him. One day on a fan he penned these lines:

Three visits to the thatched cottage for advice on matters
of State,
Under Two rulers, the old minister has furthered the power.

Thus Kuo Ni took himself for Kongming (Choukeh Liang). [. . .] One summer I went to Setchow and I noticed that the fans reserved for the guests bore the above lines. It was then I realized that what I had heard was not an idle rumor. After the defeat of Kuo Chou at Fuli, then of Kuo Chouan at Yitchen, Kuo Ni, in a state of despair that he was powerless to remedy the situation, began to cry in the presence of his hosts. Peng Fa-chouan, a judge, was witness to it. A man of wit, he declared to his friends: "What we have here is a 'Weeping Choukeh Liang.' " The witticism was much repeated and much appreciated. When it came back to him, Kuo Ni was furious and wanted to punish Peng. But Kuo Ni was stripped of his functions before he had had an opportunity to put his plan into action.

The Weeping Choukeh Liangs like Kuo Ni are simply ridiculous and nauseating. Still, the story shows that he who passes himself off as Choukeh Liang intimidates no one, and will finally be revealed under his true guise and be the laughingstock of one and all.

("Three Kinds of Choukeh Liang," from
Evening Chats at Yenshan, Vol. IV, p. 12,
first appeared in *Peking Evening News*, March
1, 1962.)

COMMENT: To whom is Teng T'o referring when he fulminates against what he calls "Weeping Choukeh Liang," and by saying that "he who passes himself off as Choukeh Liang" will inevitably "be revealed in his true guise"? If he is alluding to the bourgeoisie and the landowners, there is no point in resorting to such ambiguous terms. The only conclusion one can draw is that these insults are aimed at the Party leadership.

2. Wherein Complaints Are Made About Injustice to the Rightist Opportunists Who Were Dismissed from Office, Praising Their Anti-Party "Inflexibility" and Encouraging Them to Make a Comeback.

Speech for the Defense of Li San-tsai, Minister of the Interior and Minister of Finance, Who Was Dismissed from Office.

Among the historical figures of Peking, Li San-tsai of the Ming Dynasty, a native of Tingchow, has long fallen into oblivion. *This is regrettable* for students of local history.

When I recently talked with a few friends, all historians, his name happened to crop up. When I returned home, I looked into a few tomes of history and only then did I discover that the verdict rendered by old historians on Li San-tsai is very questionable and *should be reassessed.*

Li San-tsai (also known under the names Tao Fu and Hsiu Wu) earned his doctor's degree in the second year of the reign of Wan Li. He served successively as "Deputy Imperial Prosecutor," "Governor of Fengyang," and "Secretary of the Board of Census." He opposed the prevalent methods of collecting the mining tax and was an active supporter of the Tunglin Party. He is a well-known figure in the *History of the Ming Dynasty*.

The *History of the Ming Dynasty*, compiled early in the Ch'ing Dynasty by Chang Ting-yu and others, contains a biography of Li San-tsai which concludes with the following sentences by way of summing up: "A man of great talents, San-tsai was fond of stratagems and adept at ingratiating himself with court officials. During the thirteen years he served as governor of Fengyang, he made friends all over the country. Being unable to keep away from corruption, he was attacked by others. Those who later censured San-tsai, like Shao Fu-chung and Hsu Chao-kuei, were all followers of Wei Ching-hsien whose names were on the list of traitors, while those who recommended him, such as Ku Hsien-cheng, Tsou Yuan-piao, Chao Nan-hsing, and Liu Tsung-chou, were all distinguished high officials. Therefore, the public regarded San-tsai as a wise man."

The *History of the Ming Dynasty* characterized Li San-tsai as a man "fond of stratagems and adept at ingratiating himself with court officials." This is not a complimentary remark. If that had been true Li San-tsai would have been a political schemer and intriguer. But the facts tell another story. According to *The Truthful Record of Emperor Shen Tsung*, in the twenty-seventh and twenty-eighth years of the reign of Wan Li (Emperor Shen Tsung) Li San-tsai time and again memorialized the emperor on the abuses perpetrated in taxing mines. He boldly exposed the crimes committed by the eunuchs in collecting such taxes, their wholesale extortions and transgressions of the law. In the thirtieth and thirty-first years of the reign, he again repeatedly memorialized the emperor, expressing his opposition to the mining tax and proposing the prevention and control of the floods and droughts by dredging rivers, digging canals, and building sluice gates. The emperor accepted none of these proposals; on the contrary, he punished Li San-tsai by "depriving him of his salary for five months." How could he be described as being "fond of stratagems and adept at ingratiating himself with court officials"?

As he had repeatedly memorialized the emperor to no avail, Li San-tsai begged to resign from office and retire home.

Of course, the "Tunglin Party" also emerged at the time to attack feudal politics, and "San-tsai maintained intimate connections with its members." For this reason, the corrupt diehard forces violently attacked Li San-tsai as well as the members of the Tunglin Party such as Ku Hsien-cheng and Kao Pan-lung. Small wonder that subsequently Wei Ching-hsien and his gang should have regarded Li San-tsai together with the Tunglin Party as their sworn enemies.

It was only natural that, incited by the eunuchs, the corrupt diehard forces represented by Shao Fu-chung and Hsu Chao-kuei should have heaped abuse on Li San-tsai. They accused him of being "a great villain feigning loyalty and a big hypocrite feigning uprightness," and "listed his four major crimes of corruption, guile, deception, and tyranny." Even after Li San-tsai had finally retired home, they again trumped up the charge against him of "stealing imperial timber to build his private mansion." Perhaps this was the factual basis of the statement in the *History of the Ming Dynasty* that he was "unable to keep away from corruption." But Li San-tsai repeatedly memorialized the emperor, asking that "eunuchs be sent to conduct a trial," that "court officials come to investigate," and that "the emperor personally hear my case." He seemed to be in the right and self-confident, but the court of Emperor Wan Li did not dare make a thorough investigation of the facts. Isn't that as clear as day?

Judging by the facts about Li San-tsai during his lifetime and those facts which came to light after his death, we should regard him as a positive historical figure, though we cannot say that his character was entirely blameless.

> ("In Defense of Li San-tsai," from *Evening
> Chats at Yenshan*, Vol. V, pp. 1, 2, 104,
> first appeared in *Peking Evening News*,
> March 29, 1962.)

COMMENT: Li San-tsai was an insignificant historical figure. He was a butcher who suppressed peasant uprisings. But Teng T'o described him as a good official who spoke out for the people and worked for their welfare. He defends him because of his dismissal from office, saying that he was "in the right and self-confident." Why was he? It is easy to see that Li San-tsai was a man of the type of Hai Jui. The truth is, under the guise of defending Li San-tsai, Teng T'o is really demanding justice on behalf of the rightist opportunists.[1]

---

[1] The expression refers to P'eng Teh-huai and those who supported him.

2.

The May 16 Circular

Early in this volume[1] I described the circumstances under which the following key document of the Cultural Revolution appeared. Although not signed by any individual, it was probably the product of Mao's pen, as indicated by his characteristic style and a number of individual touches. In fact, in Appendix 4, we shall see that the Party Chairman admits to being the author of this Circular of the Central Committee of the Chinese Communist Party of May 16, 1966.

To all regional bureaus of the Central Committee, all provincial, municipal and autonomous region Party committees, all departments and commissions under the Central Committee, all leading Party members' groups and Party committees in government departments and people's organizations, and the General Political Department of the People's Liberation Army:

The Central Committee has decided to revoke the Outline Report on the Current Academic Discussion Made by the Group of Five in Charge of the Cultural Revolution which was approved for distribution on February 12, 1966, *to dissolve the "Group of Five in Charge of the Cultural Revolution" and its offices, and to set up a new Cultural Revolution Group directly under the Standing Committee of the Political Bureau.* The so-called Outline Report by the "Group of Five" is fundamentally wrong. It runs counter to the line of the socialist cultural revolution set forth by the Central Committee and Comrade Mao Tse-tung and to the guiding principles formulated at the Tenth Plenary Session of the Eighth Center Committee of the Party in 1962 on the question of classes and class struggle in socialist society. While feigning compliance, the Report actually opposes and stubbornly resists the great cultural revolution personally initiated and led by Comrade Mao Tse-tung, as well as the instructions regarding the criticism of Wu Han which he gave at the Working Conference of the Central Committee in September and October of 1965 (that is, at the session of the Standing Committee of the Political Bureau of the Central Committee which was also attended by the leading comrades of all the regional bureaus of the Central Committee).

The so-called Outline Report by the "Group of Five" is actually the Report of Peng Chen alone. He concocted it according to his own ideas behind the backs of Comrade Kang Sheng, a member of the "Group of Five," and other comrades. In handling a document of this kind regarding important questions which affect the overall situation in the socialist revolution, Peng Chen held no discussion or exchange of views at all within the "Group of Five." He did not ask any local Party committee for its opinion, nor did he make it clear that the Outline Report would be sent to the Central Committee for examination as an official document, and still less did he get the approval of Comrade Mao Tse-tung, Chairman of the Central Committee. Employing the most dishonest methods, he acted arbitrarily, abused his powers and, usurping the name of the Central Committee, hurriedly issued the Outline Report to the whole Party.

The main errors of the Outline Report are as follows:

1. Proceeding from a bourgeois stand and the bourgeois world outlook, the Report completely transposes the enemy and ourselves, putting the one into the position of the other, in its appraisal of the situation, and the character of the present academic criticism. Our country is now in an upsurge of the great proletarian cultural revolution which is pounding at all the decadent ideological and cultural positions still held by the bourgeoisie and the remnants of feudalism. Instead of encouraging the entire Party boldly to arouse the broad masses of workers, peasants and soldiers and the fighters for proletarian culture so that they can continue to charge ahead, the Report does its best to turn the movement to the Right. Using muddled, self-contradictory and hypocritical language, it obscures the sharp class struggle that is taking place on the cultural and ideological front. In particular, it obscures the aim of this great struggle, which is to criticize and repudiate Wu Han *and the considerable number of other anti-Party and anti-socialist representatives of the bourgeoisie (there are a number of them in the Central Committee and in the Party, government, and other departments at the central as well as at the provincial, municipal and autonomous region level).* By avoiding any mention of the fact repeatedly pointed out by Chairman Mao, namely, that the heart of Wu Han's drama *Hai Jui Dismissed from Office* is the question of dismissal from office, the Report covers up the serious political nature of the struggle.

2. The Report violates the basic Marxist thesis that all class struggles are political struggles. When the press began to touch on the political issues involved in Wu Han's *Hai Jui Dismissed from Office*, the authors of the Report went so far as to say: "The discussion in the press should not be confined to political questions, but should go fully into the various academic and theoretical questions involved." Regarding the criticism of Wu Han, they declared on various occasions that it was impermissible to deal with the heart of the matter, namely, the dismissal of the Right opportunists at the Lushan

Meeting in 1959, and the opposition of Hu Han and others to the Party and socialism. Comrade Mao Tse-tung has often told us that the ideological struggle against the bourgeoisie is a protracted class struggle which cannot be resolved by drawing hasty political conclusions. However, Peng Chen deliberately spread rumors, telling many people that Chairman Mao believed political conclusions on the criticism of Wu Han could be drawn after two months. Peng Chen also said that the political issues could be discussed two months later. His purpose was to channel the political struggle in the cultural sphere into so-called pure academic discussion, as frequently advocated by the bourgeoisie. Clearly, this means giving prominence to bourgeois politics, while opposing giving prominence to proletarian politics.

3. The Report lays special emphasis on what it calls "opening wide." But, playing a sly trick, it grossly distorts the policy of "opening wide" expounded by Comrade Mao Tse-tung at the Party's National Conference on Propaganda Work in March 1957 and negates the class content of "opening wide." It was in dealing with this question that Comrade Mao Tse-tung pointed out, *"We still have to wage a protracted struggle against bourgeois and petty-bourgeois ideology. It is wrong not to understand this and to give up ideological struggle. All erroneous ideas, all poisonous weeds, and all ghosts and monsters, must be subjected to criticism; in no circumstance should they be allowed to spread unchecked."* Comrade Mao Tse-tung also said, *"To 'open wide' means to let all people express their opinions freely, so that they dare to speak, dare to criticize, and dare to debate. . . ."* This Report, however, poses "opening wide" against the proletariat's exposure of the bourgeoisie's reactionary stand. What it means by "opening wide" is bourgeois liberalization, which would allow only the bourgeoisie to "open wide," but would not allow the proletariat to "open wide" and hit back at the bourgeoisie; in other words, it is a shield for such reactionary representatives of the bourgeoisie as Wu Han. The "opening wide" of this Report is opposed to Mao Tse-tung's thought and caters to the needs of the bourgeoisie.

4. Just when we began the counteroffensive against the wild attacks of the bourgeoisie, the authors of the Report raised the slogan: "Everyone is equal before the truth." This is a bourgeois slogan. Completely negating the class nature of truth, they use this slogan to protect the bourgeoisie and oppose the proletariat, oppose Marxism-Leninism and oppose Mao Tse-tung's thought. In the struggle between the proletariat and the bourgeoisie, between the truth of Marxism and the fallacies of the bourgeoisie and all other exploiting classes, either the East Wind prevails over the West Wind or the West Wind prevails over the East Wind, and there is absolutely no such thing as equality. *Can equality be permitted on such basic questions as the struggle of the proletariat against the bourgeoisie, the dictatorship of the proletariat over the bourgeoisie, the dictatorship of the proletariat in the superstructure, including all the various spheres of culture, and the continued efforts of the proletariat to weed out those representatives of the bourgeoisie who have sneaked into the Communist Party and who wave "red flags" to oppose the red flag? For decades the old-line Social Democrats, and for over ten years the modern revisionists, have never allowed the proletariat equality with the*

bourgeoisie. They completely deny that the several thousand years of human history are a history of class struggle. They completely deny the class struggle of the proletariat against the bourgeoisie, the proletarian revolution against the bourgeoisie and the dictatorship of the proletariat over the bourgeoisie. On the contrary, they are faithful lackeys of the bourgeoisie and the imperialists. Together with the bourgeoisie and the imperialists, they cling to the bourgeois ideology of oppression and exploitation of the proletariat and to the capitalist system, and they oppose Marxist-Leninist ideology and the socialist system. They are a bunch of counterrevolutionaries opposing the Communist Party and the people. Their struggle against us is one of life and death, and there is no question of equality. Therefore, our struggle against them, too, can be nothing but a life-and-death struggle, and our relationship with them can in no way be one of equality. On the contrary, it is a relationship in which one class oppresses another, that is, the dictatorship of the proletariat over the bourgeoisie. There can be no other type of relationship, such as a so-called relationship of equality or of peaceful coexistence between exploiting and exploited classes, or of kindness or magnanimity.

5. The Report states, "It is necessary not only to beat the other side politically, but also truly to surpass and beat it by a wide margin by academic and professional standards." This concept which makes no class distinction on academic matters is also very wrong. The truth on academic questions, the truth of Marxism-Leninism, of Mao Tse-tung's thought—which the proletariat has grasped—has already far surpassed and beaten the bourgeoisie. The formulation in the Report shows that its authors laud the bourgeois academic so-called authorities and try to boost their prestige, and that they hate and repress the militant new forces representative of the proletariat in academic circles.

6. *Chairman Mao often says that there is no construction without destruction. Destruction means criticism and repudiation, it means revolution. It involves reasoning things out, which is construction. Put destruction first, and in the process you have construction.* Marxism-Leninism, Mao Tse-tung's thought, was founded and has constantly developed in the course of the struggle to destroy bourgeois ideology. But this Report emphasizes that "without construction, there can be no real and thorough destruction." This amounts to prohibiting the destruction of bourgeois ideology and prohibiting the construction of proletarian ideology. It is diametrically opposed to Chairman Mao's thought. It runs counter to the revolutionary struggle we have been waging on the cultural front for the large-scale destruction of bourgeois ideology. And it amounts to prohibiting the proletariat from making any revolution.

7. The Report states that "we must not behave like scholar-tyrants who always act arbitrarily and try to overwhelm people with their power" and that "we should guard against any tendency by academic workers of the Left to take the road of bourgeois experts and scholar-tyrants." What is really meant by "scholar-tyrants"? Who are the "scholar-tyrants"? Should the proletariat not exercise dictatorship and overwhelm the bourgeoisie? Should the academic work of the proletariat not overwhelm and eradicate that of the

bourgeoisie? And if proletarian academic work overwhelms and eradicates bourgeois academic work, can this be regarded as an act of "scholar-tyrants"? The Report directs its spearhead against the proletarian Left. Obviously, its aim is to label the Marxists-Leninists "scholar-tyrants" and thus to support the real, bourgeois scholar-tyrants and prop up their tottering monopoly position in academic circles. *As a matter of fact, those Party people in authority taking the capitalist road who support the bourgeois scholar-tyrants, and those bourgeois representatives who have sneaked into the Party and protect the bourgeois scholar-tyrants, are big Party tyrants who have usurped the name of the Party. They do not read books, do not read the daily press, have no contact with the masses, have no learning at all, and rely solely on "acting arbitrarily and trying to overwhelm people with their power."*

8. For their own ulterior purposes, the authors of this Report demand a "rectification campaign" against the staunch Left in a deliberate effort to create confusion, blur class alignments and divert people from the target of struggle. Their main purpose in dishing up the Report in such a hurry was to attack the proletarian Left. They have gone out of their way to build up dossiers about the Left, tried to find all sort of pretexts for attacking it, and intended to launch further attacks on it by means of a "rectification campaign," in the vain hope of disintegrating its ranks. They openly resist the policy explicitly put forward by Chairman Mao of protecting and supporting the Left and giving serious attention to building it up and expanding its ranks. On the other hand, they have conferred the title of "Staunch Left" on those bourgeois representatives, revisionists and renegades who have sneaked into the Party and are shielding them. In these ways, they are trying to inflate the arrogance of the bourgeois Rightists and to dampen the spirits of the proletarian Left. They are filled with hatred for the proletariat and love for the bourgeoisie. Such is the bourgeois conception of brotherhood held by the authors of the Report.

9. At a time when the new and fierce struggle of the proletariat against the representatives of the bourgeoisie on the ideological front has only just begun—in many spheres and places it has not even started, *or if it has started, most Party committees concerned have a very poor understanding of the task of leadership in this great struggle and their leadership is far from conscientious and effective*—the Report stresses again and again that the struggle must be conducted "under direction," "with prudence," "with caution," and "with the approval of the leading bodies concerned." All this serves to place restrictions on the proletarian Left, to impose taboos and commandments in order to tie its hands, and to place all sorts of obstacles in the way of the proletarian cultural revolution. In a word, the authors of the Report are rushing to apply the brakes and launch a vindictive counterattack. As for the articles written by the proletarian Left in refuting the reactionary bourgeois "authorities," they nurse bitter hatred against those already published and are suppressing those not yet published. *On the other hand, they give free rein to all the ghosts and monsters who for many years have abounded in our press, radio, magazines, books, textbooks, platforms, works of literature, cinema, drama, ballads and stories, the fine arts, music, the*

dance, etc., and in doing so they never advocate proletarian leadership or stress any need for approval. The contrast here shows where the authors of the Report really stand.

10. The present struggle centers around the implementation of or resistance to Chairman Mao Tse-tung's line on the cultural revolution. Yet the Report states: "Through this struggle, and under the guidance of Mao Tse-tung's thought, we shall open up the way for the solution of this problem [that is, 'the thorough liquidation of bourgeois ideas in the realm of academic work']." Comrade Mao Tse-tung opened up the way for the proletariat on the cultural and ideological front long ago, in his "On New Democracy," "Talks at the Yenan Forum on Literature and Art," "Letter to the Yenan Peking Opera Theater After Seeing *Driven to Join the Liangshan Rebels,*" "On the Correct Handling of Contradictions Among the People," and "Speech at the Chinese Communist Party's National Conference on Propaganda Work." Yet the Report maintains that Mao Tse-tung's thought has not yet opened up the way for us and that it has to be opened up anew. Using the banner of "under the guidance of Mao Tse-tung's thought" as a cover, the Report actually attempts to open up a way opposed to Mao Tse-tung's thought, that is, the way of modern revisionism, the way to the restoration of capitalism.

In short, the Report opposes carrying the socialist revolution through to the end, opposes the line on the Cultural Revolution pursued by the Central Committee of the Party headed by Comrade Mao Tse-tung, attacks the proletarian Left and shields the bourgeois Right, thereby preparing public opinion for the restoration of capitalism. It is a reflection of bourgeois ideology in the Party; it is out-and-out revisionism. Far from being a minor issue, the struggle against this revisionist line is an issue of prime importance having a vital bearing on the destiny and future of our Party and state, on the future complexion of our Party and state, and on the world revolution.

Party committees at all levels must immediately stop carrying out the Outline Report on the Current Academic Discussion Made by the Group of Five in Charge of the Cultural Revolution. The whole Party must follow Comrade Mao Tse-tung's instructions, *hold high the great banner of the proletarian cultural revolution, thoroughly expose the reactionary bourgeois stand of those so-called academic authorities who oppose the Party and socialism, thoroughly criticize and repudiate reactionary bourgeois ideas in the sphere of academic work, education, journalism, literature and art and publishing, and seize the leadership in these cultural spheres. To achieve this, it is at the same time necessary to criticize and repudiate those representatives of the bourgeoisie who have sneaked into the Party, the government, the army and all spheres of culture, and to clear them out or transfer some of them to other positions. Above all, we must not entrust these people with the work of leading the cultural revolution. In fact many of them have done and are still doing such work, and this is extremely dangerous.*

Those representatives of the bourgeoisie who have sneaked into the Party, the government, the army and various spheres of culture are a bunch of counterrevolutionary revisionists. Once conditions are ripe, they will seize political power and turn the dictatorship of the proletariat into a dictatorship of the bourgeoisie. Some of them we have already seen through, others we have not. Some are still trusted by us and are being trained as our successors, persons like Khrushchev, for example, who are still nestling beside us. Party committees at all levels must pay full attention to this matter.

This Circular, together with the erroneous document issued by the Central Committee on February 12, 1966, is to be sent, down to the level of county Party committees, Party committees in the cultural organizations and Party committees at regimental level in the army. These committees are asked to discuss which of the two documents is wrong and which is correct, their understanding of these documents, and their achievements and mistakes.

3.

The Sixteen-Point Decision

The following document is indispensable to understanding the Cultural Revolution; it is, in essence, the revolution's charter. It is said to have been written under the personal supervision of Mao himself, which is tantamount to saying that Mao is the author of at least its sum and substance. The text helps to explain why and how the Cultural Revolution unfolded as it did. In it one finds Mao's rather extraordinarily farseeing admonition on the attitude one should take in case disturbances should occur, as one finds his reminder that people should "Make the revolution while at the same time stepping up production."

The full title of the document is Decision of the Central Committee of the Chinese Communist Party Concerning the Great Proletarian Cultural Revolution. It was adopted August 8, 1966, at the Eleventh Plenum of the Central Committee of the Communist Party, which was held in Peking August 1–12, 1966, under the chairmanship of Mao Tse-tung. In China the "Decision" is often referred to as the "Sixteen Points."

1. A New Stage in the Socialist Revolution

The great proletarian cultural revolution now unfolding is a great revolution that touches people to their very souls and constitutes a new stage in the development of the socialist revolution in our country, a stage which is both broader and deeper.

At the Tenth Plenary Session of the Eighth Central Committee of the Party, Comrade Mao Tse-tung said: "To overthrow a political power, it is always necessary first of all to create public opinion, to do work in the ideological sphere. This is true for the revolutionary class as well as for the counterrevolutionary class." This thesis of Comrade Mao Tse-tung's has been proved entirely correct in practice.

Although the bourgeoisie has been overthrown, it is still trying to use the old ideas, culture, customs and habits of the exploiting classes to corrupt the masses, capture their minds and endeavor to stage a comeback. The proletariat must do the exact opposite: it must meet head-on every challenge of the bourgeoisie in the ideological field and use the new ideas, culture, customs and habits of the proletariat to change the mental outlook of the whole of society. At present, our objective is to struggle against and overthrow those persons in authority who are taking the capitalist road, to criticize and repudiate the reactionary bourgeois academic "authorities" and the ideology of the bourgeoisie and all other exploiting classes and to transform education, literature and art and all other parts of the superstructure not in correspondence with the socialist economic base, so as to facilitate the consolidation and development of the socialist system.

2. The Main Current and the Twists and Turns

The masses of the workers, peasants, soldiers, revolutionary intellectuals and revolutionary cadres form the main force in this great Cultural Revolution. Large numbers of revolutionary young people, previously unknown, have become courageous and daring pathbreakers. They are vigorous in action and intelligent. Through the media of big-character posters and great debates, they argue things out, expose and criticize thoroughly, and launch resolute attacks on the open and hidden representatives of the bourgeoisie. In such a great revolutionary movement, it is hardly avoidable that they should show shortcomings of one kind or another; however, their general revolutionary orientation has been correct from the beginning. This is the main current in the great proletarian culture revolution. It is the general direction along which this revolution continues to advance.

Since the cultural revolution is a revolution, it inevitably meets with resistance. This resistance comes chiefly from those in authority who have wormed their way into the Party and are taking the capitalist road. It also comes from the force of habits from the old society. At present, this resistance is still fairly strong and stubborn. But after all, the great proletarian cultural revolution is an irresistible general trend. There is abundant evidence that such resistance will be quickly broken down once the masses become fully aroused.

Because the resistance is fairly strong, there will be reversals and even repeated reversals in this struggle. There is no harm in this. It tempers the proletariat and other working people, and especially the younger generation, teaches them lessons and gives them experience, and helps them to understand that the revolutionary road zigzags and does not run smoothly.

3. Put Daring above Everything Else and Boldly Arouse the Masses

The outcome of this great Cultural Revolution will be determined by whether or not the Party leadership dares boldly to arouse the masses.

Currently, there are four different situations with regard to the leadership being given to the movement of cultural revolution by Party organizations at various levels:

1. There is the situation in which the persons in charge of Party organizations stand in the van of the movement and dare to arouse the masses boldly. They put daring above everything else, they are dauntless Communist fighters and good pupils of Chairman Mao. They advocate the big-character posters and great debates. They encourage the masses to expose every kind of ghost and monster and also to criticize the shortcomings and errors in the work of the persons in charge. This correct kind of leadership is the result of putting proletarian politics in the forefront and Mao Tse-tung's thought in the lead.

2. In many units, the persons in charge have a very poor understanding of the task of leadership in this great struggle, their leadership is far from being conscientious and effective, and they accordingly find themselves incompetent and in a weak position. They put fear above everything else, stick to outmoded ways and regulations, and are unwilling to break away from conventional practices and move ahead. They have been taken unawares by the new order of things, the revolutionary order of the masses, with the result that their leadership lags behind the situation, lags behind the masses.

3. In some units, the persons in charge, who made mistakes of one kind or another in the past, are even more prone to put fear above everything else, being afraid that the masses will catch them out. Actually, if they make serious self-criticism and accept the criticism of the masses, the Party and the masses will make allowances for their mistakes. But if the persons in charge don't, they will continue to make mistakes and become obstacles to the mass movement.

4. Some units are controlled by those who have wormed their way into the Party and are taking the capitalist road. Such persons in authority are extremely afraid of being exposed by the masses and therefore seek every possible pretext to suppress the mass movement. They resort to such tactics as shifting the targets for attack and turning black into white in an attempt to lead the movement astray. When they find themselves very isolated and no longer able to carry on as before, they resort still more to intrigues, stabbing people in the back, spreading rumors, and blurring the distinction between revolution and counterrevolution as much as they can, all for the purpose of attacking the revolutionaries.

What the Central Committee of the Party demands of the Party committees at all levels is that they persevere in giving correct leadership, put daring above everything else, boldly arouse the masses, change the state of weakness and incompetence where it exists, encourage those comrades who have made mistakes but are willing to correct them to cast off their mental burdens and join in the struggle, and dismiss from their leading posts all those in authority who are taking the capitalist road and so make possible the recapture of the leadership for the proletarian revolutionaries.

4. Let the Masses Educate Themselves in the Movement

In the great proletarian cultural revolution, the only method is for the masses to liberate themselves, and any method of doing things in their stead must not be used.

Trust the masses, rely on them and respect their initiative. Cast out fear. Don't be afraid of disturbances. Chairman Mao has often told us that revolution cannot be so very refined, so gentle, so temperate, kind, courteous, restrained and magnanimous. Let the masses educate themselves in this great revolutionary movement and learn to distinguish between right and wrong and between correct and incorrect ways of doing things.

Make the fullest use of big-character posters and great debates to argue matters out, so that the masses can clarify the correct views, criticize the wrong views and expose all the ghosts and monsters. In this way the masses will be able to raise their political consciousness in the course of the struggle, enhance their abilities and talents, distinguish right from wrong and draw a clear line between ourselves and the enemy.

5. Firmly Apply the Class Line of the Party

Who are our enemies? Who are our friends? This is a question of the first importance for the revolution and it is likewise a question of the first importance for the great cultural revolution.

Party leadership should be good at discovering the Left and developing and strengthening the ranks of the Left; it should firmly rely on the revolutionary Left. During the movement this is the only way to isolate the most reactionary Rightists thoroughly, win over the middle and unite with the great majority so that by the end of the movement we shall achieve the unity of more than 95 percent of the cadres and more than 95 percent of the masses.

Concentrate all forces to strike at the handful of ultrareactionary bourgeois Rightists and counterrevolutionary revisionists, and expose and criticize to the full their crimes against the Party, against socialism and against Mao Tse-tung's thought so as to isolate them to the maximum.

The main target of the present movement is those within the Party who are in authority and are taking the capitalist road.

The strictest care should be taken to distinguish between the anti-Party, antisocialist Rightists and those who support the Party and socialism but have said or done something wrong or have written bad articles or other works.

The strictest care should be taken to distinguish between the reactionary bourgeois scholar despots and "authorities" on the one hand and people who have the ordinary bourgeois academic ideas on the other.

6. Correctly Handle Contradictions Among the People

A strict distinction must be made between the two different types of contradictions: those among the people and those between ourselves and the enemy. Contradictions among the people must not be made into contradictions between ourselves and the enemy; nor must contradictions between ourselves and the enemy be regarded as contradictions among the people.

It is normal for the masses to hold different views. Contention between different views is unavoidable, necessary and beneficial. In the course of normal and full debate, the masses will affirm what is right, correct what is wrong and gradually reach unanimity.

The method to be used in debates is to present the facts, reason things out, and persuade through reasoning. Any method of forcing a minority holding different views to submit is impermissible. The minority should be protected, because sometimes the truth is with the minority. Even if the minority is wrong, they should still be allowed to argue their case and reserve their views.

When there is a debate, it should be conducted by reasoning, not by coercion or force.

In the course of debate, every revolutionary should be good at thinking things out for himself and should develop the Communist spirit of daring to think, daring to speak and daring to act. On the premise that they have the same general orientation, revolutionary comrades should, for the sake of strengthening unity, avoid endless debate over side issues.

7. Be on Guard Against Those Who Brand the Revolutionary Masses as "Counterrevolutionaries"

In certain schools, units, and work teams of the cultural revolution, some of the persons in charge have organized counterattacks against the masses who put up big-character posters criticizing them. These people have even advanced such slogans as: opposition to the leaders of a unit or a work team means opposition to the Central Committee of the Party, means opposition to the Party and socialism, means counterrevolution. In this way it is inevitable that their blows will fall on some really revolutionary activists. This is an error in matters of orientation, an error of line, and is absolutely impermissible.

A number of persons who suffer from serious ideological errors, and particularly some of the anti-Party and antisocialist Rightists, are taking advantage of certain shortcomings and mistakes in the mass movement to spread rumors and gossip, and engage in agitation, deliberately branding some of the masses as "counterrevolutionaries." It is necessary to beware of such "pickpockets" and expose their tricks in good time.

In the course of the movement, with the exception of cases of active counterrevolutionaries where there is clear evidence of crimes such as murder, arson, poisoning, sabotage or theft of state secrets, which should be handled in accordance with the law, no measures should be taken against students at universities, colleges, middle schools and primary schools because of problems that arise in the movement. To prevent the struggle from being diverted from its main target, it is not allowed, under whatever pretext, to incite the masses or the students to struggle against each other. Even proven Rightists should be dealt with on the merits of each case at a later stage of the movement.

8. The Question of Cadres

The cadres fall roughly into the following four categories:
1) good;
2) comparatively good;
3) those who have made serious mistakes but have not became anti-Party, antisocialist Rightists;
4) the small number of anti-Party, antisocialist Rightists.

In ordinary situations, the first two categories (good and comparatively good) are the great majority.

The anti-Party, antisocialist Rightists must be fully exposed, refuted, overthrown and completely discredited and their influence eliminated. At the same time, they should be given a chance to turn over a new leaf.

9. Cultural Revolutionary Groups, Committees and Congresses

Many new things have begun to emerge in the great proletarian cultural revolution. The cultural revolutionary groups, committees and other organizational forms created by the masses in many schools and units are something new and of great historic importance.

These cultural revolutionary groups, committees and congresses are excellent new forms of organization whereby the masses educate themselves under the leadership of the Communist Party. They are an excellent bridge to keep our Party in close contact with the masses. They are organs of power of the proletarian cultural revolution.

The struggle of the proletariat against the old ideas, culture, customs and habits left over by all the exploiting classes over thousands of years will necessarily take a very, very long time. Therefore, the cultural revolutionary groups, committees and congresses should not be temporary organizations but permanent, standing mass organizations. They are suitable not only for colleges, schools and government and other organizations, but generally also for factories, mines, other enterprises, urban districts and villages.

It is necessary to institute a system of general elections, like that of the Paris Commune, for electing members to the cultural revolutionary groups and committees and delegates to the cultural revolutionary congresses. The list of candidates should be put forward by the revolutionary masses after full discussion, and the elections should be held after the masses have discussed the lists over and over again.

The masses are entitled at any time to criticize members of the cultural revolutionary groups and committees and delegates elected to the cultural revolutionary congresses. If these members or delegates prove incompetent, they can be replaced through election or recalled by the masses after discussion.

The cultural revolutionary groups, committees and congresses in colleges and schools should consist mainly of representatives of the revolutionary students. At the same time, they should have a certain number of representatives of the revolutionary teaching and administrative staff and workers.

10. Educational Reform

In the great proletarian cultural revolution a most important task is to transform the old educational system and the old principles and methods of teaching.

In this great cultural revolution, the phenomenon of our schools being dominated by bourgeois intellectuals must be completely changed.

In every kind of school we must apply thoroughly the policy advanced by Comrade Mao Tse-tung of education serving proletarian politics and education being combined with productive labor, so as to enable those receiving an education to develop morally, intellectually and physically and to become laborers with social consciousness and culture.

The period of schooling should be shortened. Courses should be fewer and better. The teaching material should be thoroughly transformed, in some cases beginning with simplifying complicated material. While their main task is to study, students should also learn other things. That is to say, in addition to their studies they should also learn industrial work, farming and military affairs, and take part in the struggles of the cultural revolution to criticize the bourgeoisie as these struggles occur.

11. The Question of Criticizing by Name in the Press

In the course of the mass movement of the cultural revolution, the criticism of bourgeois and feudal ideology should be well combined with the dissemination of the proletarian world outlook and of Marxism-Leninism, Mao Tse-tung's thought.

Criticism should be organized of typical bourgeois representatives who have wormed their way into the Party and typical reactionary bourgeois academic "authorities," and this should include criticism of various kinds of reactionary views in philosophy, history, political economy and education, in works and theories of literature and art, in theories of natural science, and in other fields.

Criticism of anyone by name in the press should be decided after discussion by the Party committee at the same level, and in some cases submitted to the Party committee at a higher level for approval.

12. Policy Toward Scientists, Technicians and Ordinary Members of Working Staffs

As regards scientists, technicians and ordinary members of working staffs, as long as they are patriotic, work energetically, are not against the Party and socialism, and maintain no illicit relation with any foreign country, we should in the present movement continue to apply the policy of "unity, criticism, unity." Special care should be taken of those scientists and scientific and technical personnel who have made contributions. Efforts should be made to help them gradually transform their world outlook and their style of work.

13. The Question of Arrangements for Integration with the Socialist Education Movement in City and Countryside

The cultural and educational units and leading organs of the Party and government in the large and medium cities are the points of concentration of the present proletarian cultural revolution.

The great cultural revolution has enriched the socialist education movement in both city and countryside and raised it to a higher level. Efforts should be made to conduct these two movements in close combination. Arrangements to this effect may be made by various regions and departments in the light of the specific conditions.

The socialist education movement now going on in the countryside and in enterprises in the cities should not be upset where the original arrangements are appropriate and the movement is going well, but should continue in accordance with the original arrangements. However, the questions that are arising in the present great proletarian cultural revolution should be put to the masses for discussion at the proper time, so as to further foster vigorously proletarian ideology and eradicate bourgeois ideology.

In some places, the great proletarian cultural revolution is being used as the focus in order to add momentum to the socialist education movement and clean things up in the fields of politics, ideology, organization and economy. This may be done where the local Party committee thinks it appropriate.

14. Take Firm Hold of the Revolution and Stimulate Production

The aim of the great proletarian cultural revolution is to revolutionize people's ideology and as a consequence to achieve greater, faster, better and more economical results in all fields of work. If the masses are fully aroused and proper arrangements are made, it is possible to carry on both the cultural revolution and production without one hampering the other, while guaranteeing high quality in all our work.

The great proletarian cultural revolution is a powerful motive force for the development of the social productive forces in our country. Any idea of counterposing the great cultural revolution to the development of production is incorrect.

15. The Armed Forces

In the armed forces, the cultural revolution and the socialist education movement should be carried out in accordance with the instructions of the

Military Commission of the Central Committee of the Party and the General Political Department of the People's Liberation Army.

16. Mao Tse-tung's Thought Is the Guide to Action in the Great Proletarian Cultural Revolution

In the great proletarian cultural revolution, it is imperative to hold aloft the great red banner of Mao Tse-tung's thought and put proletarian politics in command. The movement for the creative study and application of Chairman Mao Tse-tung's works should be carried forward among the masses of the workers, peasants and soldiers, the cadres and the intellectuals, and Mao Tse-tung's thought should be taken as the guide to action in the cultural revolution.

In this complex great cultural revolution, Party committees at all levels must study and apply Chairman Mao's works all the more conscientiously and in a creative way. In particular, they must study over and over again Chairman Mao's writings on the cultural revolution and on the Party's methods of leadership, such as "On New Democracy," "Talks at the Yenan Forum on Literature and Art," "On the Correct Handling of Contradictions Among the People," "Speech at the Chinese Communist Party's National Conference on Propaganda Work," "Some Questions Concerning Methods of Leadership," and "Methods of Work of Party Committees."

Party committees on all levels must abide by the directions given by Chairman Mao over the years, namely that they should thoroughly apply the mass line of "from the masses, to the masses" and that they should be pupils before they become teachers. They should try to avoid being one-sided or narrow. They should foster materialist dialectics and oppose metaphysics and scholasticism.

The great proletarian cultural revolution is bound to achieve brilliant victory under the leadership of the Central Committee of the Party headed by Comrade Mao Tse-tung.

Mao Tse-tung Analyzes the Cultural Revolution

The following text is a compilation of remarks made by Mao Tse-tung, probably in July 1967. They were "published" in the streets of Peking in the form of posters and disseminated throughout the country as little pamphlets or handbills some two months later. Although there can be no doubt of the authenticity of the texts, it should be remembered that they do not constitute an article or a rigorous, organized collection of the Chairman's views. It is also reasonable to believe that Mao was responding to questions asked him. The posters we saw in the streets of Peking implied that Mao was addressing some foreign delegation when he made these remarks.

1. Four Stages in the Great Proletarian Cultural Revolution (GPCR)

The first year of the great proletarian cultural revolution was for making the arrangements; the second is for striving for victory, establishing temporary power structures, and the revolutionizing of thinking; the third is for tidying up. The main things to be done at present are major criticism and the achieving of great alliances and triple combinations.

The publication of Yao Wen-yuan's article was a signal. This signal was firmly opposed by P'eng Chen and others; even my suggestion that it should be printed as a pamphlet was utterly rejected. As a result I had to take charge of the drafting of the May Sixteenth Circular, in which the question of lines and the question of the two roads was clearly brought up. Most people thought at the time that my understanding was out of date, and at times I was the only person to agree with my own suggestions. Later I went with this spirit to the Eleventh Plenum of the Eighth Central Committee, where I was supported by a fairly narrow majority, though many comrades did not accept it: Li Ching-ch'uan didn't, and Liu Lan-t'ao didn't either.[1] We'll see how things work out. From the publication of Yao Wen-yuan's article to the Eleventh Plenum was the first stage of the Great Proletarian Cultural Revolution.

After the working meeting of the Central Committee the emphasis was on criticizing the bourgeois reactionary line. As the criticism of this line aroused the revolutionary enthusiasm of many revolutionaries, the revolutionary intellectuals and the young students were the first to achieve consciousness, which is in accordance with the laws of revolutionary development. In January of this year the Shanghai workers rose, as did the workers of the whole country and the peasants too, when the January Storm swept across the country. The development of the movement showed that the workers and peasants are still the main force—the soldiers are only workers and peasants in uniform, so that workers, peasants and soldiers are, at root, workers and peasants. Only when the broad masses of workers and peasants arose was all that bourgeois stuff thoroughly smashed; while the revolutionary intellectuals and the young students had to fall back into a subsidiary place.

Isn't that so? As soon as the workers rose they smashed reactionary economism, seized power from the people in authority taking the capitalist road, and hastened revolutionary great alliances and triple combinations. The triple combination is a law of the development of a revolutionary movement: it was in the democratic revolution and it is too in the great proletarian cultural revolution. In the May Fourth Movement[2] of the democratic revolution the revolutionary intellectuals were the first to be awakened and the first to set things going, but very soon afterward the workers and peasants were the main force in the revolutionary storms of the Northern Expedition[3] and the Long March.

From the Eleventh Plenum of the Eighth Central Committee to the January Storm can be regarded as the second stage. From the January Storm, the power seizures, the great alliances, and the triple combinations onwards can be taken as the third stage. Although the broad masses of the workers and peasants gave an impulse to the great alliances, and although the Central Committee also hoped that great alliances would be rapidly achieved, yet the proletariat has to follow the proletarian world outlook in changing the world. The bourgeoisie has to change the world in accordance with its own world outlook. The petty-bourgeois and bourgeois ideology that was in full spate among the intellectuals and the young students, however, wrecked this situation. Each class still wants to express itself stubbornly. As

[1] Leaders, respectively, of Szechuan and Shensi.

[2] A student-inspired movement that began on that date with a historic demonstration in Peking, followed by strikes throughout the country. A wide variety of political, economic, social, and nationalistic feelings coalesced in the May Fourth Movement, which was tragically defeated in 1927.

[3] In 1926 and the early part of 1927 the armies of the Kuomintang, then allied with the Communists, drove northward from Canton to rid the country of warlords.

the laws of class struggle can't be changed in accordance with men's subjective wills, we have been unable to form alliances, and the alliances that were formed have split apart very quickly and don't hold together any more. We will have to slow our pace somewhat.

After the publication of Ch'i Pen-yu's "Patriotism or National Betrayal?" and of "Betrayal of Proletarian Dictatorship Is Essential Element in the Book *On Self-Cultivation*" the movement moved into the fourth stage. This is a crucial moment in the struggle between the two lines and the two classes. Here, by the way, I have something to say on the question of attitudes to those who have been deluded. Most of them are workers, peasants and key cadres of the Party and League. We must have confidence in over 95 percent of the masses and the cadres; consequently we must also have confidence in those who have been temporarily deluded. This is a question everyone really ought to think about.

The workers, peasants and soldiers have no direct contacts with counter-revolutionary revisionists. On top of this, these counterrevolutionary revisionists all wave the red flag to attack the red flag. They go under the colors of Central Committee directives. Yet again the masses of workers, peasants and soldiers as well as the cadres who are the mainstay of the Party and the League have strong proletarian emotions. Thus they were easily put upon; but once they reform that will be all right.

The lid has now been taken off the class struggle. The masses of workers and peasants have really been armed with Marxist-Leninism; this is a powerful material force. The intellectuals have always been quicker on the uptake than the workers and peasants, and they are also rather more flexible and adaptable, but they often have a definite tendency to opportunism. If revolutionary intellectuals want to carry revolution through to the end they must continually reform themselves through labor. This is because the education that they, including the young students, have received over several decades is basically bourgeois; bourgeois thinking has blended into their bloodstream, and unless they make big efforts to change their world outlook things will start turning into their opposites. I still think that the great majority of intellectuals, whether inside or outside the Party, remain basically bourgeois. Please will you all consider whether or not this view is out of date. In this crucial moment of the class struggle we must stress the reform of our own world outlook.

2. The Great Strategic Disposition at Present is Achieving Great Alliances and Triple Combinations through Major Revolutionary Criticism

The present great cultural revolution will not end soon. It will develop even more deeply and on an even larger scale. The small handful of the biggest power holders in the Party taking the capitalist road must be criticized with even more concentrated forces. We must make propaganda about the Eleventh Plenum; we must talk about our achievements and our line. If we are to overthrow the small handful of the biggest power holders taking the capitalist road we must do so not only organizationally but also politically, ideologically, and in the realm of theory. This is a vital issue for the country and the world. If revisionism is not overthrown it will stage a restoration. This is a great historical task. Looking forward, it is very far indeed from being completed.

In this great struggle we must turn the spearhead toward the power holders taking the capitalist road, toward revisionists. Some of these people have infiltrated the Party and usurped positions of leadership. They are the supporters and protectors of all the ghosts and monsters. They are all ambitious scheming hypocrites from the exploiting classes. They pretend to comply when they are inwardly disobeying. They are two-faced and treacherous, talking like people to your face and like devils behind your back. They often raise Marxist-Leninist phrases as their standards while making a great commotion over a "but." Those who wave the red flag are even more dangerous. We must be very much on our guard against this.

Personally, I think we can see the first signs at present of giving up the struggle against the enemy, the struggle against the biggest power holders in the Party who are taking the capitalist line. When I raised this question in the last discussion forum here I said that we ought to make a program aimed at the biggest of the power holders in the Party taking the capitalist road. At present this contradiction is not concentrated; it is widely dissipated. This means it is very hard to criticize the biggest of the power holders inside the Party until they are utterly exposed.

In the cataclysmic changes that have developed over the past year there has naturally been chaos everywhere. There is no connection between the chaos in one place and that in another. Even violent struggle is very good, because once contradictions are exposed they are easily solved. The losses in this great cultural revolution have been minimal and the achievements huge.

The great advantage of the army supporting the left is that it makes the army itself get educated. They understand this question through actual struggles. In supporting the revolutionary masses and the left-wing organizations not only do they see the struggles between the two lines that exist in all aspects of society and the class struggle; they also see that the struggles between the two lines and class struggles exist in the army as well. When the army supports the left this problem is similarly exposed, with the result that the army is strengthened and the ideological level of our troops is raised.

We must not be afraid of rows. The bigger they are the better. With seven or eight rows things are bound to be sorted out properly and to some effect. No matter what sort of rows there are we must not be afraid of them, because the more afraid we are the more trouble there will be. But we must not shoot. It is bad to shoot at any time.

The whole country is involved in a big row. If you have a boil it contains germs and it is bound to burst. Opposing the thinking of the bourgeois academic authorities is a case in point—it amounts to smashing it. If it is not smashed, socialism cannot be established and struggle-criticism-transformation is impossible.

If a cart is driven too fast it will overturn. You have to listen to those who greet you. The main things at present are great alliances and triple combinations; digging out bad people, ghosts and monsters; and the revival of the

Party organizations. In my opinion Party congresses at all levels, including the Ninth National Congress, can be called at about this time next year. You should not all be feeling tired or wanting to get out of things.

The obstacles to great alliances come at present from two sources: the persons in authority in the Party taking the capitalist road on the one hand; and, on the other, mountain-top-ism,[4] showing off, and unwillingness to form great alliances among the rebels. When revolutionary committees have been founded, petty-bourgeois revolutionaries need to be very well led. As for the Liberation Army, we need the slogan "Support the Army and Cherish the People." If one looks at the very detailed reports on the problem of armed struggle that have come in from throughout the country, one can see that there has not been so much. There is some armed struggle, but some of the reports are unfounded—rather like reports of natural disaster intended to get extra relief grain. On the question of cadres, we must criticize "attacking the many to protect the few," which is still happening throughout the country. Great alliances, triple combinations and supporting the left are immutably fixed principles. Seizing power, the army, and the cadres are the three big problems at present. Where power has already been seized, holding it is the current big problem. If these problems are grasped the main line of policy can be achieved; otherwise it will fail. We must also grasp major criticism, grasp things of substance. *Red Flag* has published an article of substance.

At present we must carry major criticism to a new high tide, making it the central task with priority over everything else. We should integrate criticism of the small handful of top power holders in the Party taking the capitalist road with that of power holders taking the capitalist road in our own localities and departments. The overall emphasis in papers and journals must be on Liu Shao-ch'i, Teng Hsiao-p'ing, T'ao Chu, P'eng Chen, Lo Jui-ch'ing, Lu Ting-yi, and Yang Shang-k'un. In the army the emphasis of criticism is on Liu Shao-ch'i, P'eng Teh-huai, Ho Lung, and Lo Jui-ch'ing.

3. Revolutionary Rebels Must Work Hard at Remolding Their World View

In this crucial moment in the class struggle we must stress the remolding of our own world view. Revolutionary leftists are under an even stronger obligation to eliminate the bourgeois and promote the proletarian. Otherwise bourgeois ideology will not be cleaned up for a long time and will even go toward the negative side of things. You don't believe it? I would like to ask you all how, after all, we are to move from socialism to communism. Have you thought about this carefully? If we are to guarantee that the mistake of taking the capitalist road will never be repeated and if we really concern ourselves with the affairs of the nation, we must work hard at remolding our world view.

It looks as though two preconditions are essential for a great alliance. One is that only an alliance created through struggle can be strong, because struggle is absolute while unity is relative. Some say that the Chinese people

---

[4] The tendency of some revolutionary groups to act independently and in their own self-interest, to the detriment of strategic and tactical considerations.

are passionately fond of peace. I don't think they are so fond of it. The Chinese people are pugnacious.

"Revolution is no crime, rebellion is justified" should not be wildly applied at present. Revolution and protecting both have the strongest class nature. Revolutionary cadres must be protected, and protected with full justification and boldness. It is better to be left than rightist. Apparent "leftism" that is really rightism looks even more revolutionary on the outside than does being realistic, but we do not advocate it. It is in the bourgeois domain, it is clique-ish.

Distinguished and influential figures of the May Fourth period included then leftists like Hu Shih,[5] who later became a running dog of U.S. imperialism. Ch'en Tu-hsiu,[6] who was famous in the May Fourth Movement, became a counterrevolutionary. Li Ta-chao[7] did not write many articles at the time, but he devoted himself to his work and became a revolutionary leftist. Then there was Lu Hsun,[8] who stressed social investigation and independent thought at that time and later became a great Marxist. We learn from history. We should not be flashes in the pan. We should work hard, be good at thinking, and have close links with the masses. We must be good at putting the petty-bourgeois thinking in our ranks back on the proletarian revolutionary track. This is a key problem in winning victory in the great proletarian cultural revolution.

4. China Must Become the Arsenal for the World Revolution

Modern weapons, guided missiles and atom bombs were made very quickly, and we produced a hydrogen bomb in only two years and eight months. Our development has been faster than that of America, Britain and France. We are now in fourth place in the world. Guided missiles and atom bombs are great achievements. This is the result of Khrushchev's "help." By withdrawing the experts he forced us to take our own road. We should give him a big medal.

U.S. imperialism is even more isolated. All the peoples of the world know that U.S. imperialism is the chief cause of war. The peoples of the whole world, even the American people, are against it. Soviet revisionism has been further exposed, particularly in this Middle East affair. The Soviet revisionists used Khrushchev's tricks again. They sent over 2,000 military experts to the UAR. First they went in for adventurism and sent warships in. Then they persuaded the UAR not to be the first to attack, and at the same time told Johnson on the hot line—there was no hot line in Khrushchev's day. Johnson

[5] An intellectual who had an American-style education and was an admirer of John Dewey. He was China's ambassador to the United States.

[6] Founder of the Chinese Communist Party and its first general secretary. He is held responsible in China for the 1927 disaster.

[7] A former leader of the Chinese Communist Party, Li was assassinated in 1927. A history professor and librarian at Peking University, Li obtained a post there for the young Mao Tse-tung.

[8] Lu Hsun (1881–1936) is often considered the greatest modern Chinese writer. His independent, combative position has always given him a special place in Mao's affections.

lost no time in telling Israel to launch a surprise attack. Sixty per cent of the UAR's aircraft was destroyed on the ground. Soviet aid to the UAR amounted to 2,300,000,000, but in the end the UAR surrendered and stopped fighting. This is another big exposure of how the nationalist states are betrayed.

A lot of places are anti-China at the moment, which makes it look as though we are isolated. In fact they are anti-China because they are afraid of the influence of China, of the thought of Mao Tse-tung, and of the great cultural revolution. They oppose China to keep the people in their own countries down and to divert popular dissatisfaction with their rule. This opposition to China is jointly planned by U.S. imperialism and Soviet revisionism. This shows not that we are isolated, but that our influence throughout the world has greatly increased. The more they oppose China the more they spur on popular revolution; the people of these countries realize that the Chinese road is the road to liberation. China should not only be the political center of the world revolution. It must also become the military and technical center of the world revolution.

5.

Press Communiqué of the Ninth Party Congress

The Press Communiqué of the Secretariat of the Presidium of the Ninth National Congress of the Communist Party of China was published April 24, 1969, at the end of the Ninth Party Congress and was disseminated in pamphlet form by the Foreign Languages Press in Peking.

The Ninth National Congress of the Communist Party of China came to a victorious close on the afternoon of April 24.

The great leader Chairman Mao attended today's session.

Vice-Chairman Lin Piao presided over today's session.

The Ninth Central Committee of the Communist Party of China was elected at the plenary session today. An extremely enthusiastic, revolutionary atmosphere prevailed throughout the process of voting in the election. When the names of the great leader Chairman Mao and his close comrade-in-arms Vice-Chairman Lin Piao were read in the announcement of the list of the elected members at the session, prolonged applause resounded throughout the hall and the delegates burst into prolonged hearty cheers: "Long live the great, glorious and correct Communist Party of China!" "Long live the United and Victorious Ninth National Congress of the Party!" "Long Live Invincible Mao Tsetung Thought!"[1] "We wish our great leader Chairman Mao a long, long life!"

After the Congress took up the third item on the agenda on April 15, the delegates set to work conscientiously and with a great sense of responsibility.

---

[1] During and since the Cultural Revolution there has been a tendency to simplify Chinese names in transliteration, doing away with apostrophes and hyphens. This is especially true in this phrase.

In accordance with the rules laid down by the Presidium of the Congress, candidates for membership and alternate membership of the Central Committee were first nominated by the delegations freely. The Presidium, after collecting the opinions of the delegations, proposed a preliminary list of candidates and handed it back to the delegations and a list of candidates was worked out after full consultations. A preliminary election by secret ballot was then conducted. After such repeated, full democratic consultation from below and from above, a final list of candidates was decided upon, and it was submitted by the Presidium to the Congress for final election by secret ballot. The process of the election of the Ninth Central Committee of the Chinese Communist Party was a full manifestation of the Party's democratic centralism and mass line.

Among the 170 members and 109 Alternate Members elected to the Central Committee, there are proletarian revolutionaries of the older generation of our Party and new proletarian fighters who have come forth during the Great Proletarian Cultural Revolution; there are leading cadres from the various fronts of the Party, the government, and the army, outstanding Party members working at production posts in factories and rural areas, combat heroes of the People's Liberation Army safeguarding our Motherland, Communists engaged in cultural and scientific work and outstanding men and women communist fighters of various nationalities. The delegates said that the composition of the Ninth Central Committee forcefully shows the unprecedented vitality and revolutionary unity of our Party under the great red banner of Mao Tsetung Thought.

Seated in the front row of the rostrum today were: Comrades Chou En-lai, Chen Po-ta, Kang Sheng, Chiang Ching, Chang Chun-chiao, Yao Wen-yuan, Hsieh Fu-chih, Huang Yung-sheng, Wu Fa-hsien, Yeh Chun, Wang Tung-hsing, and Wen Yu-cheng.

Also there were: Comrades Tung Pi-wu, Liu Po-cheng, Chu Teh, Chen Yun, Li Fu-chun, Chen Yi, Li Hsien-nien, Hsu Hsiang-chien, Nieh Jung-chen, and Yeh Chien-ying.

The delegates happily said: Holding high the great red banner of Marxism-Leninism-Mao Tsetung Thought, the Congress has seriously and concientiously studied Chairman Mao's theory of continuing the revolution under the dictatorship of the proletariat, summed up the great victories and basic experience of the Great Proletarian Cultural Revolution of our country and decided upon our Party's tasks and policies for both domestic affairs and international activities, and it has elected the new Central Committee today. Both politically, ideologically and organizationally, it has successfully realized Chairman Mao's call to make the Congress "*a congress of unity and a congress of victory*." The Congress will surely have a most far-reaching influence on the history of our Party. We are certain that after the conclusion of the Congress, "*still greater victories will be won throughout the country*" under the leadership of the great leader Chairman Mao and of the Ninth Central Committee with Chairman Mao as its leader and Vice-Chairman Lin as its deputy leader.

The Congress holds that it is essential to further unfold a great mass movement for the living study and application of Mao Tsetung Thought throughout the country, to study conscientiously the extremely important speeches made by Chairman Mao on several occasions at the Congress, the political report made by Vice-Chairman Lin and the Constitution of the Communist Party of China, and to study the historical experience of the struggle between the two lines within the Party over the past forty-eight years, particularly since the beginning of the period of the socialist revolution. Through such study, a clear understanding of the situation, tasks and policies should be acquired, Liu Shao-chi's counterrevolutionary revisionist line further criticized and its pernicious influence eliminated, so that *unity in thinking, policy, plan, command and action* will be achieved under the great red banner of Mao Tsetung Thought by the whole Party, the whole army and the people of all nationalities throughout the country. This is the fundamental guarantee for the realization of the various tasks set forth by the Congress and for the achievement of still greater victories.

The Congress calls on the whole Party, the whole army and the people of all nationalities in our country resolutely to carry out Chairman Mao's proletarian revolutionary line, continue to strengthen and consolidate the dictatorship of the proletariat, carry through to the end the revolution in the superstructure including every sphere of culture such as education, literature and art, the press and health, and fulfill all the tasks of struggle-criticism-transformation as set forth in Vice-Chairman Lin's political report. We should trust the masses, rely on them and respect their initiative. We should fulfill those tasks in every single factory, every single school, every single commune and every single unit step by step and in a deep-going, meticulous, down-to-earth and appropriate way. We should make concrete analyses of the conditions in different places and, taking into account the unevenness in the development of the movement, draw up the necessary plans in order to fulfill the tasks for all the stages in struggle-criticism-transformation throughout the country.

The Congress calls on the leading cadres at all levels in the Party and the army and on the broad revolutionary masses to bear firmly in mind Chairman Mao's teaching that *policy and tactics are the life of the Party* and conscientiously carry out all Chairman Mao's proletarian policies. We should, under the leadership of the proletariat, consolidate the worker-peasant alliance, reeducate the intellectuals and win over and unite all people that can be united with to fight concertedly against the enemy. We should pay attention to the trends in the class struggle between the proletariat and the bourgeoisie, fight against the handful of counterrevolutionaries who vainly attempt to stage a comeback, fight the "Left" or Right erroneous tendencies which run counter to Chairman Mao's policies and combat all manifestations of the bourgeois world outlook.

The Congress urges all the comrades of the Party and the revolutionary committees at all levels conscientiously to carry out the mass line, adhere to the Marxist scientific method of investigating and studying social conditions initiated by Chairman Mao, and analyze and resolve contradictions by means of materialist dialectics of one dividing into two. We should be good at distinguishing between the two different types of contradictions, those between ourselves and the enemy and those among the people, and should properly handle the different types of contradictions by different methods. In solving a problem, we should note both its positive and negative aspects; when taking notice of one main tendency, we should also pay attention to the other tendency which may be covered up; we must take full notice and get firm hold of the main aspects and at the same time solve problems of the minor aspects one by one. Leading comrades at all levels must understand the whole situation, be good at grasping typical examples, sum up experience, closely follow the trends, do their work in a deep-going and meticulous way and overcome the tendency of falling into generalities. In a victorious situation, comrades must maintain the style of arduous struggle and plain living and the style of being modest, prudent and free from arrogance and rashness, and must guard against the sugar-coated bullets of the bourgeoisie and its attempts to corrupt and split our Party and the revolutionary ranks.

The Ninth National Congress of the Communist Party of China extends a warm proletarian revolutionary salute to the working class, the poor and lower-middle peasants, the Red Guards, the revolutionary cadres and the revolutionary intellectuals all over the country who have made remarkable contributions in the Great Proletarian Cultural Revolution, and to the commanders and fighters of the People's Liberation Army who have done meritorious service in safeguarding the sacred territory of our motherland and in the work of supporting industry, supporting agriculture and supporting the broad masses of the Left and exercising military control and giving political and military training. The Congress sends warm regards to the broad sections of the patriotic overseas Chinese and our patriotic compatriots in Hongkong and Macao, to our compatriots in Taiwan who are under the oppression and exploitation by the U.S.-Chiang reactionaries and to all those who support socialism and love the motherland and have for many years done useful work for the revolution and the construction of the motherland. The Congress calls on the working class, the poor and lower-middle peasants and the people of all nationalities in our country to persist in building socialism *independently and with initiative in our own hands and through self-reliance*, and by going all out, aiming high and achieving greater, faster, better and more economical results, help bring about a new high tide in revolution and production by taking the concrete action of *grasping revolution, promoting production and other work and preparedness against war* and score new achievements in the three great revolutionary movements of class struggle, the struggle for production and scientific experiment.

The Ninth National Congress of the Communist Party of China extends a warm and militant salute to the heroic Albanian Party of Labour and the genuine fraternal Marxist-Leninist Parties and organizations all over the world, to the revolutionary people of the five continents who are waging valiant struggles against imperialism headed by the United States, modern revisionism with the Soviet revisionist renegade clique as its center and the reactionaries of various countries, and to the heroic Vietnamese people who persist in carrying through to the end the war of resistance against U.S. aggression and for national salvation. The Congress solemnly declares: The Communist Party of China, nurtured by the great leader Chairman Mao, always upholds proletarian internationalism and firmly supports the revolutionary struggles of the proletariat and the oppressed peoples and nations of the whole world. We are determined to unite with the genuine Marxist-Leninists all over the world and the broad masses of the proletariat and of the revolutionary people in all countries, thoroughly smash the plot of U.S.-Soviet collusion to redivide the world and carry through to the end the great struggle against imperialism, revisionism and all reaction.

U.S. imperialism, Soviet revisionism and the reactionaries in the world are all paper tigers. They cannot escape their doom. Their difficulties are insurmountable. The revolutionary cause of the people the world over will definitely triumph. We are fully aware: There will still be difficulties and twists and turns on our way forward, and the reactionaries at home and abroad will still put up a last-ditch struggle. But all this cannot stop the victorious advance of our great cause of socialism. Armed with Mao Tsetung Thought, the Chinese people and the Chinese People's Liberation Army are invincible. We are determined to liberate Taiwan! We are determined to defend the sacred territory and sovereignty of our great motherland! All the schemes, sabotage and shameless aggression by U.S. imperialism, Soviet revisionism and the reactionaries abroad and all the schemes and sabotage by the domestic reactionaries are bound to be smashed to smithereens by the iron fist of the Chinese people and the Chinese People's Liberation Army who are fully prepared! Ours is an era in which imperialism is heading for total collapse and socialism is advancing to worldwide victory, a great era in which Marxism-Leninism-Mao Tsetung Thought triumphs all over the world. Let us closely follow the great leader Chairman Mao and advance valiantly to win new and greater victories!

Long live the victory of the Ninth National Congress of the Party!

Long live the victory of the Great Proletarian Cultural Revolution!

Long live the dictatorship of the proletariat!

Workers of all countries, unite!

Proletarians, oppressed peoples and nations of the world, unite!

Down with U.S. imperialism! Down with Soviet revisionism! Down with the reactionaries of various countries!

Long live the great unity of the people of all nationalities in our country!

Long live the great unity of the people of the world!

Long live invincible Marxism-Leninism-Mao Tsetung Thought!

Long live the great, glorious and correct Communist Party of China!

Long live our great leader Chairman Mao! A long, long life to Chairman Mao!

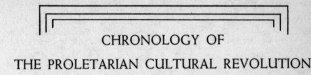

CHRONOLOGY OF
THE PROLETARIAN CULTURAL REVOLUTION

First Phase
November 10, 1965, to April 1966:

The attack on Wu Han, and P'eng Chen's resistance

November 10: Publication in Shanghai of the article "On the New Historical Play *Hai Jui Dismissed from Office*"

P'eng Chen's "Outline Report" of February 1966

April-June 1966:

Criticism of P'eng Chen and the "Black Gang"

The "May 16 Circular" of the Central Committee

The Cultural Revolution begins to take hold in the universities

May 27: First Marxist-Leninist *ta-tzu-pao* (big-character poster) at Peking University

June and July 1966:

Period of the work teams directed by Liu and Teng; The "fifty days" of Mao's absence

July 17: Mao Tse-tung returns to Peking

August 1-12, 1966:

The Eleventh Plenum of the Chinese Communist Party's Central Committee is held in Peking

The work teams are condemned, and Liu Shao-ch'i and Teng Hsiao-p'ing are downgraded

August 8: The Central Committee adopts the Sixteen-Point Decision

Second Phase

August-September 1966:

Appearance of the Red Guards, and T'ao Chu's maneuvering	August 18: Mass meeting at T'ien-an-Men, the Gate of Heavenly Peace; more then a million young Chinese gather in Peking to hear Mao and other leaders
Revolutionary exchanges	
Red Guards fan out all over the country	
The Cultural Revolution begins to spread to the factories	

October-December 1966:

The working class enters the Cultural Revolution	October 3: Publication of editorial in *Red Flag* No. 13 calling for struggle against the Liuist line
Attacks on Liu and Teng begin	
Resistance by the Liuist faction	October 23: Liu Shao-ch'i makes his first self-criticism
A split in the unity of the Red Guards	
Incidents in Shanghai	November 9: The incident at Anching
The revolutionary counteroffensive	
Big-character posters attacking T'ao Chu	

Third Phase

January-February 1967:

The January Revolution in Shanghai	January 31: Creation of the Revolutionary Committee of Heilungkiang
Power transfers inaugurated in Shanghai and spread throughout China	February 5: The Shanghai Commune
Revolutionary Committees develop	February 13: Creation of the Revolutionary Committee of Kweichow
Appearance of "spontaneist" tendencies	

February-March 1967

Rectification campaign of mass organizations	February 22: Congress of the Red Guards
The rightist countercurrent of February	March 2: Creation of the Revolutionary Committee of Shantung
The revolutionary counterattack	
The authorities call for the Great Alliance and for unity	March 18: Creation of the Revolutionary Committee of Shansi

Conflict within the Group in Charge of the Cultural Revolution

Mid-March: Important meeting of Party leaders to debate the problems that have arisen so far

End of March through April 1967

The official Party press attacks Liu by inference

March 22: Workers' Congress

Attacks on Liu's book *How to Be a Good Communist*

April 1: Publication of "Patriotism or National Betrayal?"

Start of mass revolutionary criticism

April 20: Creation of the Revolutionary Committee of Peking

May 1–June 15, 1967:

Conflict within the leadership of the Group in Charge of the Cultural Revolution, between the ultraleftists on the one hand and the Chou En-lai line on the other; division of Maoist forces

Splits in the mass organizations

July–August 1967:

Development of the "spontaneist" trend within both the GCCR and the mass organizations

July 20: The Wuhan Incident

August 5: Liu Shao-ch'i makes another self-criticism

Widespread political schisms

August 20: Outbreaks of violence reach their peak in Canton

Attacks against the army

Posters attacking Chou En-lai appear in Peking

August 22: The British Legation in Peking is burned

September 1967:

After a tour through the provinces, Mao Tse-tung returns to Peking and issues a number of important directives: he backs Chou En-lai and the army; the ultraleftists are ousted from the GCCR; it is announced that the Liuist faction has been decisively defeated

Fourth Phase
September 1967–February 1968:

The restoration of order

October 1: Lin Piao, in a speech, announces the formation of groups to study Chairman Mao's teachings

Reinforcement of revolutionary vigilance

November 1: Creation of the Revolutionary Committee of Inner Mongolia

324 CHRONOLOGY

Creation of study groups to concentrate on Mao's teachings

Creation of new revolutionary committees and bolstering of those already set up

The struggle against factionalism

The call to reshape the Party organizations

Start of the new educational programs

Fifth Phase

February-April 1968:

The second February countercurrent

Hsieh Fu-chih, attacked by various groups in Peking and defended by others, receives the backing of the Party leaders

Under the pretense of combating leftism, a rightist countercurrent develops aimed at rehabilitating revisionists

April-July 1968:

Struggle against the second countercurrent

Factionalism resurfaces in the universities

Teams of workers arrive to keep order in the universities, then do the same in the administration offices and cultural services

July-October 1968:

Revolutionary committees take root

By October 1, the country is covered with a network of revolutionary committees

The Twelfth Plenum of the Central Committee announces the formal ouster of Liu Shao-ch'i, and draws up a balance sheet of the Cultural Revolution

January 20, 1968: Creation of the Revolutionary Committee of Wuhan

February 21: Creation of revolutionary committees in Canton and the province of Kwangtung

January 28: Editorial in the *Liberation Army Daily*, "Support the Left but Not Any Particular Faction"

Early February (?): The ousting of Ch'i Pen-yu

March 18: *People's Daily* publishes a photograph of Hsieh Fu-chih on the front page

Mid-March: Three important military leaders ousted: Yang Ch'eng-wu, Yu Li-chin, and Fu Ch'ung-pi

End of April-Beginning of May: Mao's appeal to the people to defend the revolutionary committees and not to fear factionalism, which he says is part of class struggle

April 27: *People's Daily* publishes an article entitled "Make a Class Analysis of Factionalism"

Mid-July: The first workers' team arrives at Tsinghua University

September 5: Creation of Revolutionary Committees of Sinkiang and Tibet

September 7: Mass celebration held in Peking

Mid-October: *Red Flag* publishes an article entitled "Absorb New Blood from the Proletariat"

October 13-31: The Twelfth Plenum of the Central Committee

October 1968-April 1969:

Preparation for the Ninth Party Congress, and restructuring the teaching, administrative, and management organizations of the country

Reorganization of the Party; reinforcement of the revolutionary committees

April 1969:

The Ninth National Congress of the Chinese Communist Party; election of a new, enlarged Central Committee, and adoption of a new Party Constitution

April 1: The Ninth Party Congress opens

April 14: New Constitution is ratified

April 23: New Central Committee is named; close of the Ninth Party Congress

INDEX

About the Author

JEAN DAUBIER was born in Algeria in 1939. He went to the People's Republic of China in April 1966 and worked there as a teacher and with the French section of the *Peking Review*. He followed, and later participated in, the Cultural Revolution. He returned to France in 1968. He has taught at the University of Paris on the political life in China during the Cultural Revolution.

VINTAGE HISTORY—WORLD